MYSTERIES AND SECRETS OF NUMEROLOGY

OTHER WORKS BY LIONEL & PATRICIA FANTHORPE

The Oak Island Mystery: The World's Greatest Treasure Hunt

Satanism and Demonology

The Big Book of Mysteries

Secrets of the World's Undiscovered Treasures

Mysteries and Secrets of Voodoo, Santeria, and Obeah

Mysteries and Secrets of Time

Mysteries and Secrets of Masons

The World's Most Mysterious Castles

Mysteries and Secrets of the Templars: The Story Behind the Da Vinci Code

Unsolved Mysteries of the Sea

The World's Most Mysterious Murders

The World's Most Mysterious Objects

Death: The Final Mystery

The World's Most Mysterious Places

The World's Most Mysterious People

The World's Greatest Unsolved Mysteries

MYSTERIES AND SECRETS OF NUMEROLOGY

LIONEL AND PATRICIA FANTHORPE

DUNDURN
TORONTO

Editor: Britanie Wilson
Design: Jesse Hooper
Printer: Webcom

Library and Archives Canada Cataloguing in Publication

Fanthorpe, R. Lionel
Mysteries and secrets of numerology / by Lionel and Patricia Fanthorpe.

Issued also in electronic format.
ISBN 978-1-4597-0537-1

1. Numerology. I. Fanthorpe, Patricia II. Title.

BF1623.P9F26 2013   133.3'35   C2012-904629-9

1   2   3   4   5   18   17   16   15   14   13

We acknowledge the support of the **Canada Council for the Arts** and the **Ontario Arts Council** for our publishing program. We also acknowledge the financial support of the **Government of Canada** through the **Canada Book Fund** and **Livres Canada Books,** and the **Government of Ontario** through the **Ontario Book Publishing Tax Credit** and the **Ontario Media Development Corporation.**

Printed and bound in Canada.

VISIT US AT
Dundurn.com | Definingcanada.ca | @dundurnpress | Facebook.com/dundurnpress

Dundurn	Gazelle Book Services Limited	Dundurn
3 Church Street, Suite 500	White Cross Mills	2250 Military Road
Toronto, Ontario, Canada	High Town, Lancaster, England	Tonawanda, NY
M5E 1M2	L41 4XS	U.S.A. 14150

This book is dedicated to all of our family and friends who are interested in mathematics and numerology.

CONTENTS

FOREWORD

The writer of this foreword was once described by his grandson as being almost technologically illiterate. There was no sense in taking umbrage as he was only stating the truth. He could have gone even further. He could have called me almost numerically bankrupt and he wouldn't have been far from wrong. Numbers, as far as I am concerned, if they have secrets or ramifications, or influences on characters or events, others can have them. My apathy towards numbers goes back a long way in my life and I can trace its roots. As a very small child I was privileged to go to a very select fee-paying school. Every morning we did sums using a slate and pieces of chalk and every child who got all his sums right was rewarded with a piece of pink coconut ice. If my teeth came to suffer premature decay it was not due to excess of coconut ice! Like most of us, I learnt to struggle with maths enough to pass essential exams, but even today, faced with the choice of a cryptic crossword or sudoku, it will be the crossword every time. Words I love; numbers I gladly leave to others.

Why then, you may wonder, have I agreed to write the foreword to a book dealing exclusively with numbers, what they portend, their secrets, their influences on character or events, be they imaginary or real? The answer is simple: I read the book in proof form for my two author friends as I have done for many of their other works. Even at that stage, two reasons for recommending it to a wider reading public were immediately apparent.

First, unlike myself, some have always immersed themselves in numerology as a duck takes to water. It becomes their lifelong interest. It is well such people exist as it was their expertise that helped us win the last war. Numerical experts conspired to crack the enigma code and thus gain access to messages that the enemy deemed secret. All through-out the ages there have always been such gifted men and women, for whom all secrets are a challenge. Some spend a lifetime studying the stars above us. Others plumb the depths of the world's great oceans. Some scholars devote their lives to seeking out and then deciphering the world's most ancient manuscripts. Numerologists are just such like-minded people and there are many of them. To them, at least, this book is offered, and the authors hope it will cause many others to take interest in some of the mysteries it uncovers. The book, in some ways, is beyond me. It is not beyond others who will enjoy every page of it.

My second reason for endorsing the book is the immense volume of research it reveals. How do the Fanthorpes do it? Co-author Lionel works full-time, and yet, somehow, he and Patricia find time and energy to uncover so much hitherto known only to the few. They write about all sorts of people from so many countries and so many ages, often, seemingly, telling stories the rest of the world seem never to have heard.

Their scholarship is immense and meticulous and deserves to be shared with others. I hope that their labours get the support they deserve.

— Stanley Mogford, Cardiff, 2012

(The authors are deeply grateful to Canon Mogford for his help with proofreading and supplying this foreword. He is rightly regarded as one of the foremost scholars in Wales.)

INTRODUCTION

Numbers play an essential, integral part in all of our lives. The time and space in which we live and move are measured in hours, minutes, and seconds, kilometres and metres. How long until the next appointment? The next meal? The next day off? How far to New York, Toronto, London? We calculate with numbers, we work out the cost of everything using numbers, and we weigh and measure using numbers.

But there are other less obvious aspects of numbers. What do we mean when we think of "lucky" or "unlucky" numbers? Can numbers influence the environment? Can certain numbers make things happen? Can numbers warn us against dangers or lead us towards positive events?

These are the mysteries and secrets of numerology. This is the quest to discover what numbers really are and what they can really do. From a history of mathematics and numerology we explore the mysterious Fibonacci series, which has an enigmatic tendency to turn up in nature where it is least expected.

The more we investigate chemistry and physics at the macrocosmic and microcosmic levels, the more intriguing the numbers become.

Numerology goes back millennia. There were numerologists in ancient Egypt, and the great Greek Pythagoras was a numerologist as well as a brilliant, pioneering mathematician. The early Babylonians were numerologists, as were the philosophical Indians and fearless Norsemen. The wise men responsible for the Kabbalah and the writers and redactors who compiled the Bible were also deeply into the mysteries and secrets of numerology.

The Gnostics, in their relentless pursuit of wisdom, explored their own numerological mysteries and made exciting discoveries there.

Numerologists look for specific links with the numbers associated with names, places, and dates. When all 3 — such as a person's name, the town where he was born, and the time of his birth — point in the same direction, the insight that these particular numbers reveals is hard to ignore.

Numerology also explores a person's character type and looks for compatibility — or otherwise — between people. Would numerological analysis have warned Desdemona away from Othello, the husband who killed her? Cleopatra might have avoided Antony, and Belle Elmore might not have married Hawley Crippen.

The mysteries and secrets of numerology are closely linked with the mysteries and secrets of the Zodiac and astrology. There are also strange secret connections between tarot cards and numerology. The numbers of the major arcana can reveal a great deal to the skilled numerologist.

There are also persistent numerical features in folklore, legend, and mythology. These, too, would seem to have numerological significance.

Music, and especially folksongs, also have numerological associations.

So the persistent numerological questions remain mysterious and unanswered: do numbers influence people, places, times, and events?

— Lionel and Patricia Fanthorpe, 2012

1

WHAT ARE MATHEMATICS AND NUMEROLOGY?

O ur broad understanding of mathematics is that it is a system of communication, calculation, and problem solving involving the use of numbers and allied symbols that represent processes such as addition, subtraction, multiplication, and division. It may be described as a language or code. Its more advanced concepts include the measurement of single linear dimensions, areas, volumes, structures, and changes. Further extensions of its definition include special fields such as algebra, trigonometry, statistics, and calculus. Mathematicians look for patterns and then base conjectures on the patterns they have observed. Mathematics lies at the heart of understanding the amazing complexities of the universe, from subatomic particles to the unimaginably vast spaces between the galaxies. Sir James Jeans once suggested that the universe is a thought in the mind of a great mathematician.

In their earliest days, mathematics and numerology were practically indistinguishable. The power of numbers, and the power of those who understood more about numbers than most of their contemporaries, seemed close to magical. Numerology may be regarded as the fundamental idea that numbers, mathematical symbols, quantities, measurements, and statistical analyses have yet *further* powers than those which they display when we use them to solve mathematical problems. Inside their straightforward mathematical box, numbers and symbols answer questions that have been posed in numbers and symbols. Outside their mathematical box, numbers and symbols are believed to have powers far beyond mere calculating. Numerology suggests that certain digits can affect the universe around them and can influence human behaviour, success, and failure. To the mathematician, numbers and symbols solve problems of quantity, measurement, and numerical changes. To the numerologist, numbers and symbols are like the words of magical liturgies and the ritual movements of enchanters, sorcerers, and magicians. To the numerologist, numbers and symbols have the power to influence people and things in paranormal ways. They also have the power to predict likely outcomes.

The Greek word μάθημα (*mathema*), from which the English word *mathematics* is derived, originally meant "knowledge, learning, or study." Having studied patterns and derived conjectures from them, mathematicians look for proofs of their conjectures. There are several forms of mathematical proof, and a very basic example of the type called "direct proof" can be seen in the fact that the sum of any 2 even numbers will always be another even number. The term *integer* is used in mathematics to define a whole number with no fractional parts attached to it. Integers can be positive or negative: -3, -2, -1, 0, 1, 2, and 3 are all integers. The proof begins by calling any 2 even integers "x" and "y." Because they are even — that is, they can be divided by 2 — it can be argued that $x=2a$ and $y=2b$. Putting a number next to a letter in mathematics signifies that the number multiplies the letter adjacent to it. So, if x and y are both even, each of them will be made up of 2 other integers, which we call "a" and "b." Suppose that we decide that $x=8$ and $y=12$. Then $8=2\times a$ and $12=2\times b$. This means that a must be equal to 4 ($8=2\times4$) and b must be equal to 6 ($12=2\times6$). This then leads to the next step in the proof, which is the following equation:

$x+y=2a+2b$ or $8+12=2(4)+2(6)$

This can be written as 2(a+b), or 2(4+6). The "2" outside the bracket multiplies everything inside the bracket. What has been done so far shows that x+y has 2 as a factor, and the definition of an even integer is that it can be divided by 2. This then constitutes the mathematical proof that the sum of any 2 even integers is another even integer.

It is an essential part of mathematics to set out to prove or disprove mathematical conjectures by using mathematical proofs like the one above. Unlike that basic example, it can sometimes take many years to establish an advanced mathematical proof.

Two very great philosophical mathematicians, Giuseppe Peano (1858–1932) and David Hilbert (1862–1943), made outstanding contributions to mathematical proof theory and mathematical logic.

Of even greater mathematical stature than Peano and Hilbert was the outstandingly brilliant Johann Carl Friedrich Gauss (1777–1855). He was justifiably known as *Princeps mathematicorum*, a Latin title meaning "Prince of Mathematicians" or "Foremost Mathematician." Gauss was also known in his own day as the greatest mathematician since antiquity, and he himself referred to mathematics as "the queen of sciences." He spread his academic and intellectual net widely, making massive contributions to astronomy, statistics, number theory, geophysics, and electrostatics. Gauss's theories are at the forefront of the debate about whether mathematics is a science, and so much of that debate hinges on the definition of what constitutes a science as opposed to a field of knowledge.

Sir Francis Bacon (1561–1626) combined philosophy with statesmanship and a deep knowledge of legal matters, but his contribution to science and the scientific method may be reckoned as his most worthwhile memorial.

The Baconian method of studying science aimed to investigate the cause of a phenomenon, especially what made it different. He advised researchers and investigators to make lists of where the phenomenon occurred and where it did not occur. The lists were then ranked in order according to the strength of the influence of the phenomenon being studied. From Bacon's underlying principles came the idea of natural science as distinct from other fields of knowledge and the various methods of making progress within them. The natural sciences were closely concerned with experimental procedures, and this gave rise to the controversy over whether mathematics could be classified as a science if it was capable of functioning without a reliance on experimentation. Einstein, who had an amazing gift for summarizing major facts succinctly, said that when mathematical laws referred to reality, they were not certain, and when they were certain, they didn't refer to reality.

Francis Bacon

Sir Karl Raimund Popper (1902–1994), undoubtedly one of the greatest philosophers of science of all time, argued that mathematics was much closer to the natural sciences than it seemed. The outstanding physicist John Ziman (1925–2005) held the view that science is best defined as public knowledge, and must, therefore, include mathematics. Different philosophers and scientists hold varying views, but the weight of evidence, and the increasing importance of experimental mathematics, would favour the idea of including mathematics among the sciences. It is undeniable that it forms the solid rock foundation upon which many sciences are built, especially physics and chemistry.

Mathematics and numerology can be thought of as originating rather like a pair of conjoined Siamese twins, but they have separated over the millennia. Just as academic mathematics can be seen to belong in the vicinity of the natural sciences, so numerology belongs in the vicinity of magic. Magic can be defined and described as what are believed to be methods of altering and manipulating the environment (people and things) by supernatural means. These so-called supernatural means can be thought to include knowledge of occult causes and effects that are unknown to science. It is an essential part of science to rely on observation and logical analysis; it is an essential part of magic to believe that there are inexplicable forces beyond logical cause and effect.

There are ways in which magic resembles religion. Although heavily criticized by later thinkers, Sir James George Frazer (1854–1941), author of the monumental work on anthropology *The Golden Bough* (1890), worked out a succession in which the earliest peoples tried to control nature by using magic, which gave way first to religion and then to science. Fundamentally, Frazer argued, humanity had attempted to control the environment by using what were believed to be the inexplicable and illogical powers of magic. When these palpably failed so frequently, and were clearly seen to be ineffective, our remote ancestors turned to religion. When their magical activities — rituals, liturgies, spells, and incantations — did not control the environment, they thought that they must appeal to the gods to help them. In due course, as millennia passed, it became clear that appealing to the gods was also ineffectual. Along with the decline in religious belief came the realization that science could succeed far more often than either magic or religion. If making magical gestures and reciting curses failed to kill the enemy, and if prayers to divine beings also failed to halt the advance of the foe, then the invention and employment of superior weapons based on scientific principles would bring an opponent down. Where magic and prayer had failed to accomplish the desired results, scientifically designed Gatling and Maxim guns could cut the enemy down very effectively.

There are contemporary magicians — numerologists among them — whose theory of magic regards it as some strange kind of bonding with largely unknown universal powers. They believe that if some magical act is performed, through manipulating numbers, reciting incantations, making magical passes with the hands, or flourishing a magic wand, then a result will occur elsewhere in the universe. If it is benign white magic, the magician believes that a sick person will recover, or a lost person will be found alive and well. If it is dark, negative magic, the black magician believes that someone will suffer financial loss, a healthy person will become ill, a sick person will die, or someone previously honest and well-balanced will delve into criminality, vice, or drug misuse. Another view of magic held by some contemporary magicians is that it is not itself a controlling or directing phenomenon, but a way of contacting powerful spirit beings who will carry out the magician's will when asked to do so.

Numerology can also be thought of as the search for a link between some measurement, or counting process, and life itself — a link that numerologists believe can be used advantageously. The number may be thought to control the environment, or individuals within the environment, or to predict what has been revealed by the supposed environmental link. Put in its simplest and most basic form: the number "7," for example, may be thought to *cause* good things to happen, or it may be thought to *predict* the good things that are about to happen without having any causative influence over them. Theory number 1, the causative theory, likens the magical, influential number to a hand and arm that can manipulate events. Theory number 2, the predictive theory, likens the magical number to an eye that can see and predict, but cannot influence or manipulate events.

In his book, *Numerology: Or What Pythagoras Wrought*, highly analytical mathematician Underwood Dudley discusses the Elliott Wave Principle used for analyzing the behaviour of stocks and shares. The Wave Principle was the creation of a professional accountant, Ralph Nelson Elliott (1871–1948). It's a form of technical analysis that investors can use to analyze cycles in financial markets, and so make substantial gains by buying and selling at appropriate points in those stock market cycles. Market trends can be analyzed by studying investor psychology and the ways in which stock market prices change. Elliott's book, *The Wave Principle*, came out in 1938. A later book, *Nature's Laws: The Secret of the Universe*, appeared in 1946, just 2 years before Elliott's death. In it he argued that humanity was rhythmic by nature and human behaviour was therefore also rhythmic and cyclical. From this basic idea Elliott deduced that human behaviour could be predicted with remarkable accuracy, and that those who knew how to understand and use this wave information could make a success of buying and selling on the stock exchange.

An interesting suggestion regarding wider and deeper aspects of numerology follows from this preliminary look at the Elliott Wave. Scientists recognize that series, cycles, and rhythms are part of natural life, including human life, and that they are also susceptible to numerical analysis. Series, cycles, and rhythms can also be observed and recorded. It could perhaps be suggested that where numerology appears to produce positive results it is because the numerologist has linked up, either knowingly or unknowingly, with a natural rhythm, series, or cycle. Examples include circadian rhythms and the so-called "body clock." These biological mechanisms control human times of activity and inactivity. Scientific and medical research has observed that these body clocks and circadian rhythms operate on an approximate period of 24 hours. Reflection on our own physical and mental experiences indicates that there are times in the 24-hour cycle when we feel alert and energetic, while at other times in the cycle we feel sleepy and lethargic. For many self-observers, there are perceptible high points of mental alertness between 8:00 and 10:00 in the mornings and again between 8:00 and 10:00 in the evenings. Physical strength and energy peaks later than the mental summit in the mornings — on average, about an hour later. In the evenings, however, the peak of physical strength and energy comes an hour or so before the mental peak is reached.

Medical scientists and expert neurologists have located an area in the hypothalamus containing approximately 20,000 neurons. This is known as the SCN, or suprachiasmatic nucleus, and acts as the body's super-clock, or biological pacemaker. The external stimuli, which appear to stimulate its activities, are generally thought to be associated with sunlight or bright daylight. As light decreases at the end of the day, the eyes and associated visual system transmit messages to the suprachiasmatic nucleus, which signals another gland to produce more melatonin. This, in turn, produces a feeling of tiredness and sleepiness. Lengthy experiments with subjects being deprived of light tend to indicate that without the natural 24-hour light and darkness cycle the body clock moves to a 25-hour cycle. Numbers and time measurement are at the core of any understanding of circadian rhythms, and this can provide essential data for numerologists.

The seasons of spring, summer, autumn, and winter are a major example of a natural cycle that can be assessed and analyzed numerically. Rather less obvious than the cyclic nature of the 4 seasons are the biogeochemical cycles, yet they are very real and are subject to numerical, scientific analysis. Some of these cycles are gaseous and others sedimentary. Gaseous cycles store the element that is being analyzed and followed in the earth's atmosphere. Sedimentary cycles store the element that is being tracked within the earth's crust. The carbon cycle provides an important example. Plants absorb carbon dioxide from the air. Herbivores, such as rabbits, eat the plants. The carbon absorbed from the plants creates tissue for the herbivore. Carnivores then eat the herbivores, and use the carbon they have ingested. Carbon dioxide is returned to the air when the animal breathes, and to the earth when the animal dies and decomposes. Plants can then take carbon from the soil and the whole cycle continues. The carbon in the cycle can be weighed and measured, and therefore is subject to numerical analysis.

The water cycle provides another useful example of a natural cycle that can be analyzed numerically. Water evaporates from the surfaces of lakes, seas, and oceans and forms clouds. When the meteorological conditions are right, it falls again as rain, sleet, hail, or snow. It is then evaporated again, and so the cycle continues. Precipitation and evaporation can be weighed, measured, and analyzed numerically.

Later chapters will deal in full with the meanings of different integers as understood and used by numerologists. At this early stage, however, it will be useful to give a broad interpretation of the basic meanings assigned to numbers, as this allocation of meanings marks a clear distinction between scientific mathematics and the "magical" aspects of numerology. The "0" is one of the most powerful of all numerological symbols. It can represent everything from the entire universe to nothingness. It can signify ascent and descent. The "0" is unlimited and eternal. The figure "1" stands for individuality. It can also indicate aggression and assertiveness, determination and drive. It also has a masculine aspect. The figure "2" stands for balance and unity, receptiveness and understanding. Opposite to number "1," the "2" has a feminine aspect. Number "3" symbolizes fairness, objectivity, and good judgement. There is a sense in which numerologists regard it as the symbol of neutrality. The figure "4" represents creativity, originality, inventiveness, ingenuity, resourcefulness, vision, and inspiration, whereas "5" can be problematic. Many numerologists think of "5" as indicative of vigorous action, movement, restlessness, and an inability to find calmness and peace. "Six" symbolizes responsibility, dependability, and trustworthiness. The figure "7" is one of the very best. It means thoughtfulness, wisdom, knowledge, and insight. "Seven" can signify a careful attention to detail, consideration, and contemplation. Number "8" stands for power, but can also entail sacrifice. "Eight" is sometimes thought of as a heroic number;

it signifies gallantry and noble courage. The "9" signifies change of a major type: movement from one lover to another, from one religious faith to another, from one philosophical persuasion to another.

It should be noted that numerology is known and practised globally, and the list of numbers and their meanings can vary considerably from one location to another.

One important Chinese system is associated with the sounds of certain letters and numbers. In this system, "1" represents certainty; "2" is ease, comfort, facility, and simplicity. Number "3" is life, self-awareness, and existence, whereas "4" is associated with water, which is considered to bring wealth and good luck. In a different Chinese system, however, "4" is thought to be a warning of impending death. The number "5" is the self, the individual, the person, the self-conscious entity. In this system, "6" is thought of as a stronger version of "2." It represents ongoing easiness and smoothness, a situation that is pleasant all the way, and enduring happiness. Whereas "7" is a supremely good number in Western numerology, it is regarded as being negative, crude, and vulgar in this Chinese system. The "8" has some similarities in both systems. Here, it symbolizes the prosperity and good fortune that arise from the exercise of power and energy. Number "9" in Chinese symbolism is almost the direct opposite of its significance in Western numerology where it means a major change. In the Chinese system it represents longevity, endurance, and persisting for a very long time.

Over and above the values and meanings, which the Chinese system allocates to single-digit integers, there are certain number combinations that are thought to be very significant by Chinese numerologists who use this system. The number "99," for example, stands for eternity, or a good thing that is everlasting. The numbers "148," "168," and "814" are thought to be especially lucky in China, and "168" is the number used by a chain of motels there. The personal prosperity number is "518," which is believed to bring great success and financial rewards to those who use it. Triple prosperity is allegedly attached to "888," which signifies infinite riches and wealth. A long and happy life verging on immortality is associated with the number "1314," while "289" is almost as powerfully fortunate. It means always having enough, and having it throughout an entire lifetime.

Just as there are wide differences of interpretation between Western and Chinese numerologists, there are similar distinctions between both those systems and the ancient Indian system. In the Indian system, the numbers "1," "10," "19," and "28" are regarded as being ruled by the sun. When their digits are added, they all reach the total of "1." So, adding the digits of "10" together equals 1 (1+0); the digits of 19 added together come to 10 (1+9), which then reduces to 1 (1+0=1); and adding the digits of "28" also comes to 10 (2+8), which again reduces to 1 (1+0=1). Applying the system further, the numbers "2," "11," "20," and "29" all represent the moon, and all add up to 2. For example, the digits of "11" add together to 2 (1+1), the digits of "20" add together to 2 (2+0), and the digits of "29" add together to 11 (9+2), which then reduces to 2 (1+1). Letters are also allocated their own special number values in this system. "A," "I," "J," "Q," and "Y" all carry the value "1," and "B," "C," "K," and "R" all carry the value "2."

The Mayans and Aztecs were expert astrologers and calendar-makers. They achieved a highly commendable level of mathematical efficiency, which was especially evident in their amazing calendars.

Mayan calendar

They could justifiably be described as expert numerologists, but their systems varied from our contemporary Western numerology, and from Indian and Chinese techniques and interpretations.

The numerological process of adding digits to arrive at a single figure features in almost all numerological systems throughout the world, but it may not always be performed in the familiar base-10 system of Western mathematics. For example, because "9" has certain peculiarities, what is called a nonary system, or base-9, may be employed for some numerological processes. Instead of using the digits from 1–9 as in base-10, the digits 1–8 are employed; and "9" is written as "10," signifying 1 in the nines column and no units. The columns in nonary systems are: units, 9s, 81s, and 729s, instead of the decimal system's columns of: units, tens, hundreds, and thousands. For example, a numerologist using the nonary system would add up the digits of "578685" as 5+7+8+6+8+5=43 and then add the digits of the number "43" (4+3) to yield a single nonary digit of "7." This is because the digits add to 39 in the normal decimal-based system, but "39" in normal decimal notation has to be written in nonary as "4" in the 9s column and "3" in the units column. This is because 4×9=36, hence the "4" in the 9s column accompanied by "3" in the units column. The same 6 digits in normal decimal notation add to 39, and the resulting 3+9 gives 12, which, in turn, can be reduced to 3 by adding the digits of 12 together like so: 1+2=3. The numerologist working in the nonary system finishes with a single digit of "7" from 4+3=7, whereas the numerologist working in decimal-base finishes with a single digit of "3" from 1+2=3. This can cause differing opinions and outcomes as the numerals "7" and "3" have very different interpretations in numerology.

The comparison of nonary and decimal systems is shown in the following table:

NORMAL (BASE-10) DECIMAL NOTATION

Thousands	Hundreds	Tens	Units
5	6	7	8

NONARY (BASE-9) NOTATION

729s	81s	9s	Units
7	7	0	8

So what *are* mathematics and numerology? Scientific mathematics enables us to understand the minute mysteries of the subatomic microcosm and the almost infinite vastness of the cosmos. Mathematics is a superbly accurate number and symbol code that enables us to communicate, calculate, and solve problems.

If the numerologists are right about their mysterious fields of study, numerology might prove to be more breathtakingly exciting than scientific mathematics. Can numerology tell us about human characters and dispositions, personalities, and relationships? Can it reveal whether certain locations are favourable, while others are negative and hazardous? Can it suggest which dates and times are better than others for achieving our goals? Can it explain the immense complexity of the structure and function of plant and animal life and the mysteries of the interactions of the entire biosphere? Can it predict future events? Can it show us how to understand the mysterious influence that some numbers appear to exert over the environment?

If the mysteries of numerology could be interwoven and reconciled with pure scientific mathematics, if numerology could be shown to have a logical, rational, and scientific basis as well as a seemingly "magical" one, where would that new unified area of study take us? What if James Jeans was right in asserting that the universe is a thought in the mind of a Supreme Mathematician?

In the next chapter, we examine the long and complex history of mathematics in detail, examining in particular those areas where it comes closest to numerology.

2

HISTORY OF MATHEMATICS

The earliest artifacts relating to mathematics were various tally sticks, some dating back nearly 40,000 years. As with ancient cave paintings, which are believed to have been magical in the eyes of the early peoples who created them, the ancient mathematical tally sticks may well have had a magical numerological significance as well as a purely practical, numerical one.

The Lebombo bone is estimated to be 35,000 years old — or perhaps more. It was found in the Border Cave in the Lebombo Mountains of Swaziland in East Africa. Originally the fibula of a baboon, it has 29 distinct notches, which has led some archaeologists to believe that it was intended as a lunar calendar.

Lebombo bone

The Wolf bone was discovered in Moravia by Karl Absolon in 1937. Estimated at approximately 35,000 years old, it was found close to a Venus figurine. The bone has 55 marks carved into it. Its association with the Venus figurine suggests some kind of numerological or magical function as well as a straightforward counting or measuring function. Was this a situation in which mathematics and numerology overlapped?

The Ishango bone is rather younger, dating back some 20,000 years. It was discovered in 1960 by a Belgian explorer named de Braucourt in what was then known as the Belgian Congo, near the upper reaches of the Nile. Like the Lebombo bone, the Ishango bone was once the fibula of a baboon. At one end there is a piece of quartz, which suggests that the Ishango bone was used for marking or engraving things. It is thought that the clusters of marks cut into the bone are more complex than those on the Lebombo bone, which might indicate that the Ishango bone is something more mathematically complicated than a basic tally stick or calendar.

Mathematical historians are of the opinion that mathematical thinking started when our earliest ancestors began to form concepts of number, magnitude, and form. What precisely do we mean by number? Although there is still some controversy over whether to include "0," what are described as natural numbers are the following: 0, 1, 2, 3, 4, 5 … and so on. Integers include negative numbers and can be illustrated

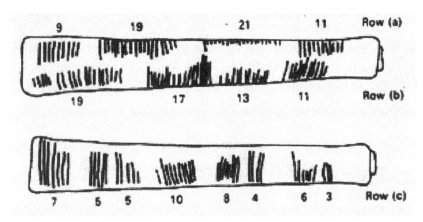

Ishango bone

28

as -5, -4, -3, -2, -1, 0, 1, 2, 3, 4, 5...and so on — the positive integers being the same as the natural numbers 1, 2, 3, 4, 5.... Rational numbers are able to be written as "*a/b*" but neither "*a*" nor "*b*" can be "0." Irrational numbers cannot be written as rational *a/b* expressions. They are numbers such as π (*pi* in the Greek alphabet), which represents the number 3.14159, with an infinite decimal trail. Pi is the ratio of a circle's circumference to its diameter.

The earliest mathematical thought was also concerned with magnitude — the size of an object compared to other objects of the same kind. To Palaeolithic hunter-gatherers, how many objects there were and how big they were was an important piece of survival data, as was form. This refers to the configuration of an object, its visual appearance, and, basically, its shape.

Recent studies of animal intelligence have reached very interesting conclusions about the basic levels of mathematical ability of this elementary type that some animal species seem to share with human beings. Numerous "counting" dogs and horses have featured as circus and vaudeville acts, and they certainly seem to show some basic number skills.

An impressive university study on animal mathematical ability was conducted by Dr. Naoko Irie in Tokyo. Elephants from the Ueno Zoo watched as apples were dropped into buckets, and the elephants were then offered their choice of the buckets. Human subjects were also involved in the experiment to compare their results with those of the elephants. The elephants scored 74 percent while the human beings scored only 67 percent. The experiment suggested that when more than a single apple was dropped, the elephants had to carry out the equivalent of running totals in their heads.

The history of mathematics indicates that as civilizations developed, the demand for mathematics increased. The old commercial civilizations, such as Sumer in the region of the Tigris and Euphrates, needed to make careful records of commercial transactions: jars of oil, measures of corn, units of cloth, slaves and animals bought and sold. The Sumerians developed writing, irrigation, agriculture, the wheel, the plough, and many other things. Their writing system, known as cuneiform, used wedge-shaped characters cut into clay tablets that were then baked. As a consequence, they have lasted thousands of years and archaeologists have studied them closely for centuries. In the Sumerian civilization there was the need to measure areas of land and to calculate taxes. Sumerians developed calendars and were keenly interested in observing and recording the stars and planets in their courses. They developed the use of symbols to represent quantities. A large cone stood for "60." A clay sphere stood for "10," and a small cone was a single unit. In addition to these developments, they used a simple abacus.

Just as the popular base-10 decimal system of numbering is almost certainly based on the fact that we have 10 fingers, so it is suggested that the Sumerian and later Babylonian sexegesimal system (base-60) is based on the 12 knuckles of 1 hand and the 5 fingers of the other, which create 60 when multiplied together. Five hands would be thought of as containing 60 knuckles.

This base-60 system had many advantages. For example, "60" is the smallest number into which all numbers from 1–6 will divide exactly. The number "60" is also divisible by 10, 12, 15, 20, and 30. The convenience of "60" can still be seen in the concept of having 60 seconds in a minute, and 60 minutes in an hour. The 360 degrees of a circle is based on 60 multiplied by 6.

The Babylonians also used an early version of the "0," although they seem to have employed it more as a place marker than as a symbol representing nothing. Five thousand years ago the Sumerians and Babylonians were making complicated tables filled with square roots, squares, and cubes. They could deal with fractions, equations, and even algebra. They got as close to π as regarding it as 3 1/8, or 3.125, which isn't far from our contemporary 3.14159....

They also had the square root of 2 (1.41421) correct to all 5 decimal places. The square root of 2 is very useful for calculating the diagonal of a square. The formula is:

side of square×$\sqrt{2}$=the diagonal of that square

As a maths tutor, co-author Lionel passes that useful shortcut to his students along with the square root of 3 multiplied by the side of a cube to calculate the diagonal of a cube. The formula is:

√3×side of cube=diagonal of cube

Other Babylonian tablets provide the squares of numbers up to 59 (59×59=3481): a major achievement for mathematicians without calculators or computers!

The rich leisure culture of Babylon had numerous games of chance, and the dice they designed for these provided further archaeological evidence of their mathematical knowledge. This would seem to suggest an area of early thought where mathematics and numerology share the territory. Gamblers enjoy using systems of "lucky" numbers to try to beat the odds. In the old Babylonian games of chance, players may well have played their luck with numbers that they hoped would prove to be influential in moving the odds in their favour. Outstanding mathematicians like Marcus du Sautoy have examined these theories and suggested among other things that picking consecutive numbers can increase a gambler's chances of winning a lottery.

Their buildings were also geometrically interesting, and the Sumerians and Babylonians had no problems calculating the areas of rectangles, trapezoids, and triangles. Volumes of cuboids and cylinders were also well within their mathematical capabilities.

One of many interesting problems in the history of mathematics and numerology is the famous Plimpton 322 tablet. It came from Senkereh in southern Iraq, and Senkereh was originally the ancient city of Larsa. The tablet measures 5 inches by 3.5 inches, and was purchased from Edgar J. Banks, an archaeological dealer. In 1922, he sold the mysterious tablet to George Plimpton, a publisher, after whom it was named. Plimpton placed it in his collection of archaeological treasures and finally bequeathed them all to Columbia University.

Written some 4,000 years ago, the tablet contains what seem to be Pythagorean triangle measurements — written centuries before Pythagoras lived! The classical "3, 4, 5" Pythagorean triangle is right-angled because $3^2+4^2=5^2$, also expressed as 9+16=25. Any triangle with those ratios will also be right-angled, for example "6, 8, 10" produces 36+64=100. Whoever carved the Plimpton 322 tablet millennia ago seems to have been well aware of that.

Evidence for the development of mathematics in ancient Egypt was found in a tomb at Abydos, where ivory labels with numbers on them had been attached to grave goods. The famous Narmer Palette was discovered in 1897 by J.E. Quibell at Hierakonpolis, the capital of Predynastic Egypt.

The palette reveals the use of a 10-base number system and accounts for thousands of goats, oxen, and human prisoners. Inscriptions on a wall in Meidum, near one of the mastaba (a low-lying, flat-bench-shaped tomb), carry mathematical instructions for the angles of the walls of the mastaba. These inscriptions involve the cubit as the unit of measurement. This was a unit based on the size of parts of the body, from the elbow to the fingertips, approximately 18 inches.

The Rhind Mathematical Papyrus, which is well over 3,500 years old, was acquired by Alexander Henry Rhind in Luxor in 1858 and is now in the British Museum. It was copied from a much older papyrus by a scribe named Ahmes, who described it as being used for "Enquiring into things … the knowledge of all things … mysteries and secrets." It would seem from this that Ahmes had a numerological view of the power of numbers. They were not merely of use to solve mathematical problems: they had magical powers as well.

The Rhind Papyrus contains a number of problems in both arithmetic and algebra, which has led some antiquarians to suggest that it was perhaps intended as a teaching document. One interesting example shows how the Egyptian mathematicians of that period took the numbers from 1–9 and divided them by 10. They worked out that $7 \div 10$ could be expressed as $2 \div 3 + 1 \div 30$. The papyrus continues with interesting practical problems such as dividing loaves of bread among 10 men. There are then algebraic examples of linear equations such as $x + 1 \div 3x + 1 \div 4x = 2$ in modern notation. When the equation is solved, $x = 1$ and $5 \div 19$ or approximately 1.263157894. The Rhind Papyrus goes on to provide methods of finding the volumes of cylindrical and cuboid

The Narmer Palette

granaries. The Rhind Papyrus also contains formulas for division and multiplication and its contents infer that the Egyptians of that period knew about prime numbers and the Sieve of Eratosthenes, which is a technique for finding prime numbers.

A prime number is a natural number that has only 2 factors: itself and 1. They are, of course, also its only divisors. Oddly enough, "1" is not a prime number because it has only 1 factor, which is itself. The Sieve of Eratosthenes, who was an early Greek mathematician — not an Egyptian — will find all the prime numbers up to and including the end number of the specified range. This end number, the highest number, is always referred to as "n." To use the Sieve of Eratosthenes, begin by writing out all the numbers in your list from 2 up to and including "n." Now introduce the term "p," which stands for "prime." It has the starting value of "2," which is the lowest prime number. Beginning with p itself, go through the list and cross off all the numbers that are multiples of p. Those numbers will be $2p$, $3p$, $4p$ … and so on. Now look for the lowest number that has not yet been crossed off. This will be the prime immediately above 2, which is "3." The next step is to give "p" the value of this number ("3"), and repeat the process as often as necessary with each succeeding prime. Finally, when you have used all the known primes (2, 3, 5, 7, 11, 13 …) any unmarked numbers remaining will be primes.

As a very short, simple example, suppose we are trying to find whether 17 is a prime. Call "17" "n" and begin with "p" as "2":

2, 3, 4, 5, 6, 7, 8, 9, 10, 11, 12, 13, 14, 15, 16, 17

Delete all the multiples of "p" when $p=2$:

3, 5, 7, 9, 11, 13, 15, 17

Therefore, "p" now becomes the next prime, which is "3."

Delete all multiples of 3:

5, 7, 11, 13, 17

In turn, "p" now becomes "5," then "7," then "11," then "13."

This leaves only "17" — our original target — so "17" is a prime.

The Rhind Papyrus certainly creates a high degree of respect for the Egyptian mathematicians who created it some 4,000 years ago.

Another very interesting piece of evidence for the mathematical developments in early Egypt is found in what is known as the Egyptian Mathematical Leather Roll. This dates from well over 3,500 years ago and comes from Thebes. It found its way to the British Museum in 1864, but was not unrolled and deciphered until 1927. The roll contains numerous fractions added together to form other fractions. Examples include 1/30+1/45+1/90=1/15 and 1/96+1/192=1/64 together with 1/50+1/30+1/150+1/400=1/16. The Roll makes it clear that fraction calculations of this type were highly significant for the Egyptian mathematicians of this period. They regarded certain fractions as "Eye of Horus" numbers.

In the legendary battles between the evil god Seth and Isis and Osiris, who were Horus's parents, Seth tried to blind Horus, who was later healed by the good and wise Thoth. One piece of his eye, however, was missing, and Thoth used magic to make up for the missing piece. The Horus eye numbers were 1/2, 1/4, 1/8, 1/16, 1/32 and 1/64. These add to 63/64, leaving the missing piece of Horus's eye with a value of 1/64. The eye legend combined with the missing fraction brings mathematics and numerology close together in Egyptian thought. Each Pharaoh thought of himself as Horus during his earthly reign, but at death he was transformed into Osiris.

On the other side of the world, in South America, the ancient Mayans were developing a mathematical system using the vigesimal number base-20 instead of 10. This suggests to historians that the Mayans used toes as well as fingers in their counting system. Their basic numbering system was clear and effective: dots were used up to "5," which was a short horizontal line. Dots were then added above the line until the sum of "9" was reached, illustrated as a horizontal bar, for "5," with 4 dots above it. "Ten" was expressed with 2 of the short horizontal lines, worth 5 each. "Eleven" was the 2 lines that stood for "10," with a single dot above it. The system continued in this way as far as "19," which was represented with 3 of the horizontal 5-lines, 1 above the other, and then there were 4 dots above them.

The Mayan calendar is made up of 20 sets of 13-day cycles, leading to 260 total days. These 13-day periods are known as *trecena* cycles, and are comparable to months in our modern calendar. Religious ceremonials are based on this unique system, and it is also used to predict the future. Mayan calendar mathematics also involves the numerology of divination.

Over the centuries, various fundamentalist sects and cults — as well as some of the major religions —have preoccupied their thinking with eschatology and trying to find dates for the end of the world. Mayan calendar numerology is a case-in-point, and one which causes more unnecessary alarm than many of the others. According to what is referred to in the Mayan system as "Long Count," a period of 5,126 years will come to an end on December 21, 2012. On that day, the winter solstice sun will be more or less in conjunction with what approximates to the galactic equator. The Maya regarded this as some sort of mystical sacred tree. Some pessimistic end-of-the-world enthusiasts are convinced that the event will mean the end of civilization as we know it.

A similar end-of-the world obsession happened in July 1999. Co-author Lionel was then making the television program called *The Real Nostradamus*, and a great many Nostradamus readers had convinced themselves that the old French soothsayer had forecast terrible disasters for July 1999. One very sad interviewee on the show was totally convinced that everything was ending. He had given up a good professional job and his London home so that he could go back to the village where he had been born in order to await the end there. That is the kind of serious damage that misguided eschatological obsessions can induce. The authors — with over 50 years' experience of investigating the paranormal and the anomalous — are totally confident that nothing bad will happen to our Earth in December 2012. Mayan mathematics was exceptionally advanced for its time, but well-designed as it was, their Long Count Calendar certainly does not herald the end of all things.

Thales of Miletus lived from 624–546 BC. He was a pre-Socratic philosopher and a master of mathematics and astronomy, who also had a keen interest in ethics and metaphysics. Experts regard him as one of the traditional 7 Sages of Greece. He set out to explain natural phenomena through causes and effects, as opposed to the mythological explanations so prevalent at the time. It was characteristic of popular Greek thought during this period to depend upon exegetical myths — those that attempted to explain the origins of everything. For example, the changing of seasons was thought to be a result of the Greek earth goddess, Demeter, searching for her missing daughter, Persephone. Numerology features here in the myth of Persephone and the 6 pomegranate seeds that she ate out of temptation, leading to her curse of having to spend 6 out of every 12 months with Hades in the Underworld, which corresponds to the number of winter months we experience each year. Another example is provided by Aeolus, or Aiolos, who was appointed by Zeus to take charge of the storm winds. These were released when the gods wanted to cause damage and disaster. Instead of relying on these myths to explain the natural phenomena happening around him, Thales looked instead for rational explanations that he did his best to examine open-mindedly and objectively. This gave him the title of the Father of Science, although supporters of Democritus felt that he deserved the title instead.

One of Thales's excellent ideas was to calculate the height of a tall building, such as a pyramid, by standing in a position where he could measure his own shadow and the shadow of the target building. When his shadow coincided exactly with his own height, he measured the pyramid's shadow and argued that if his shadow gave his height, then the pyramid's shadow would reveal its height. He was also responsible for a number of important theorems: that any diameter bisects a circle; that the angle from the diameter to the circumference in a semi-circle is a right-angle; that the base angles of an isosceles triangle are equal; that the opposite angles formed by 2 intersecting straight lines are equal; and that triangles are congruent if 1 side and 2 angles are equal.

Pythagoras lived from approximately 570–495 BC and was the leader of a group known as the Pythagoreans. He and his followers in Croton (what is now Crotone in southern Italy) lived like a monastic brotherhood and were all vegetarians. All their joint mathematical discoveries were attributed to Pythagoras, so it is impossible to tell how much of the work was his alone. Because of this cult aspect of his life, it may be more appropriate to think of him as a numerologist than as a scientific mathematician. The safest conclusion is that he was both. The theorem associated with him is that in any right-angled tri-angle the square on the hypotenuse is equal to the sum of the squares on the other 2 sides. The proof of this theory is a very interesting one. Draw a right-angled triangle with sides a, b, and c as shown below. The longest side, the hypotenuse opposite the right-angle, is side c. What has to be proven is that $a^2+b^2=c^2$. Now draw the square of side c as shown in the diagram, and draw the original 90-degree triangle, "a, b, c," in the 4 corners as illustrated here.

The big square with the c^2 inside it has the area $(a+b)^2$, or we can say: A (the area of the big square)$=(a+b)(a+b)$.

The area of the tilted internal square is c^2.

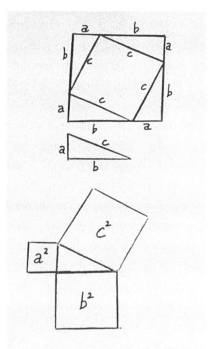

Diagram of Pythagoras' Theorem

Each of the right-angled triangles has the area $1/2ab$. There are 4 of these, so their total area is: $4(1/2ab)$. We can re-write this as $2ab$. The entire area of the tilted square and the 4 right-angled triangles is $A=c^2+2ab$. This then becomes $(a+b)(a+b)=c^2+2ab$. The term $(a+b)(a+b)$ can be multiplied out to produce $a^2+2ab+b^2$, further resulting in the equation $a^2+2ab+b^2=c^2+2ab$. The next step is to subtract the $2ab$ from each side. This leaves $a^2+b^2=c^2$, which is the proof that we were looking for!

One of Pythagoras's most able disciples was Parmenides, who applied his mathematical skills to cosmology and came up with the idea of a spherical Earth inside the spherical universe. One of his disciples, Zeno of Elea, devoted his mathematical and philosophical skills to creating paradoxes, and some of these shaped the development of mathematics for centuries after his death. One of Zeno's best-known paradoxes is called Achilles and the Tortoise. Zeno argued that a fast runner like Achilles could never overtake the tortoise. If it started 16 metres ahead of Achilles, but could run at only half his speed, by the time he covered those 16 metres, the tortoise would have gone 8. By the time he had covered those 8 metres, the tortoise would have gone another 4. By the time he had covered those 4, the tortoise would have gone another 2 ... and so on indefinitely.

Another important early Greek mathematician was Hippocrates of Chios (470–410 BC) who, like many others since his day, attempted to square the circle: that is, to construct a square with the same area as a given circle. It is impossible to do this with perfect accuracy because π (3.14159…) is not a rational number.

The curve, known as the "quadratrix," or "trisectrix," was the work of Hippias of Elias around about 430 BC. It can be used to trisect an angle, or to divide an angle into a given number of equal parts. He, too, was one of the early mathematicians involved in unsuccessful attempts to square the circle.

Eudoxus of Cnidas (410–350 BC) developed a system of geometric proofs, based on what became known as the exhaustion method. When he attempted to show that 2 areas, a and b, were equal, he would begin by trying to prove that a was greater than b.

When that proof failed (was exhausted) he would attempt to prove that *b* was greater than *a*. When that proof also failed (was also exhausted) Eudoxus argued that as neither area was bigger or smaller than the other, they must be equal.

Eudemus of Rhodes (350–290 BC) was not so much a great early mathematician in his own right as an *historian* of mathematics. His 3 very informative books in this genre were histories of arithmetic, geometry, and astronomy. He also wrote another volume dealing with angles.

Euclid of Alexandria (325–265 BC) has gone down in mathematical history as the greatest mathematical teacher of all time. His ideas are still quoted authoritatively today. In addition to all his well-known work on geometry, his theory of the infinite number of prime numbers has stood the test of time.

Aristarchus of Samos (310–230 BC) was a remarkably able mathematician and astronomer, who came up with a well-argued heliocentric theory of the universe. Nearly 2,000 years later, Copernicus delved into Aristarchus's work and agreed with his conclusions.

Apollonius of Perga (262–190 BC) focussed his mathematical skills on cones and the curves that are derived from slicing them. His book on conics introduced the terms "parabola," "ellipse," and "hyperbola."

Hipparchus of Rhodes (190–120 BC) worked mainly as the pioneer of trigonometry. Every angle has a sine, a cosine, and a tangent, and these can be used to find angles or sides in a 90-degree triangle. The 3 sides are referred to as the hypotenuse, the adjacent, and the opposite. The basic trigonometrical formulae are:

sine=opposite÷hypotenuse

cosine=adjacent÷hypotenuse

tangent=opposite÷adjacent

These formulae make it clear that whenever any 2 of the measurements are known, the third can readily be calculated.

Claudius Ptolemy (85–165 AD) enjoyed, as his name implies, a rich mixture of Greek and Roman culture and learning. His mathematical works, principally on astronomy, were honoured with the Arabian title *Almagest*, meaning "The Greatest."

Diophantus (200–284 AD) did remarkable early work on number theory, and his book *Arithmetica* provided a great deal of inspiration for Pierre Fermat (1601–1665). Fermat's Last Theorem states that if we call 3 positive integers a, b, and c, then the equation $a^n+b^n=c^n$ will only be possible if n is not greater than 2. Proving it became a leading mathematical problem for centuries, and even made its way into the Guinness Book of Records!

A brilliant Persian mathematician named Al-Khowarizmi (780–840) was also a gifted scientist and astronomer. His additional interest in astrology made him something of a numerologist — like Pythagoras — as well as a scientific mathematician. The modern word *algebra* was transliterated from his book *Hisab al-jabr w'al-muqabala*, where it was rendered as "*al-jabr*."

Francesco Pellos (1450–1500) was the inventor of the decimal point — a tremendously useful part of contemporary mathematics. The gifted Scots theologian John Napier (1550–1617) indulged in mathematics more or less as a hobby when he wanted a break from theology. He was largely responsible for creating logarithms, which were perfected by Henry Briggs. At around the same period, Sir Isaac Newton (1642–1727) published his epoch-making *Principia* — a masterpiece of mathematics and science. There is some justification for those who regard him as the greatest scientist who has yet lived. His work on gravitation and the 3 laws of motion are unforgettable.

Another important milestone in the history of mathematics was William Jones's (1675–1749). He used the Greek symbol "π" to show the result of dividing the circumference of a circle by its diameter. This feat was published in his book, *New Introduction to Mathematics*, in 1706.

Calculus was the particular brainchild of the Italian maths genius Maria Agnesi (1718–1799). Her famous textbook on it, *Istituzioni Analitiche*, was an authoritative teaching aid on calculus for many years.

David Hilbert (1862–1943) was one of the most outstanding mathematical leaders in the late nineteenth and early twentieth centuries. His great contributions were to invariant theory and the axiomatization of Euclid's geometry. One of his other theories that was essential to functional analysis was named after him as the theory of Hilbert spaces. Tragically, he and a number of other brilliant academic mathematicians at the University of Göttingen were persecuted by the Nazis.

Benoit B. Mandelbrot (1924–2010) was a superb French-American mathematician whose name is associated with the mathematical idea of fractals. The word comes from the Latin *fractus*, which means broken. A fractal could be described as a rough or fragmented geometric shape that can be divided repeatedly into smaller and smaller parts. These smaller parts resemble — not always exactly — the original larger whole. This characteristic is described as self-similarity. Fractals play a large part in such varied sciences as soil chemistry, seismology, and medicine. After a lifetime dedicated to mathematics, Mandelbrot became the oldest professor at Yale. One of the great things about Mandelbrot's work was the way in which his fractals extend throughout nature. His demonstration of them appearing in natural environments in so many ways prompts the thoughtful reader to wonder about the extent to which fractals are numerological as well as scientifically mathematical.

Andrew Wiles, working at Princeton University in the 1990s, finally succeeded in proving Fermat's Last Theorem from the seventeenth century, stating that the equation $an+bn=cn$ will only be possible if n is not greater than 2. The gap of 300 years between its formulation and its proof emphasize the sequential nature of mathematical history. Contemporary mathematicians so often depend upon, and build upon, the work of their founding fathers.

3

HISTORY OF NUMEROLOGY

W hen we were distinguishing between mathematics and numerology in the first chapter, an important difference was that numerology was concerned with magical or mystical bonds between numbers and their environment. Certain significant numbers are believed by numerologists to have the power to make things happen or to predict what will happen to particular people in given circumstances at specific dates and times. The point was that numerologists believe that numbers have powers over, above, and beyond what might be termed their everyday use to calculate solutions using normal scientific mathematics. The earliest numerologists felt that, as potent as numbers were for solving calculation problems such as which army was likely to win a battle, how to build a stable pyramid, how much food was needed to feed a given population for a prescribed period, or how many days it would take to cover a given distance on foot, they could do other, stranger, more powerful things as well. Numerology parts company with scientific mathematics when numerologists argue that certain numbers are mysteriously influential, dominant, and predictive. Numbers, to a numerologist, are what spells and incantations are to a magician.

But how and when did these numerological beliefs begin?

There are expert historians and pre-historians who would argue that the history of numerology goes back to the ancient carvings found on bones and antlers as well as to the ancient drawings and paintings on cave walls. It is widely agreed by pre-historians that ancient cave drawings and paintings were often intended to act as a form of sympathetic magic: draw an edible animal being slain, and such an animal will be influenced by the magic in the painting to be available and vulnerable to the huntsmen on whose skill the tribal food supply depended. Were primitive attempts to use numbers cut into sticks, bones, and antlers an allied form of sympathetic magic? Did 3 notches mean that 3 animals were needed to feed the huntsman's family? Did 4 notches mean that they would be found in 4 days' time? Did 5 notches mean that the prey would be encountered after a 5 days' journey? This is pure speculation at this distance in time and culture from the hunter-gatherers who carved the notches, but it's a real possibility all the same.

The ancient systems of everyday mathematics — what we might term "ordinary" mathematics, used for simple, basic calculating — were examined in detail in the previous chapter. Very probably, those earliest counting and calculating systems had mysterious numerological purposes as well as scientific ones. Religion and magic seem to have played an integral part in human culture from the earliest prehistoric times, and on through the Stone Age, Bronze Age, and Iron Age. As early civilizations dawned there is evidence that something akin to modern numerology, something that might well have been the ancestor of contemporary numerology, originated in ancient Babylon and in ancient Egypt. The earliest Hebrew systems began in the same Chaldean area. Different versions of numerology were also being practised in Japan, China, and India. In addition, it was growing up and developing more complex and sophisticated forms in ancient Greece and Rome.

On the far side of the Atlantic, indigenous Americans like the Hopi people were exploring numerology for themselves and allocating significant values to numbers. It is particularly interesting that wise old Hopi elders, like Floyd Red Crow Westerman, who are expert numerologists, translate the 2012 date as "5" by adding its digits together, and in their system "5" signifies momentous change: the end of one era and the start of another. It is another interesting aspect of ancient Hopi numerology that there are 4 elements: earth, air, fire, and water, but there is another element — spirit — that transcends the other 4 and completes them.

In Norse mythology, numerology is recognizable because of the focus on magical numbers "3" and "9," and their product, "27," which is the cube of 3. There are, for example, 3 very different giant races: fire giants, frost giants, and mountain giants. The Norse universe began with 3 entities: the great cow, known as Audhumia; the primordial giant, Ymir; and Odin's grandfather, Buri, who was the first of the gods. A giant named Hrungnir had a stone heart that was 3-sided, and it is noteworthy in this context that the valknut symbol consists of 3 interlocking triangles with 9 corners. The name *valknut* means "The Knot of the Dead" and the symbol was carried by warriors as a talisman — those devoted to Odin who died bravely in battle would be taken to Valhalla, the paradise of Norse warriors.

The great world tree Yggdrasil has 3 roots and joins 9 worlds together. There are 3 holy wells under Yggdrasil's roots. The dreaded wolf, Fenrir (or Fenris), was secured with 3 chains, but only the final one held. Gullveig is killed 3 times and reborn 3 times. Ragnarok is heralded by the crowing of 3 cockerels: 1 for the gods, 1 for the dead, and 1 for the giants. The rainbow bridge, known as *Bifrost*, has 3 colours and 3 names. Nine magical charms were given to Svipdag by his mother, the enchantress Groa, and 9 beautiful maidens sit at the knees of Menglod. It is also significant that Aegir has 9 daughters. There are 9 locks securing the chest that belongs to Laegjarn. In another piece of Norse mythology, one of the magical fires can be lit only if 9 different types of wood are used. Thrivaldi was a giant with 9 heads.

The ancient Egyptians had a profound influence on the history of numerology. The Egyptian goddess Seshat had 2 major attributes. She was revered firstly as the inspirer of writings, and seen from this perspective as a sort of divine archivist. She was also honoured as a kind of instructor-goddess of building and construction. Numbers were another vital part of her work, which led to her being given the title of "the Enumerator."

To get inside ancient Egyptian thought, it is necessary to look at everything in the universe from the point of view that it is alive and animated. Objective twenty-first-century science has the underlying assumption that when we work in a laboratory with sulphur, lithium, magnesium, bromine, and chlorine, we are working with something dead or inanimate. Egyptian thinkers did not look at their environment that way 5,000 years ago. They might not have been familiar with the term *animism*, as such, but they still subscribed to the idea that everything in their environment was impregnated with living forces, and that such forces energized it and gave it its characteristics.

On this basic concept of an animated universe, the Egyptians based their numerology — their magical and mysterious ideas about numbers. For them, numbers were not mere quantities, or units of fruit, vegetables, and meat. Numbers were *more* than the length of a line or the area of a pyramid's base. Numbers were *more* than measurements of the volume of corn stored in a granary (thanks to Joseph's inspiration and prudence). Numbers were expressions of the world around them and the animated spirit that it contained. If a waterfall was seen as alive and powerful, numbers expressed its power in terms of the volume of water that roared down it. The plunging of a war-horse; the spinning wheels of a chariot; the great block of stone being dragged by sweating slaves: these were all *alive*. These were *animated*. Numbers could clothe objects and events and make them more comprehensible. Numbers — in the hands of a skilled numerologist — could actually *control* the environment.

For the ancient Egyptians, numbers had personalities. They were as alive and as powerful as the objects they measured and quantified. They were male and female, not neutral.

Plutarch (45–120 AD) had very interesting comments to make on this idea of gender in the natural and mathematical universes. Born at Chaeronea in Boeotia, in the centre of Greece, he studied in Athens and then moved to Rome as a teacher of philosophy. Both Trajan and Hadrian liked and admired him. In his work, *Moralia: Volume Five*, Plutarch referred to the genders of the parts of a 90-degree triangle. The "3, 4, 5" triangle was an essential part of Egyptian design and measurement. Plutarch said that the base of a right-angled triangle was female; the upright that formed the 90-degree angle against the female base was masculine, and the hypotenuse — greater than either of its parents — was the son or daughter of the 2 shorter sides. Plutarch incorporated the Egyptian legend of Isis, Osiris, and their son, Horus, into his 90-degree triangle thinking. Isis was the horizontal base of the triangle, Osiris was its upright. Their great son, Horus, the hypotenuse, avenged his noble father's death by destroying the evil god, Set.

One famous old Egyptian numerological papyrus, dating from nearly 4,000 years ago, declares that it contains methods for inquiring into "everything that exists: all mysteries and all secrets." This passage sums up the amount of faith the ancient Egyptians had in the power of numbers. The Leiden Papyrus was procured by the Leiden Museum

The Norse Valknut symbol

of Antiquities in 1829 from J. d'Anastasy. It confirms the major importance of numbers and numerology for the Egyptians of its time. The
27 stanzas within this papyrus are numbered from 1–9 as units, then
from 10–90, and finally from 100–900. The 3 groups of 9 thus cover all
27 stanzas.

The designs of Egyptian temples and pyramids were all dependent on the Egyptian numbering system and, most importantly to the
ancient Egyptians, on the numbers "3," "9," and "27." In accordance
with the numerological elements of the early Egyptian belief systems,
each number had a magical power or mystical significance.

Just as "3," "9," and "27" were milestones in the history of numerology as far the ancient Egyptians were concerned, "7" was of more
significance to the ancient peoples of the Middle East. "Seven" is frequently encountered in the *Epic of Gilgamesh*. Gilgamesh was the fifth
king of Uruk, which is modern-day Iraq, and according to some of the
ancient chronicles such as the Sumerian King List, he reigned there
for more than a century. His father was a semi-deified king named
Lugalbanda; his mother was the goddess Rimat Ninsun. Such ancestry
gave Gilgamesh tremendous physical strength and qualified him as a
demigod. In Gilgamesh's story there is a gate with 7 bolts, and 7 mountains have to be climbed on the way to the Cedar Forest. Gilgamesh
then cuts down 7 of the great cedars to reach the lair of their guardian,
the fearsome giant Humbaba, whom he tricks with 7 gifts (including his
sisters, as wife and concubine) before decapitating the giant. Gilgamesh
also meets the wise old sage, Utnapishtim, the Babylonian equivalent of
Noah, and stays with him for 7 nights. In the account of the flood that
Utnapishtim survived, the waters subsided on the seventh day.

There are scholars who would argue that the ancient Chaldean
systems of numerology are, in fact, the oldest of all. Its extreme is
disguised to some extent by the comparative secrecy in which it was
kept for millennia. Chaldean numerology assigned meanings to the
various numbers, beginning with "0." To them, the "0" represented
nothing and everything because in their mystical thinking everything began from nothing. It is the symbol of all potential things.

Ancient Middle Eastern winged figure

For the Chaldean experts, the number "1" was masculine. It stood for independence, individuality, aggression, and dominance. There were also aspects of creativity and originality associated with "1." "Two" represents the female aspect: cooperation, adaptability, understanding, tact, gentleness, and caution. "Three" represents expansion and development. It is the number of communication and diversification. The number "4" in the Chaldean system represents the 4 seasons and the virtues of control and self-discipline. "Four" is stable and enduring. "Five," by complete contrast, stands for adventure, travel, freedom, and versatility. "Five" means change. "Six" is an excellent number. It is associated with teaching, counselling, healing, and loving. The number "7" is philosophical and metaphysical. It looks for the deep eternal answers to the great questions of the universe. "Eight" is an authoritarian symbol: it quests for power and control over the environment and other people. In the Chaldean system, "9" is regarded as the ruler of all the other numbers except for the originating "0." "Nine" is the symbol of patience, tolerance, universality, and compassion. The number "11" was of great importance in the old Chaldean system of numerology. Does that mean that the Basques, who also have the highest regard for "11," may have come from the ancient Chaldean peoples? In the Chaldean system, "11" was thought of as the number of light. It is the number of wisdom and the wise. "Eleven" represents altruism, inventiveness, and tremendous strength of both mind and body.

There are also very interesting historical connections between the old Chaldean system outlined above and the ancient African system, which could very well be of similar age. Brought to America in the days of the slave trade, and carefully researched by academic African Americans in our own time, this African numerology resembles its Chaldean counterpart in some aspects, but differs from it significantly in others. In the old African system, "0" is thought of as the origin of everything else. It is considered a representation of God. The "1" is, again, male, and the "2" is female, just as in the Chaldean system. "Three" is also the number of creativity and growth. In the African system, "4" symbolizes the entire universe, having 4 corners or quadrants. It also represents the 4 stages of human life: conception, birth, existence, and death. Whereas the Chaldean "5" stood for change and resourcefulness, in the African system, "5" symbolizes religion and groups of the faithful. It also represents a combination of femininity ("2") and creation ("3"), as well as family and tribal life. "Six" symbolizes something very similar in the African system, so "5" and "6" can almost be taken together in terms of meaning. If they are, of course, they create the all-powerful and highly desirable "11." In the African system, "7" symbolizes deep thought, spirituality, and philosophy. This is closely comparable to the Chaldean meaning of "7" as the symbol of truth-seeking. In the Chaldean system, "8" stood for power and control. In the African system, it represents balance, poise, and equilibrium. For the ancient African numerologist, "9" is the symbol of nature, whereas in the Chaldean code it ruled over all the other numbers except for the "0." The Chaldean "9" meant patience, tolerance, and compassion. In the ancient African system of numerology, "10" is the perfect number. It brings together the "1" of man and the "0" of God. It unites humanity and divinity.

The ancient Japanese numerology was especially focused on "3," "5," and "7." Children younger than 3 had their heads shaved or had very short haircuts. At age 3 they were allowed to grow hair. Five-year-old boys were permitted to wear a *hakama* for the first time. When girls reached the age of 7 they were allowed to fasten their *kimonos* with an *obi*. At ages 3, 5, and 7 children were taken to a shrine to pray for long life, good health, and to be protected against evil spirits.

Chinese numerology differed from most other systems because it was a homophonic system, meaning the *sound* of the number, when spoken aloud, gave it its significance. In Chinese symbolism, "2" was a good, helpful, and lucky number because the sound of "2" in Cantonese was a homophone for the word *easy*. The favoured number "2," therefore, made difficult tasks easy to perform. "Three," in Chinese, sounds like the word for birth, so "3" is also considered a good, positive symbol in the old Chinese system. "Six" represented liquid, or fluidity, because of its homophonic partner in Mandarin. This meant it was a good number for business. In Cantonese, the same sound meant a blessing, so that also brought good luck. "Seven" is favoured among many systems of numerology, and the Chinese system, at this juncture, falls in with the majority. "Seven" symbolizes togetherness, friendship, and a happy community. "Eight" represents wealth and great prosperity. It is particularly interesting to note that a famous international banker has a string of "8"s as a telephone number. This seems to work well and bring prosperity. Chinese and Asian clients are especially keen to use this bank's services. In the ancient Chinese system, the number "9" was always associated with the Emperor. His robes were decorated with 9 dragons, and in the old mythology, the dragon had 9 children. "Nine," in the Chinese system, also symbolizes endurance and length of time, so it is conventionally used at weddings. As well as all these good and positive numerical homophonic associations, there are some negative ones. "Four" is avoided scrupulously, for example, because it sounds like the word for death.

There is a tradition that the first so-called "magic square" appeared in China about 4,000 years ago. In the legend it appeared on the shell of a turtle that had been sent by the river god to assist the emperor. The essence of these numerological magic squares is that all the columns and rows in the square, as well as the diagonals, add up to the same number. Chinese traders who visited India with spices also seem to have carried numerological concepts with them. According to the form of numerology that developed in India, every person is endowed with 3 numbers. The first of these is the psychic number, which is related to the person's date of birth. Anyone born on a date from the first to the ninth day of a month has a psychic number between 1 and 9. Someone born on the fifteenth of the month, for example, has a psychic number of "6" (1+5). A birth date on the twenty-ninth works in 2 stages: first, the numerals in the number 29 are added together (2+9=11), then, the numerals from whatever the sum of the first equation was, are added together (1+1=2).

The next number is referred to as the person's destiny number. This is found by adding the sum of the numerals for the year of their birth to the sum of the numerals for the day and month of their birth. For instance, co-author Lionel was born on 9/2/1935. Since the numerals for the day and month (9 and 2), are singular, we leave them as is. The year, however, needs to be calculated into a number below 10 using the reduction method we have previously demonstrated. So, first we add together the 4 numerals of the year (1+9+3+5), which comes to the sum of 18. We then add together the numerals of this sum, 18, which equals 9 (1+8). We now can add the 9 (representing the year of Lionel's birth) to the numerals representing his day and month of birth: 9 (day)+2 (month)+9 (year)=20. Finally, we add together the numerals of the sum 20 (2+0). This comes to 2, whereas his psychic number is "9." The destiny number refers to the way that other people see you, whereas the psychic number represents who you actually are. The third number, known as the name number, is rather more complicated.

There are several ways in which the name number can be calculated. The simplest and best known technique is to use a number for each letter, but different numerologists would tend to allocate different numbers. One school of numerologists might say: A=1, B=2, C=3, and so on until I=9; but that would mean J=10, so the reduction of 10 (1+0) reverts to "1" again, like the "A." The next letter, "K," becomes "11," which is reduced to "2" — the same number as allocated to the letter "B." There are also complications about which name the person prefers, and which name he or she is best known by. This again distinguishes between the introspective self and the public self. In some systems the capital letter with which the name begins may be allocated additional weight and numerical value. Therefore, 2 equally well-qualified and experienced numerologists working with slightly different systems could reach very different conclusions.

In the sixteenth century, Albrecht Dürer (1471–1528), the mathematician, painter, and engraver, brought the old Chinese art of magic-square-making to its zenith. In his engraving entitled *Melancholia*, which he completed in 1514, there is a magic square in the top right-hand corner. The theme of the engraving is a proto-scientist, an alchemist in all probability, who is surrounded by unused equipment. His posture and the position of his head suggest that he is deep in melancholic thought.

16	3	2	13
5	10	11	8
9	6	7	12
4	15	14	1

The magic square that he has created contains each of the numbers from 1–16. When added vertically, horizontally, or diagonally, they total 34. This has the numerological significance of "7," which is found by adding the numerals of the sum 34 together (3+4). Each of the 4 corners adds to make 34 as well, as do the 4 centre squares. Dürer has even managed to incorporate the date of his work, 1514, by placing the numbers "15" and "14" together at the bottom of his magic square. It is a truly amazing piece of numerology.

Basque numerology has significant contributions to make to the general history of the subject. Their language is not related to the old Indo-European, and their ancient origins are the subject of much speculation. Were the Basque people the original inhabitants of Europe prior to the arrival of the Indo-European peoples? Or were they from Chaldea? Interestingly, "11" has special significance in the Chaldean system. The Basques were certainly written about in Roman times. There are numerological references that suggest that the number "11" was of great significance in Basque numerology. In the Basque language, "11" is *hamaika*; "7" is *hazpi*, and "3" is *hiru*. Their interest in "11" as having special numerological significance relates to "11" being the first number that cannot be counted with the hands alone. In the sequence of prime numbers, it is the fifth: 2, 3, 5, 7, *11*. There are some very strange calculations connected with the number "11." For example, to check whether a number is exactly divisible by 11, add every alternate digit, then add the remaining digits and subtract one total from the other. If the answer is "0," or a multiple of 11, the large number will divide by 11.

For example, consider 2,592,821. Consider the equation 2+9+8+1=20 followed by 5+2+2=9. Subtract 9 from 20, resulting in 11. This reveals that the large number 2,592,821 is divisible by 11. When the division is done, the answer is 2,592,821÷11=235,711 — an answer that consists of the first 5 prime numbers.

A polygon with 11 sides is called an "undecagon" or a "hendecagon," and has special significance for numerologists. A regular hendecagon can have a spindle placed through its centre, so that it can be used as a spinner — the equivalent of a miniature roulette wheel. The numbers 1–9 are marked on 9 of its sides, and two extra "1"s fill the last 2 sides to represent "11." When the undecagon settles on any of the "1"s it is considered to be very positive and to bring good fortune to the person who spun it. If this occurs on 3 consecutive occasions, it is thought to bring either great fortune or deep and lasting romantic fulfilment.

There are points throughout the history of numerology at which numerology blends into general magic involving spells and charms: so many movements of the hands, so many repetitions of an incantation, so many portions of each ingredient, the dates and times at which the spell can be enacted with the greatest likelihood of success. The same is true of the interaction between alchemy and numerology: for the alchemical processes to work, the alchemist believed that a particular blend of ingredients had to be assembled, and that the numbers of each, and the temperatures reached, were all significant for the work.

The history of numerology, with its global ramifications and its intertwining with scientific mathematics, is a difficult path to follow, but it can be summed up as the route that perceptive and thoughtful numerologists have followed in order to reach the interesting forms of numerology that are practised today.

4
THE MYSTERIOUS FIBONACCI NUMBERS AND THE GOLDEN MEAN

Two of the most intriguing sets of numbers that are of interest to scientific mathematicians as well as numerologists are the Fibonacci numbers and the golden mean, which are closely bonded to one another.

The brilliant Italian mathematician and numerologist generally known as Fibonacci was born in 1170 and died at the age of 80 in 1250. His full name was Leonardo Pisano Bigollo, and he was referred to by a few different names, including Leonardo of Pisa, Leonardo Fibonacci, and Leonardo Bonacci. Historians of numerology and mathematics regard him as the outstanding genius of the Middle Ages in those allied fields.

Fibonacci's father, Guglielmo Fibonacci, was a very prosperous Italian merchant who was in charge of a busy trading post in Bugia, which was then a port belonging to the Almohad Sultanate in what is now Algeria. Bugia is currently known as Bejaia. As a youngster, Fibonacci travelled with his father to assist him with the demanding work of the trading post, and in the process, the young and gifted mathematician learned all about the numerals used by Hindus and

Arabians. He saw almost immediately that these were much easier to manipulate than the Roman numerals that he had grown up with in Italy.

Captivated by the relative ease and simplicity of using the Hindu-Arabic numerals, young Fibonacci went in search of the top mathematicians and numerologists in the whole of the Mediterranean area. In his early 30s he came back from these extensive study-travels and set down his findings in an exceptionally important mathematics textbook called *Liber Abaci*, which translates as "*The Book of Calculations*." It was largely due to the circulation of Fibonacci's treatise that the Hindu-Arabic numerals spread all over Europe. This was close to the start of the thirteenth century.

Scholars and academics such as Fibonacci depended on the sponsorship of friendly and enlightened rulers like the Emperor Frederick II, who was himself interested in numerology, mathematics, and science. Frederick and Fibonacci became friends and Fibonacci lived as Frederick's guest for some time. When he was 70, Fibonacci was honoured with a salary given to him by the Republic of Pisa and a statue to him was erected during the nineteenth century: a fitting tribute to an outstanding mathematician and numerologist.

Indian mathematicians had already devised the mysterious series of numbers that bears Fibonacci's name as early as the sixth century, but it was his popularizing of it in the twelfth century that made it widely known to numerologists and mathematicians in Europe. In his book, *Liber Abaci*, Fibonacci created and then solved a mathematical problem involving an imaginary population of rabbits. What Fibonacci came up with was a series of numbers for succeeding generations of his imaginary rabbits, which was created by starting with 0, followed by 1. Each subsequent number is found by adding its 2 predecessors together. This gives the start of the Fibonacci numbers as: 0, 1, 1, 2, 3, 5, 8, 13, 21, 34, 55, 89, 144, 233, 377, 610, 987, 1597, 2584, 4181 … and so on.

There is an equally important and closely allied series, which is referred to as the Lucas Numbers. These were the work of Edouard Lucas (1842–1891), a brilliant French mathematician, who is probably best remembered for inventing his Tower of Hanoi puzzle, consisting of 3 columns and discs of varying sizes that have to be moved from 1 column to another while observing the rules of the game, which are that only 1 disc may be moved at a time and no disc may ever be placed on top of a smaller disc. He observed the Fibonacci principle of adding 2 preceding numbers to obtain the next number in the sequence. However, where Fibonacci started with 0, 1, 1, 2, 3, 5, and so on, Lucas began with "2" followed by "1," then "3," then "4," "7," "11," "18," and so on. When 2 consecutive Lucas numbers are divided they will also give φ, or its reciprocal. Just as with the Fibonacci series, the higher up in the series the numbers are, the more closely will their divisions approximate to the φ ratio and its reciprocal. The Greek letter φ (*phi*) is the twenty-first letter of the Greek alphabet, and is used in the same way as π (*pi*), the sixteenth letter, to express an irrational number such as 1.6180339 ... or 3.1416....

The Fibonacci series has a very close link with the equally mysterious ratio represented by the Greek letter phi. This ratio can be written as 1.61803398874.... Geometrically, it refers to 3 lines, which are divided so that the ratio of the full line to the longer of its 2 sections is the same as the ratio of the longer section to the shorter section.

_____Whole line *A*

_____Longer section *B*

Shorter section *C*   _____

The ratio of *A* to *B* is the same as the ratio of *B* to *C*.

That ratio is φ which is 1.61803398874 ...

This ratio has been used for centuries in art, architecture, and design work. It has even been found in some musical compositions.

Phi (φ) can be found by dividing 2 adjacent Fibonacci numbers. The higher up the Fibonacci series we go, the closer the result is to φ.

$8 \div 5 = 1.6$

$13 \div 8 = 1.625$

$21 \div 13 = 1.61538$

$34 \div 21 = 1.619$

$4181 \div 2584 = 1.618034$

This can also be expressed algebraically: $a+b$ divided by $a=a$, divided by $b=\phi$.

The expression $1+\sqrt{5}$, all divided by 2, also gives ϕ.

The choice of the Greek letter ϕ to represent this very important mathematical ratio was the work of Mark Barr, the American mathematician, who thought it would be appropriate as it was the first letter in the name of Phidias in Greek, and Phidias was a brilliant sculptor from the fifth century BC. Barr almost certainly had in mind that Phidias's outstanding work owed its beauty and balance to his use of the golden mean.

Mario Livio, an outstanding astrophysicist, has written in depth about the mysterious ϕ and has commented that some of the greatest mathematicians of history have been fascinated by it for millennia.

Johannes Kepler (1571–1630), the great German astronomer and mathematician, was extremely interested in ϕ, and in our present century it has attracted the attention of the brilliant award-winning mathematician, physicist, and astronomer, Sir Roger Penrose.

Interesting examples of painters' and designers' use of ϕ can be seen in many places, one of which is Georges Pierre Seurat's *The Parade*, in which ϕ dominates the picture. Seurat was born in 1859 and died in 1891. Along with his fascination with ϕ, he was famous for his development of a technique known as "pointillism" or "divisionism," which grouped small dots of colour to create very effective impacts on viewers of his paintings.

Another clear example of the ϕ ratio in artwork is *The Baptism of Christ* by Piero della Francesca (1415–1492), who was also a mathematician, numerologist, and geometer. He employed the golden mean extensively in his picture *The Baptism of Christ*. Another of his great paintings that involves the use of the ϕ ratio is called *The Legend of the True Cross*, which resides in the Church of San Francesco in Arezzo, Tuscany.

Nicolas Poussin (1594–1665) painted his famous *The Shepherds of Arcadia*, depicting 3 shepherds and a shepherdess beside a tomb, on which one of the shepherds is tracing out the inscription "*Et in*

Arcadia ego." Various art experts have analyzed this curious composition and concluded that it is based on Poussin's expert knowledge of geometry and numerology. If the shepherd's staff is regarded as a key measurement, various sophisticated geometric features are revealed — including the Golden Section with its φ ratio. Another interesting feature is that the dimensions of the tomb in the painting — an exact replica of which once stood at Arques near Rennes-le-Château — also approximate to the golden mean.

Another aspect of the Rennes-le-Château mystery connects with a pentagonal pattern of landmarks in the area around the village. The golden mean can also be associated with the pentagon.

The line XQ is the same length as one of the sides of the regular pentagon U, V, W, X, Y. Begin by joining XU. Mark the point Q along the line XU so that XQ is the length of a side. Then from the point Q draw a line at 90 degrees that is half the length of XQ. Join the point X to this new point R to form a 90-degree triangle — XQR. Place the point of the compass on R and draw an arc with the radius RQ intersecting XR at a new point, S. Place the point of the compass on X and draw an arc with radius XS so that it intersects XQ at the new point T. This has now made the Golden Section along the line XQ. The ratio of the length

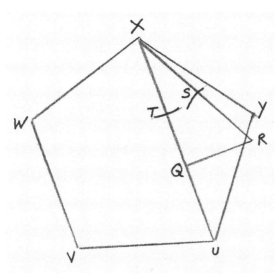

Pentagon diagram

TQ (the shorter part) to *XT* (the longer part) is the same as the ratio of *XT* to *XU*. In both cases, the longer line divided by the shorter line produces ɸ, which is 1.61803398874…. Dividing the shorter length by the greater length produces 0.618033989 … which is the reciprocal of ɸ.

Poussin's involvement in the Rennes-le-Château mystery of Father Bérenger Saunière's control of inexplicable wealth at the end of the nineteenth century may tie in with some coded numerological messages that the painter hid in *The Shepherds of Arcadia*, and, perhaps, in some of his other paintings as well. Art experts who are also familiar with the scenery in and around Rennes-le-Château have suggested that the background to *The Shepherds of Arcadia* is the range of hills near Rennes-le-Château. There is a technique known as "taking back bearings," which orienteers and other outdoor adventurers are familiar with. Standing on a spot, which the observer wishes to identify, a bearing is taken of a clear, distant landmark such as a mountain peak. A second bearing is taken in a different direction by looking at another prominent landmark. Tracing those back-bearings on a map will show the observer the point at which he is standing. It has been theorized that the Rennes-le-Château treasure is buried at a point that can be located by tracing the back-bearings from the mountain scenery in 2 of Poussin's canvases. One is almost certainly *The Shepherds of Arcadia*. The other is possibly Poussin's 1648 canvas entitled *Landscape with a Man Washing His Feet at a Fountain*. Could the background mountain ranges in both canvases indicate back-bearings that would lead the treasure hunter to a very significant location near Rennes-le-Château?

At Shugborough Hall in England there is a carved copy of the tomb from Poussin's painting of the shepherds, and this bears a short but mystifying inscription. Shugborough was, at one time, the property of the immensely wealthy Anson family. The letters on the Shugborough memorial are:

O.U.O.S.V.A.V.V.

D. M.

Despite numerous interesting possibilities, this code has never been satisfactorily or definitively deciphered. However, this mysterious

Shugborough code may be accessible to a numerological approach. To the best of our knowledge this has not yet been attempted.

Exploring the English alphabet with its numerological values, we get:

A=1

B=2

C=3

D=4

E=5

F=6

G=7

H=8

I=9

J=10=1+0=1

K=11=1+1=2

L=12=1+2=3

And so on up to Z=26=2+6=8

If we apply the numerical values to each number in this inscription, starting with the "D" on the lower line, we get:

O.U.O.S.V.A.V.V.

D. M.

4+6+3+6+1+4+1+4+4+4=37=3+7=10=1+0=1

The "1" is particularly significant as it suggests that the entire code indicates a strong, independent, and energetic leader, a pioneer, and an outstanding achiever.

Could this coded reference then indicate Admiral Anson of Shugborough? Is the code saying that Anson possessed some great secret — perhaps hidden treasure — and the code, when analyzed in depth, could indicate where that treasure is concealed?

George Anson (1697–1762) went to sea at the age of 14 and became a naval lieutenant in 1716. He later commanded his own warships and circumnavigated the world. After many hardships and desperate battles, he eventually sailed home with treasure that was almost too valuable to count accurately! Although after coming home from the sea, he lived mainly in Hertfordshire, he was also a frequent visitor to Shugborough. He could easily have been the "1" of the secret code on the Shepherd Memorial there.

Poussin was certainly a party to some deep and sinister secrets, which he shared with Nicolas Fouquet, Superintendent of Finance in France from 1653 until 1661, and Nicolas's younger brother, Louis. A letter written by Louis to Nicolas is still in existence. Part of it reads:

> I have given to Monsieur Poussin the letter that you were kind enough to write to him; he displayed over-whelming joy on receiving it. You wouldn't believe, sir, the trouble that he takes to be of service to you, or the affection with which he goes about this, or the talent and integrity that he displays at all times. He and I have planned certain things of which in a little while I shall be able to inform you fully; things which will give you, through M. Poussin, advantages which kings would have great difficulty in obtaining from him and which, according to what he says, no-one in the world will ever retrieve in the centuries to come; and furthermore, it would be achieved without much expense and could even turn to profit, and they are matters so difficult to enquire into that nothing on Earth at the present time could bring a greater fortune nor perhaps ever its equal.

Was this mysterious secret that Poussin controlled a *numerological* secret like the geometrical secret that he hid in *The Shepherds of Arcadia*?

There is a further layer to this mystery involving the Fouquet brothers and Nicolas Poussin. When Fouquet senior fell from power as a result of Colbert's plotting against him, there is a possibility that Fouquet became the Man in the Iron Mask. Suppose that there was a standoff between Fouquet and King Louis XIV? If Fouquet had some secret that the king desperately wanted, Louis XIV could hardly kill him. If he did, the all-important secret would die with him. If it was Fouquet who was imprisoned in an iron mask in the custody of King

Louis's trusted jailer, Bénigne Dauvergne de Saint-Mars, it was essential from the king's point of view that Fouquet could not communicate the vital secret to anyone. Regulations surrounding the masked prisoner were particularly strict. Fouquet also knew perfectly well that if he gave in and revealed his secret to the king, he would be executed to silence him. Poussin, Fouquet, Louis XIV: what did they all know that was so valuable and so secret? Could that strange numerological secret have gone all the way back to ancient Greece?

One of the earliest and most famous examples of the use of the golden mean expressed in the ratio of φ — the Parthenon in Athens — is renowned throughout the world. Built during the fifth century BC as a temple to the goddess Athena, it comprises a series of Golden Rectangles based on φ. The particular use of golden mean rectangles in this sacred building suggests a numerological significance as well as an architectural one. What does "5" signify numerologically? Activity, energy, freedom, adventure, and constant movement and change.

The Parthenon

The goddess Athena, also known as Pallas Athena, is the goddess of courage, wisdom, and skill. Also known as Minerva to the Romans, she was their goddess of justice, strength, and strategy, and was an inspirer of heroes. Wisdom, which is one of her greatest attributes, includes the mysteries of mathematics and the strange secrets of numerology. She is traditionally associated with the owl, the bird of wisdom, and some numerologists would associate the owl with the number "7" as indicative of wisdom and thoughtfulness.

The Golden Section ratio φ was very important to early Greek mathematicians and numerologists because it featured prominently in pentagrams and pentagons. Pythagoras and his followers most certainly gave it a great deal of attention. The pentagram with a pentagon inside it was their Pythagorean symbol. Euclid's book, *The Elements*, contains what may well be the earliest description of the golden ratio in words. In describing it, he said that the golden ratio was found when the whole of a line to its greater segment was the same as the relationship of the greater segment to the lesser segment. Some of the proofs that Euclid used in *The Elements* reveal that the golden mean φ is an irrational number — a number that cannot be expressed as a fraction with 1 integer above another.

Michael Maestlin (1550–1631) worked out a decimalized approximation for the reciprocal of φ in 1597 and came up with 0.618034. This was incredibly close. Maestlin worked at the University of Tübingen and his calculations appeared in a letter to Kepler, who had been one of his students.

Le Corbusier, the Swiss-born French architect, whose real name was Charles-Édouard Jeanneret (1887–1965), produced magnificent buildings, often based on the harmonies and proportions of the golden mean and the Fibonacci numbers. He is quoted as saying that the rhythms of the golden mean and the Fibonacci series were at the "very root of human activities." He felt that there was a great inherent mystery in them which placed them somehow in the minds of "children, old men, savages and the learned" — a point of view that many numerologists would share.

The outstandingly brilliant Leonardo da Vinci (1452–1519) was well aware of the golden mean and the Fibonacci series. His amazing picture of the so-called Vitruvian Man testifies to this. Named after the old Roman architect Vitruvius (80 BC–15 BC), the 2 superimposed human figures in the drawing are in perfect artistic proportion. Le Corbusier was a great admirer of da Vinci's work and seems to have modelled some of his finest architecture on da Vinci's principles.

Prince Matila Ghyka (1881–1965) influenced Salvador Dali, who undoubtedly used the golden ratio in his superb work *The Sacrament of the Last Supper*. There is a vast dodecahedron behind the central figures and its edges are in golden ratio to one another.

Over and above the works of these artists and architects, the psychology of the golden mean attracted the attention of Gustav Theodor Fechner (1801–1887), the pioneering German experimental psychologist. Fechner wanted to find out whether the Golden Section was correlated with the human ideas of what constituted beauty. His research concluded that there was a distinct preference for rectangles that were built on the golden mean.

Musicians and advanced music theorists like James Tenney (1934–2006) applied the numerical theories of the golden mean and the Fibonacci series to their musical compositions with striking results. Musicologist Roy Howat, who is also an excellent pianist, has found musical pieces that correspond to the golden mean.

The golden mean and the Fibonacci series are among the most intriguing mysteries of mathematics and numerology. They even overflow into the flora and fauna of the Earth's biosphere, which are the subject of the next chapter. Nature, it seems, is the product of special numbers and special numerical sequences.

5
NUMBERS IN FLORA AND FAUNA

One of the strangest things about the power of numbers, as disclosed by both scientific mathematics and the mysteries of numerology, is their persistence throughout the biosphere. Animals, plants, fungi, and insects — in fact, *all* life forms — are surprisingly and persistently numerical. Why is there this persistent correlation between numbers and the multitude of organisms, from whales to bacteria, that fill the biosphere along with us? The component parts of most of these living things have inexplicable numerical sequences. They often line up with the Fibonacci series and with φ. What have life and mathematics and numerology to do with one another? It all seems to make numerology far more viable and significant. It raises the major question, yet again: is the mind of the Creator the mind of a mathematician?

Adolf Zeising (1810–1876) was a remarkable German psychologist, mathematician, and philosopher, who was convinced that he could trace the mathematical principles of φ and the golden ratio in plant stems and the arrangements of veins in their leaves. He pursued his research into animal skeleton formations and other zoological details such as the cardiovascular system, arteries, veins, neurones, and the lymph system. He also looked into the shapes and relative sizes of crystals, and he applied his favourite mathematical theories to chemical compounds. Wherever Zeising looked, he found indications of ɸ. For him, the golden ratio was a kind of universal law that he claimed he could detect in every phenomenon in the universe. Zeising didn't just find significant number series in living organisms — he found them everywhere. In his view, the Fibonacci mystery permeated everything: organic and inorganic, acoustic and optical, forms and structures, movements and perspectives — and it found its ultimate perfection in human beings. Zeising can be thought of as the ultimate numerologist in terms of his belief in the power and ubiquity of numbers and number patterns. A great many examples are there to be examined.

Take the case of a hardy, drought-tolerant plant, usually called by the popular name of sneezewort (*achillea ptarmica*). It is also known as "fair-maid-of-France," "white tansy," "wild pellitory," and "goose tongue." It blooms through June until August and provides the researcher with a particularly clear example of the Fibonacci series of numbers. The sneezewort produces its growing points in the Fibonacci sequence, and these can clearly be observed: none to start with, then 1, then another, then 2, 3 … and so on.

Daisy petals

70

In addition to the Fibonacci numbers of growing points on plants, such as the sneezewort, the series occurs again when petals are counted.

Daisies can have as many as 89 petals, although 55 and 34 are more usual totals. All 3 of these totals are Fibonacci numbers. Buttercups are members of the *ranunculaceae* family — an interesting name that comes from the Latin for "little frog," which has about 1,700 species worldwide. Buttercups produce 5 petals, "5" being a member of the Fibonacci series, and so do pinks, larkspurs, columbines, and wild roses. This fundamental link between plants and the Fibonacci numbers continues powerfully with many additional examples. The iris and the lily have 3 petals. Delphiniums have 8. Asters have 21 and corn marigolds have 13, as do cineraria. When the Lucas numbers are accepted as a parallel series, very similar in principle to the Fibonacci numbers, the fuchsia can be included with its 4 petals because 4 fits the Lucas series: 2,1,3,4,7,11.... Asters and chicory have 21 petals; plantains and pyrethrum have 34. Rose petal formations also comply with the Fibonacci numbers.

The technical botanical term *phyllotaxis*, also rendered as *phyllotaxy*, refers to the way that leaves are arranged on the stem of a plant. The word was coined in 1754 by a Swiss naturalist named Charles Bonnet (1720–1793). He derived it from 2 ancient Greek terms: *phyllon*, meaning a leaf, and *taxis*, meaning the way that things are arranged, set out, and displayed. A few years later, other naturalists discovered that each new leaf on a plant is set at a particular angle (137.5 degrees) from the one that preceded it. This is called the "angle of divergence." It can also be described as the fraction of a circle differentiating a new leaf from its immediate predecessor. When the 137.5-degree angle is calculated, it turns out to be in the ratio of $1 \div \phi$, and this leads straight back to our Fibonacci series and the golden mean: 1.618033 and its reciprocal 0.618033.

The spirals in a pinecone are designed according to Fibonacci numbers, and sunflowers are especially geared to the series. Some have 34 spirals, some have 55, and others have as many as 89.

Other Fibonacci phenomena can be seen when studying broccoli and cauliflowers. When the spirals are counted on a ripe cauliflower, the Fibonacci number "5" can be detected. There are 13 spirals (another Fibonacci number) on Romanesque broccoli. A slice through a banana reveals 3 sections; a slice through an apple shows 5. The Fibonacci numbers are there again.

The *echinocactus grusonii* cactus fits in well with the Lucas series and displays 29 ribs to the world. Best known by its popular name of the "golden ball," or "golden barrel," it grows in central Mexico.

These Lucas- and Fibonacci-based numbers in living things, however, are not confined to plant life such as cacti, cauliflowers, and broccoli — far from it. Other examples are found in natural spirals, such as those of snails.

Theoretically, there is no limit to the size of this spiral. It could fill anything from a galaxy to a garden trowel. Each new square will have a side that is the same length as the 2 previous sides added to each other — the construction technique for the Fibonacci series. If we now consider

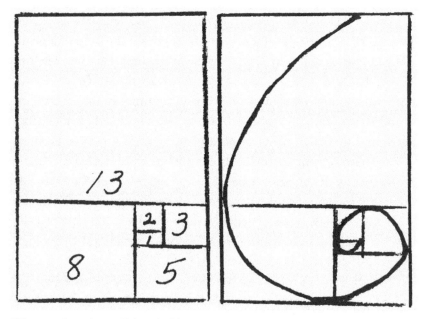

Fibonacci and snail's shell

the importance of φ and apply it to the spiral constructed from the Fibonacci-sided squares, it becomes clear that every quarter-turn of the spiral has rotated in such a way that each line drawn from the spiral to its centre will be approximately 1.618 times longer than its predecessor. The humble little garden snail is not alone in possessing a Fibonacci-based spiral shell: a great many other shells exhibit it both on land and sea. There has been some controversy between naturalists, mathematicians, and numerologists over the exactness of this coordination between spiral shell measurements and the Fibonacci series. Nautilus seashells seem to vary between about 1.9 and 1.6, nevertheless they seem to come close enough to φ to be worth serious consideration. But how powerfully, and how consistently, does nature conform to the Fibonacci series and the mysterious golden mean? And what does that conformity imply about mathematical structures and its mysterious first cousin, numerology?

The cochlea of the human ear also forms a Fibonacci spiral. From the complexity of these spirals to the simple but equally impressive zoological example that can be found in the human arm, the whole question becomes closer and more familiar. Begin by considering the humerus bone: just one single bone from shoulder to elbow. At the elbow, 2 bones begin: the ulna and the radius. The hand has 5 digits, and each digit possesses 3 small bones. The arm clearly illustrates the Fibonacci series: "1," "2," "5," and "3" are all Fibonacci numbers. The golden mean can also be demonstrated by measuring the hand, from the wrist to the fingertips, and comparing it to the length of the forearm from the elbow to the wrist. The ratio of the forearm to the whole distance from elbow to fingertips (which is the same as the ancient cubit, the unit used to give the dimensions of Noah's ark in the flood story) is the same as the ratio of the forearm (elbow to wrist) to the hand (wrist to fingertips).

Dolphins also comply with the Fibonacci numbers. If lines are measured from the eyes, fins, and tail, they all combine to make the golden section. Strange to think that a dolphin has the same beautiful proportions as classical Greek architecture. The simple starfish with its 5 "arms" provides yet another instance — "5" being a significant Fibonacci number.

The beautiful and intricate body shape of the marine angel fish also complies with the golden section: members of the *pomacanthidae* family, they live on shallow reefs in the Indian Ocean, the tropical Atlantic, and the western Pacific.

Going down into the depths of life's mysteries, inside the nucleus of the living cell, is DNA. The nucleus of a living cell contains "X"-shaped chromosomes and each of them can contain thousands of genes. Each gene is the blueprint of an inherited characteristic. The mysterious DNA (deoxyribonucleic acid) is a weird double-helix shape, and, when measured, it turns out to be in the ratio of 21:13 angstroms, which boils down to φ. Therefore, Fibonacci's awesome numbering system is even found in the depths of genetics and DNA, which can be thought of as one of life's foundation stones.

Other number mysteries concern the amazing cicada insects. They have 2 large eyes, 1 on each side of the head, as do thousands of other species — "2," of course, is a Fibonacci number — but the cicadas also have 3 small eyes, known as ocelli, situated between the 2 large ones and matching their colour. "Three" is a Fibonacci number, and when all a cicada's eyes are added they make a total of 5 eyes. That, too, is a Fibonacci number. Equally remarkable numerically is that some cicadas emerge from the ground after 17 years, and "17" is a prime number. Science has not yet come up with a modus operandi for how the cicadas know that 17 years have elapsed. The great majority of animals and plants seem to operate on recognition of solar and lunar patterns and seasons. Certain temperatures and certain amounts of light and darkness stimulate particular daily or seasonal functions. The cicada is busily getting on with its life underground, unaware of surface lighting or surface temperatures. Then after 7 years, 13 years, or 17 years — up it pops! All of these timeframes are prime numbers. A numerologist might well suggest an answer that is not within the current range of the scientific principles of cause and effect.

The 17-year cicada phenomenon is strange enough, but it seems even stranger that some others should work on a 7- or 13-year plan. "Thirteen" is also one of the Fibonacci numbers, as well as having strange numerological significance. "Thirteen" is the sixth prime number after 2,3,5,7, and 11. Curiously, and of interest to numerologists, "13" is also the smallest emirp — a prime number that becomes a different prime when it is reversed; "31" and "13" are therefore both reversible primes and, as such, are both in the small, select group of emirps. Just as the numbers "3," "4," and "5" form a Pythagorean triangle — always of special interest to numerologists — because 3^2 added to 4^2 is equal to 5^2 (9+16=25), so "5," "12," and "13" *also* form a Pythagorean triangle. This is because 5^2 added to 12^2 equals 13^2 (25+144=169).

"Thirteen" has deep religious significance as well because the visions of the Virgin of Fatima were believed to have occurred on the thirteenth day of 6 consecutive months. Saint Anthony of Padua has his Feast Day on June 13.

In addition to all the number mysteries associated with the cicada, the familiar honeybee is entangled in the Fibonacci series as well. This can be seen by tracing the family tree of a male bee. The rather strange thing about these honeybees is that males have only 1 parent — the queen bee. Females are produced after the queen has mated with a male, but males are produced by the queen on her own. If we try to create a family tree for any male bee it will seem rather strange because he has 1 parent, 2 grandparents, 3 great-grandparents, 5 great-great-grandparents, and 8 great-great-great-grandparents. This puts his family tree into the Fibonacci series: 1, 2, 3, 5, and 8.

Oliver Goldsmith (1730–1774), author of *The Vicar of Wakefield* and *She Stoops to Conquer*, also wrote *A History of the Earth and Animated Nature*. In this volume, Goldsmith's careful reference to honeybees is particularly interesting. He comments on the rings on the bee's body, which can overlap one another, so that they some-times appear as 6 rings and sometimes as 5. "Five" is a member of the Fibonacci series, and "6" is the sum of the first 3 Lucas numbers added together: 2+1+3=6.

Another Fibonacci number that is particularly significant in the biosphere is "8," and "8" has a number of interesting properties in addi-tion to its importance in the biosphere. In number theory there is a

75

curious thing referred to as a "sphenic" number. It takes its name from the ancient Greek word for "wedge." A sphenic number, by definition, has to be the product of 3 different prime numbers. For example, in the equation 2×3×5=30, the product "30" is a sphenic number. Curiously, all sphenic numbers have 8 divisors. "Thirty," for example, has the following divisors: 1, 2, 3, 5, 6, 10, 15, and 30, making 8 divisors in all. Another simple example can be found in the equation 3×5×7=105. This also has 8 divisors: 1, 3, 5, 7, 15, 21, 35, and 105, again making 8 divisors for a sphenic number.

The Fibonacci number "8" is particularly significant in the biosphere. For instance, spiders have 8 legs, as do all arachnids. The Areneidae spiders also have 8 eyes. The octopus is one of the cartoonist's favourite life forms because its 8 tentacles can be used to signify many kinds of social, political, and financial concepts. A moth known as the "alypia," a member of the *zygaenidae* family, is also referred to as the "8-spotted forester" because there are 8 white spots on its wings. Human beings and a majority of mammals have 8 cervical nerves on each side, and an adult human being with a full set of teeth has 8 in each quadrant of the mouth.

The characteristic 8 legs of the highly dangerous and predatory scorpion are again an interesting numerical feature, and scorpions are involved in a wide range of myths and legends. In legend and mythology, the scorpion — or rather, 7 scorpions — are associated with the Egyptian goddess Isis. These 7 scorpions were said to guard Isis from outsiders that may hinder her work. Each of her scorpions has a name: Tefen and Befen walk behind her; Mestet and Mestetef walk on each side of her; and Petet, Matet, and Thetet travel ahead of her to clear the way. The holy guardian scorpions of Isis are fierce but ethical and moral. They never harm children or small innocent animals.

The existence of all these special Lucas and Fibonacci numbers in nature adds strength and credence to the underlying beliefs of numerologists — that numbers are powerful and purposeful. However, the great open question arises: as numbers seem to be everywhere in nature, do they influence the natural environment of the biosphere?

If they do exert an influence, how does it work and how powerful is it? Do the powers of different numbers sometimes contradict one another? If "3"s and "7"s are what might be termed *lucky* or *positive*, are there *unlucky* or *negative* numbers that can neutralize what would otherwise be a very welcome and benign influence? From numbers in nature, we move on to examine numbers in the physical sciences. Are there influential and important numbers in physics and chemistry, just as there are in biology?

6
NUMBERS IN THE PHYSICAL SCIENCES

In the previous chapter we explored numbers in nature, in flora and fauna, and in all living materials, and in doing so described their special significance in nature. The persistence of certain numbers and patterns throughout the biosphere is remarkable enough, but numbers and patterns also persist throughout the material sciences of chemistry and physics. Living matter has proven to be dependent upon the laws of physics and chemistry, and biology is, therefore, not really comprehensible without applying the principles of the physical sciences to it. It seems logical and reasonable, therefore, to find that the persistent numerical patterns that permeate the biosphere are also present in chemistry and physics. Numbers are everywhere and they exert massive power and influence over everything. Scientific mathematics and orthodox calculations approach numbers from one direction — numerologists approach from another direction.

How do numbers fit into the science of chemistry? A chemical element is defined as a pure substance, which cannot be broken down by chemical processes into other substances. The environment consists of single chemical elements and compounds of chemical elements. They can be there as gases, liquids, or solids, but they are all subject to chemical analysis, and chemical analysis depends upon numbers. Exciting new chemical elements are still being discovered — or created artificially — and the total number in existence as of November 2011 was 118. Of that total, 94 occur naturally, 80 are stable, and the others are radioactive. The radioactive elements break down or decay into other elements at varying rates. Some last for less than a second, while others can take billions of years to change.

Elements are distinguished from one another by their atomic numbers — that is the number of protons in the nucleus. For every proton in the nucleus that carries a positive electric charge there is a negatively charged electron situated in one of the electron shells outside the nucleus. These tiny electrons have only about 1/2000 of the mass of a proton or a neutron. A neutron is a particle which shares the nucleus with the protons. Protons and neutrons have similar mass, but the neutron has no electric charge.

Some elements exist in varieties with different numbers of neutrons, but as long as the protons do not change, they remain the same element. When there are different numbers of neutrons in different varieties of the element, these varieties of the same element are referred to as isotopes. Protons and neutrons together are also referred to as nucleons because both are found in the nucleus. When added together, the number of protons and neutrons is called the mass number of the element. There are, for example, 3 isotopes of carbon that are called carbon-12, carbon-13, and carbon-14. The number of carbon protons does not change. There are always 6. The 3 different mass numbers come about because, in addition to its 6 protons, carbon-12 has 6 neutrons; carbon-13 has 7 neutrons and carbon-14 has 8.

The most recently discovered element is known as "ununoctium" and it was found in 2002. It has the highest atomic number and the highest atomic mass of all the elements.

The relative atomic mass of a chemical element is measured against an atom of carbon-12. This is regarded as possessing 12 units of atomic mass. Surprisingly, the element hydrogen has an atomic mass of 1.01 rather than a simple "1." Once again, numbers are the key factor. While it seems logical to assume that elements that are whole numbers would have atomic masses, it is the presence of the isotopes that leads to the decimal fractions. Most elements have 2 or 3 isotopes, and different percentages of those that occur naturally occur as different isotopes. Chlorine provides a useful example of this: 75 percent of it exists as the isotope chlorine-35, and only 25 percent of it exists as the isotope chlorine-37. To work out the relative atomic mass of chlorine as a whole, the calculation is: 75 percent of 35 added to 25 percent of 37. In other words, 26.25 added to 9.25, giving chlorine a relative atomic mass of 35.5.

The arrangements of the electrons in their shells are also numerologically significant. For the first 20 elements, the atom can hold 2 electrons in its first shell, 8 in the second, 8 in the third, and 8 more in the fourth.

When chemical elements combine to create a compound (a substance with at least 2 chemical elements bonded together) they lose an electron, gain an electron, or share their electrons. These chemical activities almost invariably involve the number of electrons in the outer shell. Electrons can be thought of as always seeking to make groups of 8. If electrons were sentient, conscious, and capable of wanting things, they would want to be in stable groups of 8. If an atom of sodium from group 1 of the periodic table of elements encounters an atom of chlorine from group 7, they will form the compound sodium chloride, with the formula $NaCl$. The sodium atom has 1 electron in its outer shell. The chlorine atom has 7. By combining, sodium and chlorine can form a compound with 8 electrons.

Most of the early alchemists, from whose pioneering work modern scientific chemistry gradually developed, were convinced that numerology was an integral part of understanding the chemicals with which they were working. Just as some substances were understood by them to be powerfully reactive, so they came to associate these powerful substances with what they regarded as powerful numbers. For the early alchemists, sulphur was understood to be very powerful

— partly because of its readiness to burn, partly because of its penetrating odour, and partly because of its ability to react with other chemicals and change things. It was also associated with their belief in hell and the power of Satan and demons. For some alchemists who also studied numerology, sulphur was associated with the number "1." It was seen as an aggressive substance and was thought of as attacking other substances. Mercury was also of the greatest interest to the early alchemists. In many of their minds it was associated with the number "2." It would dissolve other things — even gold. It was a unifying metal. Mercury was seen as receptive because although it was recognizable as a metal, it was a metal that was liquid at ordinary temperatures.

The number "3," in its numerological sense, was sometimes associated with lead in the workings of the medieval alchemists. They saw lead as being neutral, yet it was a means of communication. Water was contained within it and ran along lead pipes and guttering. Lead facilitated that travel and communication.

Gold was associated with number "4." Gold created health as well as wealth: it was the ultimate healing metal. The golden wedding rings of married couples were a prelude to children being created, so in that sense the alchemists thought of gold as the symbol of creation, just as numerologists regarded it as having the number of creation.

The number "5" was very important to numerologists and was linked by some alchemists to *sal ammoniac*, sometimes rendered *salammoniac*, which is now known as ammonium chloride and has the chemical formula NH_4Cl. It is water-soluble, which was important to the ancient alchemists, and it forms crystals that vary in appearance from yellowish-brown to colourless. In the old world, supplies came from the Temple of *Ammon* in Egypt, hence its name. It was associated with the idea of movement, change, restlessness, and impermanence. It is used as a flux for soldering stained glass windows, and the religious themes portrayed in the stained glass were once believed to have magical and mystical significance, hence adding to the power of the numerologists' mystical and magical number "5." Sal ammoniac can also be helpful for refining precious metals. Here, too, its association with gold and silver gave it added qualities. At one time, sal ammoniac was also used by bakers to produce an extra crisp texture in what they cooked, and it is still used in the north to make a salty form of licorice known in Scandinavia as *salmiakki*. The idea of "5" as a number representing restlessness and movement is understandable in light of the many different uses — the figurative "restlessness" — to which sal ammoniac has been put over the centuries.

To some early alchemists, the number "6," which had the meaning of responsibility and importance to numerologists, was associated with *aqua regia*, also called *aqua regis*, meaning literally "the water of royalty," or "kingly water," because it was capable of dissolving gold. It is a very corrosive acid mixture and appears as a yellow or fuming red solution. Its modern name is nitro-hydrochloric acid. The usual ratio is 1:3 by volume of nitric acid (HNO3) and hydrochloric acid (HCl). Because of its powers, aqua regia acquired the numerological value of "6," signifying that great care and responsibility were essential during its use.

Gold

The number "7" is associated with silver and with silver nitrate (AgNO$_3$). The ancient alchemists referred to this compound as *lunar caustic* and recognized its value in medicine. For numerologists, "7" is associated with consciousness, wisdom, and deep thought. Silver, in ancient times, was linked with the moon, as well as various moon gods and goddesses worldwide. The owl, the traditional bird of wisdom, flew by night and also came to be associated with the moon and with silver.

Many varieties were known as "Silver Owls" because of this, and their link with the precious metal connected powerfully with the numerological concept of "7," indicating consciousness, wisdom, and thought. It is especially interesting that silver, so revered and respected by the ancient alchemists, has the highest thermal conductivity of any

Lionel with owl

84

of the metals and the highest electrical conductivity. The old alchemists knew silver was special when they allocated their special number "7" to it, but they didn't know, in early times, quite *how* special it was.

"Eight" was the number of sacrifice, and some of the old alchemists associated it with cobalt. Cobalt stood for demons and things that were evil and dangerous, and to whom sacrifices had to be made in order to placate them. Cobalt resembled silver, but was dangerous instead of wholesome and healthy. It was frequently mixed with arsenic, and in that form was especially dangerous. In some alchemical groups, "9" stood for iron sulphide, also known as "fool's gold."

In numerology, "9" represents the strongest, most traumatic level of change. For example, thinking that you have found gold only to find that it's just the deceptive iron sulphide symbolizes the kind of disappointing, negative change that the number "9" is associated with.

The great and famous Persian alchemist, Geber, whose full name was Abu Musa Jābir ibn Hayyān, lived from 721–815. In addition to his vast knowledge of alchemy, he was a competent astrologer and numerologist. Geber was the son of an Arabian alchemist belonging to the Azd tribe, who had apparently emigrated from the Yemen. Geber grew up to become an alchemist under the patronage of Caliph Harūn ar-Rashīd (763–809) who ruled from 786–809. The Caliph was very enlightened and progressive for an eighth-century ruler, and alchemy, numerology, and science all flourished under his rule. One of his greatest achievements was establishing the amazing library known as *Bayt al-Hikma*, which translates to "House of Wisdom."

The numerologists among the early alchemists were very close to finding the modern connections between numbers and chemical science. There are, undoubtedly, what might be referred to as "magic numbers" in chemistry, which surface when the structures of the nucleus and its accompanying electrons are analyzed. Those magic numbers — better, perhaps, to designate them as *significant* numbers — are 2, 8, 20, 28, 82, and 126. The isotopes are more likely to be stable when they have even numbers such as carbon-12, so that they have equal numbers of protons and neutrons.

In addition to the numerological ramifications that appeared first in alchemy and then later in scientific chemistry, there are what may well be numerological connections in physics as well. The word *physics* comes from the ancient Greek word for nature. Modern scientific physics may be defined as that branch of science that involves the study of matter and the movement of matter through space-time. Albert Einstein (1879–1955), rightly regarded as the father of modern physics, developed the theory of general relativity and the special theory of relativity. He won the 1921 Nobel Prize in Physics. An essential part of Einstein's thinking, and vital to his concept of the space-time continuum, was that nothing could exceed the speed of light. In Einstein's opinion, the speed of light was an absolute at 299, 792, 458 metres per second, or approximately 300,000 kilometres per second. But the latest research seems to indicate that neutrinos from the CERN facility in Geneva *may* have travelled through the ground to the Gran Sasso laboratory in Italy faster than the speed of light. This opens up the possibility of sending data back through time, even if human time travel is still some long way ahead of contemporary scientific development.

Some historians of science would regard physics as one of the oldest — perhaps the very oldest — branch of science. In as far as it includes astrophysics and branches of astrology and astronomy, physics may well have been the earliest set of thought patterns that had any claim to being scientific in nature. For the past 2,000 years, physics shared what was originally called natural philosophy with chemistry, mathematics (numerology), and biology. With the changes in thought that marked the scientific revolution of the sixteenth century, physics began to establish itself as a separate science in its own right. Contemporary physics cuts into many areas of research, such as biophysics and quantum chemistry. Physics also acts as a spur, or stimulus, for developments in many other sciences. When new discoveries are made in physics, they often help to explain the basic functioning of some of the other sciences. As new discoveries are made in physics — such as the recent neutrino experiments that seem to show that the speed of light can, perhaps, be exceeded

— those new discoveries make an impact on mathematics and on the philosophy of science.

Breakthroughs in physics can often herald whole new areas of technology. Nuclear physics and advances in electromagnetism made possible the development of computers and television. It can also be argued that as physics made possible the development of ever more advanced computer systems and calculators, so the investigation of numbers and the deep mysteries of numerology, as well as scientific mathematics, became increasingly accessible.

The mysteries of physics and the numbers locked inside it can be taken all the way back to the natural philosophy of ancient Greece. Philosophers like Thales, who flourished in the period before Socrates, had their feet firmly on the ground and refused all explanations of natural phenomena that involved the intervention of gods or magical beings. Thales (*circa* 624–545 BC), who seems to deserve the title of the first real physicist, came from Miletus in Asia Minor and was traditionally regarded as one of the Seven Sages of Greece. Bertrand Russell (1872–1970) always contended that western philosophy began with Thales.

The natural sciences continued to develop in China as well as India and the Middle East. Outstanding Muslim physicists, including al-Bīrūnī (973–1048) and Alhazen (965–1040), were pioneers of experimental physics and masters of mathematics and numerology.

The numerologically significant number "3" comes to the fore when considering Newton's Laws of Motion, which were the mainstay of physics until they were superseded by Einstein's theories, which also look as if they may now be in danger of being superseded in their turn! Sir Isaac Newton (1642–1727) is often considered the most influential scientist who ever lived. He was a physicist, astronomer, mathematician, alchemist, and theologian — and outstandingly good at every intellectual pursuit that he followed. Numerology was no stranger to Newton. His 3 Laws of Motion begin with the idea that an object that possesses mass will stay at rest if it is at rest, or will continue in motion in the same direction if it is in motion, *unless a force acts on it*. This is Newton's First Law of Motion. His Second Law of Motion is concerned with the *acceleration* of an object, and relates to the magnitude of the force that is being applied and the mass of the object that is being accelerated. The acceleration achieved is inversely proportional to the mass of the object that is being accelerated by the force. The same force applied to a boulder with a mass of 1,000 kilograms and a small stone with a mass of 1 kilogram will accelerate the 1-kilogram stone far more effectively than it will accelerate the 1,000-kilogram boulder. Newton's Third Law says that for every action there is an equal and opposite reaction. Standing on the floor means that the floor is pushing upwards with an equal and opposite force, otherwise the person standing on that floor would go down through it. Firing a rifle produces a kick into the rifleman's shoulder to balance the force with which the bullet is travelling in the opposite direction.

An experienced professional numerologist looking at the Laws of Motion would see in them something with certain parallels to his own special fields of study. He or she would think of numbers as having potential force within them — very mysterious force. If numbers with positive or negative influences are applied to people or objects, or to anything in the environment, the numerologist would say that they will create movement, or alter movement, in a psychic way as well as a physical one. The power of the influential number and the magnitude of the object or event will together influence what happens. The numerologist would also argue that for every good and positive number force, there is an equal and opposite negative number force. A positive, good, and lucky number can, therefore, be neutralized by the conjunction of a bad, negative, unlucky number, and vice versa.

Newton's First Law takes the observer into a consideration of centrifugal and centripetal forces and the mysteries of circular motion. The concept of circularity in its psychic and mystical sense is of great interest to numerologists. A moving body will tend to travel along a straight path at a constant speed unless some other force acts on it. If there is to be circular motion, like a weight on the end of a string that is being spun around in someone's hand, or a planet orbiting a star, there has to be some additional force pulling the circulating object towards the middle. Centrifugal force is influencing the object to zoom off in a straight line. Centripetal force, according to this argument, is pulling it in towards the centre. So centrifugal and centripetal forces are balancing each other and keeping the object in its circular path. If the object is a planet orbiting its parent star, the centripetal force is gravity. If it's a ball on the end of a string, the centripetal force is the mechanical function of the string. In the case of an electron orbiting the nucleus of its atom, the force is electrical.

A formula can be devised for this. What can be thought of as the power, size, or magnitude of the centripetal force is written as F. This is calculated as being equal to the mass of the body that is orbiting, written as m, multiplied by its velocity squared. The letter v stands for the velocity. The whole of this is then divided by the radius (r) of the orbit in which the mass (m) is travelling. The complete formula is written as:

$F=mv^2 \div r$

Newton's Third Law, however, maintains that for every action there has to be an equal and opposite reaction. Does this mean that the centripetal force — the force pulling the mass *towards* the centre of the circle around which it is orbiting — has to be balanced by a centrifugal force, a force pulling the mass *away* from the centre? According to Newton, the 2 forces have to be equal in power and opposite in direction. But the centrifugal force does not act on the mass in motion. The only force acting on it is the centripetal force! The centrifugal force acts on the source of the centripetal force so that it displaces it radially from the middle of the circular path. In the same way, when a mass such as a stone is spinning round in a warrior's sling — like the one that David used to bring down Goliath of Gath in the Biblical account — the centripetal force transmitted by the leather straps of the sling pulls *in* on the stone to maintain it in its circular path. At the same time, the centrifugal force being transmitted by the leather thongs pulls *outward* at the point of attachment, which is the small leather cup into which the slingsman's stone is fitted. Mistakenly, the centrifugal force is thought to cause the stone to deviate from its circular path once the sling is released. What actually happens is that the removal of the centripetal force allows the stone to travel in a straight line in accordance with Newton's First Law, as Goliath found to his cost. Another way of looking at the apparent paradox of circular motion is the observation that if there were a force acting to move an orbiting mass out of its circular path, then when it was released, the mass would not travel in the straight-line course that is invariably seen when a slingshot is released.

A special branch of mathematics that was invented simultaneously by Newton in the UK and Gottfried Wilhelm Leibniz (1646–1716) in Germany was known as *calculus*, from the Latin word for a small pebble. Calculus is that branch of mathematics that studies the ways in which things change over time. Change is also of major significance to numerologists, who are concerned with the influence of dates and times of events and with the changing of human personalities and attitudes over time, thus influencing events. Calculus tries to ascertain what type of change is taking place and the magnitude of the change. Numerologists are also very interested in the types of change that occur in life and the magnitude of those changes. Calculus sets out to discover what type of change it is and how big it is by using functions at the precise moment when the change is taking place. Functions are also of great significance to the numerologist, who views them as the underlying process behind numerous changes.

A numerologist would regard a function as a kind of device or machine. Raw materials go in one end and a finished product comes out the other end. A real number, having certain numerological significance, goes into the function machine, things happen to it inside the machine, and it comes out again in a modified form. The numerologist may, for example, wish to employ a function to neutralize a negative or unlucky number. He or she may also wish to make a positive or lucky number more powerful. Different function machines will enable him or her to achieve these objectives. When the function is being written as a formula, the letter f is frequently used. Take, for example, a strengthening formula that could be written as:

$f(x)=2x+5$

This formula tells us that the function, which is designated as *f*, is a function that relates to a term called *x*. When the numerologist wishes to work on a number such as 7, the "7" takes the place of the *x*. The "7" will be placed into the function formula where the *x* was before. By applying the function *f* as shown, the "7" will go through the *f* machine and be doubled first. It will then have 5 added to it. It will, therefore, come out of the function machine as 14+5=19. The machine has taken in the "7" as its raw material and has produced an output of 19. Numerologically, this can be treated as 1+9=10, followed by 1+0=1, so the original "7" has been processed into a "1" by the function *f*. For the numerologist, "7" stands for consciousness, wisdom, and thought, while "1" represents power, force, attack, and aggression. The idea of "1" is ambition and driving force. By using the function machine and adding the power of the aggressive "1" to the wisdom of "7," the numerologist is creating something of significant power.

Calculus is understood to have 2 distinct branches: differential calculus and integral calculus. Differential calculus divides things into tiny pieces and sets out to demonstrate the ways in which these minute pieces change from moment to moment. The title "differential" comes from the pieces all being *different*. Integral calculus joins, or *integrates*, small separate pieces and sets out to show what their total is and how significant the change is that has been brought about. Scientists use calculus in physics, engineering, and medicine, as well as other disciplines. Numerologists use it to study numbers, such as "9," that are conceptually associated with change. Numerology also sets out to analyze the numerical *causes* of change and the total significance of major changes to people and their environments.

Just as the previous chapter investigated numbers in the biosphere, this chapter has looked at the importance of numbers in physics and chemistry. The following chapter takes numbers to the extremes of the microcosm and macrocosm — numerologists are keenly interested in the vast stellar universe and in subatomic particles like the boson, the lepton, and the quark.

7
NUMBERS IN THE MACROCOSM AND MICROCOSM

The universe can be defined as everything that exists, and some philosophers of science might add that this definition includes everything that *has* ever existed in the past, or ever *will* exist in the future. As part of its immense mystery, the universe contains an infinite amount of numbers.

Numerologists examining the universe and its infinity of numbers will recognize the significance of the powerful number "3" once again, because there are 3 fundamental principles that are essential to any understanding of the universe. The first is space-time. The second is the alliance of matter and energy in all of their forms. The third principle surrounds the only partially understood physical laws that *appear* to integrate space-time, energy, and matter.

There are avant garde cosmologists and astrophysicists who have postulated the existence of what are sometimes termed multiverses or parallel universes. These are sometimes referred to as "the worlds of 'if.'"

If we think of some simple point, some instant, a metaphorical crossroads in time at which a number of possibilities were open, the parallel universe theory suggests that the choices that were *not* made, the possibilities that did *not* materialize, nevertheless still exist in a parallel universe. The existential universe in which we wrote this book, in which our publishers had it printed and distributed, and in which you, the reader, bought a copy and read it, is what we would all think of together as our real universe. But if we had not written it, if it had never been published and distributed, and if you had never read it in this universe, those scientists who hold the multiverse theory of parallel universes would say that corresponding worlds exist somewhere, in which the book did not exist. In some of those corresponding universes *we* might not exist because our respective parents had never met. In yet other parallel universes we exist right enough — but in very different life situations. Depending upon life-shaping events, the burglar in one world could be a police captain in another; the obese, overweight couch potato in one world could be an Olympic athlete in the next; and the barbaric, sadistic, totalitarian despot in one universe is a saint in a parallel universe.

So many different possibilities are open at every moment that the number of such parallel universes must be infinite if the multiverse theory is correct. Those numerologists who accept the idea that the "worlds of 'if'" really exist and are part of an infinite cosmos would also, perhaps, consider the idea that the magical power of numbers could be exercised throughout those parallel universes. It might be suggested that numerological power expresses itself by manipulating or influencing the environments people are in and the decisions they make, which lead them to one zone of the multiverse rather than another. Do good, positive, lucky numbers put people onto favourable probability tracks, while bad, negative, unlucky numbers put them onto unfavourable probability tracks? Can the right numbers send us to the equivalent of Heaven and the wrong numbers send us to the equivalent of Hell?

Whether there are parallel universes or not, the existential universe in which we live now and within which we can share our awareness of the environment is immensely vast. Its enormous size threatens to take it outside the realm of human thought.

As astronomy developed it became clear that the Earth and our solar system itself is an infinitesimally minute part of a galaxy composed of billions of stars, some very much larger than our sun.

One of the important discoveries about the Earth and its movements came from Jean Bernard Léon Foucault (1819–1868), a French physicist. He gave the gyroscope its name and made attempts to measure the speed of light, but was most famous for his invention of the Foucault Pendulum in 1851 — an ingenious device for measuring the Earth's rotation, which is of great interest to numerologists.

The numbers associated with rotation are significant. The 360-degree circle can be expressed as 3+6=9 and the "9" has numerological implications of giving and of creative expression. To a numerologist, the idea of a rotating Earth implies a home planet that is filled with creative power and selfless giving. Mother Earth is a generous parent to a numerologist.

This galaxy of which we are a very tiny part is known as the Milky Way, and billions of other, similar galaxies exist beyond it. The universe seems to be expanding and some of the most widely accepted theories, such as the Big Bang hypothesis, suggest that it

Foucault's Pendulum

had a definite and unique beginning. Some theorists argue that there seems to have been an extremely hot, exceptionally dense point way back in that beginning, which is now referred to as the Planck epoch. It's named after the great German scientist, Max Karl Ernst Ludwig Planck (1858–1947), who was awarded the Nobel Prize in Physics in 1918 for his pioneering work on the quantum theory. If there really was a beginning, that beginning — the Big Bang — deserves a numerological "1," carrying with it all the power that the number signifies.

As astronomers develop ever more advanced technology, theories of dark matter and dark energy begin to emerge in an attempt to explain why there seems to be much more mass in the universe than is visible, and why the galaxies seem to be accelerating away towards the edge of the universe. These 2 mysteries — dark energy and dark matter — confront cosmologists. Numerologists, however, would be quick to point out that this means that there are 2 pairs of strange phenomena in the cosmos. There is normal energy and normal matter. There is also dark energy and dark matter. They add to make 4, and when space-time is added to the equation, the total rises to 5. In numerology, "2," "4," and "5" are very significant numbers. Adding either pair to space-time brings back the all-important number "3."

One possible meaning of the "2"s here is cooperation, adaptability, and working as a united whole. For the early alchemists, with their knowledge of numerology, "2" was associated with mercury and was thought to signify a unifying power. "Two" was understood to be receptive. Does that signify that the universe, however vast, is an integrated totality? That it is receptive to all its components? That it is a totality that makes everything part of itself? The "3" is again vitally important as an expression of art, socialization, and the sheer joy of living. Number "4" represents foundation and order in some numerological tables of meaning. It can represent steady growth and continuous pressure against limits and boundaries as well, which fits in well with theories of the expanding universe. The alchemists associated the number "4" with gold and creativity. Gold, in its turn, was also associated with healing, and it is not unreasonable to view the universe as a self-healing phenomenon.

The number "5" also indicates expansiveness, visionary adventure, and the constructive use of freedom. These qualities are certainly relevant to the cosmos. Science fiction stories are full of visionary adventures and the quest for freedom in the remotest parts of the universe.

What other numbers can be associated with the mysteries of the cosmos and its strange parallel universes? The age of the universe is usually accepted to be in the region of 13 billion years. The number "13" is singularly significant for numerologists, largely because of Norse mythology and the death of Baldur because of the evil Loki, who was the thirteenth guest. There is the well-known Christian tradition of "13" (Jesus and the 12 disciples) at the Last Supper. Friday, October 13, 1307, was the date on which Philip IV attacked the noble Knights Templar. From another point of view, Baldur and Christ were both the thirteenth person — not Loki and Judas Iscariot. Zeus was recognized as the thirteenth and most powerful of the Greek gods. In ancient Egyptian folklore and mythology there were 13 rungs making up the ladder leading to eternity. There are also 13 moons in a calendar year. The Charioteer was supposedly the sign of the Zodiac, representing a driving force.

Chariot

There are some expert students of numerology who would regard "13" as being the fulfilment of "3." It should also be observed that "13" and "3" are prime numbers and members of the Fibonacci series.

As we have seen, the universe's age is approximately 13 billion years, but its size is just as numerologically significant as its age. The diameter of the universe is estimated at 93 billion light years, and "93" is a very interesting number for numerologists. Adding the "9" to the "3" produces 12, and when the "1" and "2" of 12 are added through reduction, the answer again is the highly significant "3." In some numerological tables, "3" stands for expression, explanation, art, and a celebration of life itself. The numerological association of "93" with the size of the universe suggests that the purpose of the universe may be thought of as the joy of life. In other words, the real purpose of the universe is to provide an infinite environment in which life can be expressed and enjoyed.

But will the numerological associations with what cosmologists call the universe — or the theoretical multiple universes — continue to hold if the Big Bang theory is a fallacy? There are eminent astronomers who have very serious doubts about the Big Bang theory. After all, it is only theory. It is possible that future cosmologists will look back on our twenty-first century beliefs about the Big Bang and all that goes with it, including the age and size of the cosmos, and regard them as we currently regard the flat-Earth theory and the concept of phlogiston. One problem that is difficult if not impossible to solve is how and why what is termed a *singularity* existed before the Big Bang happened. The idea of such a singularity is mathematically obscure — and that is describing it kindly. *Something* was supposed to have had 0 volume, yet within that 0 volume it also managed to encapsulate infinite matter and infinite energy. There is then the equally intriguing question as to *why* — if it ever existed in the first place — this mysterious singularity that compressed everything into 0 volume suddenly went pop and is still whizzing at ever-increasing speed towards the unknown nowhere outside the universe. Until these questions can be satisfactorily answered, the Big Bang remains an even bigger mystery.

Think about the idea of an accelerated expansion in the most distant parts of the cosmos. Is that compatible with an explosion of unparalleled magnitude that happened for no known reason some 93 billion years ago? It is much more likely, in the light of astrophysics, as we understand it today, that there is some huge, sinister force *pulling* at the boundaries of the cosmos. Could there be the equivalent of a supersized black hole — something more like a black bag, perhaps — which is affecting the red shifts? Would this create the *illusion* of a cosmos that *appears* to be accelerating outwards at its periphery? Could it be that what is really happening is that the super-gravity black bag outside the cosmos is dragging the peripheral galaxies ever faster towards their ultimate fate? Further criticism of the Big Bang and red shift theory suggests that red shifts are affected by many extraneous factors and are not of much use as measurements of time or distance. Estimates of speed, time, age, and distance can vary by factors of billions. Nothing is proven. The Big Bang and red shift calculations are only useful theories; they are not incontrovertible facts. Some recent cosmological theories involve what are referred to as "superclusters." It has been argued that these superclusters suggest the universe could be upwards of 200–300 billion years old, rather than the 13 billion years currently suggested.

Recent discoveries have revealed that a galactic structure referred to as the "Sloan Great Wall" is 1.36 billion light years long. This "1.36" is again numerologically significant. The "1" suggests individuality, independence, and attainment. It also suggests something that is pioneering. Does it argue that the cosmos is the first of its kind, but not the only one of its kind? The "3," once more, is the purpose of life and the joy of living for all life forms within the cosmos. Does it suggest that the cosmos itself is one huge living organism? The "6" represents responsibility, protection, and nurturing. Does it mean that the cosmos is nurturing and protecting the life forms within it? Adding 1, 3, and 6 together gives 10, further reduced to 1. The number "1" emphasizes individuality, independence, and attainment, yet again.

Recent advanced observations of the Sloan Great Wall and similar structures are beginning to suggest that the macrocosm is a mixture of huge walls and clusters of galaxies, which are separated by enormous, bubble-like voids. Difficulties arise with previous theories when considering that the Great Walls are so big that they could not have arisen by virtue of the mutual gravitational pull of the galaxies by themselves. This somewhat contradicts the expectations that are part of the Big Bang theory. Cosmologists who hold that theory suggest that matter *should* be evenly distributed throughout the universe, but it isn't. There shouldn't be any clusters and voids, but there are. If it didn't all start with a Big Bang, how did it start?

The almost infinite macrocosm presents mind-boggling distances and time-scapes: the infinitesimally small microcosm does the same, but at the other end of the scale.

It has been estimated that there are very strange parallels of comparative size when the dimensions of an average human being are compared to the microcosm on one side and the macrocosm on the other. Multiplying by several billion converts the smallest subatomic particle to the size of a human being. Multiplying by the same number converts a human being to the size of the universe. Have we been deliberately placed at this mid-point to enable us to observe and understand both extremes?

What strange numerological mysteries wait for us in the microcosm?

The molecule, the atom, and the subatomic particles within it, form the mysterious building blocks of the entire physical universe. As outlined in the earlier section dealing with chemistry, the nucleus contains protons with positive electrical charges and neutrons that carry no electrical charges. The electrons, which are approximately only a two-thousandth part of the mass of a proton or a neutron, move in their electron shells around the nucleus and each carries a negative electric charge equal to the positive charge on a proton. These electrons and protons are balanced — each atom has as many electrons as it has protons. Numerologically, this would seem to suggest that at the innermost heart of all matter there is balance.

Moving from these physical, chemical concepts of atomic structure to the idea of the microcosm in its philosophical sense as a human being, the hypothesis goes back many centuries. When microcosm and macrocosm are used as philosophical terms, rather than as scientific ones, the central idea is that human beings are themselves microcosms, having within them a miniaturized universe that corresponds to the macrocosm. A person is, therefore, regarded as a model, or an epitome of the universe itself. The early philosophers who put forward this hypothesis also believed that, just as a human being is sentient, so is the universe. This philosophy embraced the idea that if a human being is a microcosm of the universe, then just as a person is animated by what might be termed a "soul," so there has to be one vast world-soul animating everything.

Sextus Empiricus (160–210), the philosopher and physician, lived and worked in Alexandria. He wrote about Pythagoras and Empedocles, and explained that they believed in an early form of the philosophy of the microcosm. According to Sextus, they believed that human beings were part of one vast community, linked not only to the gods of the Greco-Roman pantheon, but also to the animal kingdom.

Terminology is vitally important in understanding philosophy, and a great deal of this early thinking about the microcosm hinged on the Greek word *kosmos*. Kosmos can mean "order," "world order," or simply "world." For these early microcosmic philosophers, the microcosm could mean a human being in relationship to the cosmos, or in relationship to the state in which he or she lived. Plato's *Republic* provided an example of this type of microcosmic thinking. There was also a sense in which the concept of microcosm in its philosophical context referred to a part of anything, especially part of a living thing, which was thought to represent the whole to which it belonged.

Cardinal Nicholas of Kues (1401–1464), also known as Nicolaus Cusanus and Nicholas of Cusa, was a brilliantly intelligent mathematician, philosopher, and theologian. He thought of individual human beings as contractions, or miniaturized versions of the universe itself. This was very much a microcosmic theory. Leibniz's theory involving monads — special types of units — saw them as living mirrors of the universe. Other microcosmic philosophers

101

saw an individual human soul as a fragment or splinter of the One Entity whom the Pythagoreans, in particular, regarded as divine and immortal. Microcosmic philosophers believed that once the owner of the individual soul had realized the ultimate truth about its being a portion of the One, then that individual soul could return to the vast Perfection from which it had come.

This idea of a human individual as a microcosm of the universe was of distinct interest to numerologists as well as philosophers. The numbers springing from names and dates affecting individuals could influence not only those individuals themselves but also the macrocosm of which each was a miniaturized model. A number affecting one person might be thought to affect the universe of which that person was a microcosm. These ideas were also held by Anaximenes of Miletus (585–528 BC), who was almost certainly a disciple of the great Greek thinker Anaximander (*circa* 610–545 BC), who also came from Miletus. Both were early scientists who looked for the laws of nature and were especially interested in origins. Another early thinker who seems to have been concerned with human beings as microcosms was Heraclitus of Ephesus (535–475 BC). He was concerned especially with the constant change that he observed both in individual people as microcosms and in the universe as a whole. One of his most famous quotations is: "No one steps into the same river twice." Heraclitus was interesting from a numerological point of view because he saw everything in "2"s. He taught a philosophy that embraced what he described as "the unity of opposites." He saw an ascending path and a descending path as one and the same. To him, everything had contrary properties. The numerological "2" meant partnering, cooperating, and mediating. For Heraclitus, "2" stood for adaptability, as it does for numerologists today.

This idea of human beings as microcosms of the entire universe is also found in the works of Empedocles (490–430 BC) of Agrigentum in Sicily. He believed in the 4-element theory — earth, air, fire, and water, and in 2 opposing powers which he referred to as Love and Strife. In his hypothesis, these 2 powers were responsible for uniting and separating the 4 classical elements. Numerologically, his 2 powers stood for cooperation, consideration of others, mediating, and partnering. His 4-element theory embraced the numerological concepts associated with "4": steady growth, struggling against limits and boundaries, order, and a solid, reliable foundation. Empedocles was also keenly interested in the origins of the universe and the beginnings of life. Among other things, he accepted the idea of reincarnation.

The doctrine of human beings as microcosms was also part of the teachings of the Stoics and Neoplatonists. Orphics, Gnostics, and the writers of the Hermetic texts also favoured the idea. These teachings persisted into the Renaissance and centred on the idea that cosmic wisdom could be found within the human mind, and especially within the human imagination. The Renaissance philosophers who were interested in this microcosmic philosophy saw in it the idea that human life and consciousness were somehow linked with the vast and mysterious powers that controlled the entire natural world, from the stars down to the tiniest insect life.

Even up until the relatively modern period of rational scientific thought, there has always been a great deal of sympathy for the idea that microcosmic human beings provided a tiny model of the order and harmony that early scientists felt pervaded the universe. If there was order and rationality in nature, if it followed certain recognizable laws and principles all the way down from the vastness of the macrocosm to one single human being, then there must be something unifying about it all — something that made sense of the cosmos.

To the numerologist, this vital, unifying principle linking the microcosm and the macrocosm is inextricably bound up with the importance of numbers and their mystical, magical meanings.

Some of the roots of such numerological beliefs can be traced clearly to the ancient Egyptians and their understanding of the individual human being and his or her place in the cosmos, which is examined in more detail in the next chapter.

8
ANCIENT EGYPTIAN NUMEROLOGY

The ancient Egyptians were convinced that numbers were very important, not only for predicting what was likely to happen in the future, but even to control and influence it to some extent. French Egyptologist René Schwaller de Lubicz (1887–1961) was born in Alsace-Lorraine, and studied the design and architecture of Luxor for many years. He was intrigued by the way that ancient Egyptian philosophy aligned with their mathematics and science. De Lubicz made a detailed study of Paracelsus, whose full name was Philippus Aureolus Theophrastus Bombastus von Hohenheim (1493–1541). This amazing sixteenth-century thinker was a redoubtable occultist, physician, alchemist, numerologist, and astrologer. His title of Paracelsus referred to his equalling — or even surpassing — Aulus Cornelius Celsus (25 BC–50 AD), the pioneering Roman physician and early writer of medicine.

De Lubicz was a great admirer of Paracelsus's work and wrote *The Temple of Man*, in which he argued that the ancient Egyptians had been deeply involved with numerology and sacred geometry, including the golden section. Although he is not in line with the ideas of many contemporary, orthodox, academic Egyptian scholars, de Lubicz's mystical thinking is popular with some hermeticists. Their religious philosophy is based on the ideas associated with Hermes Trismegistus, meaning "Hermes the Thrice Blessed." The Greek god Hermes and the Egyptian god Thoth were syncretized and worshipped at Khemnu — known to the Greeks as Hermopolis. Allegedly, the greatest of all secret ancient wisdom was said to have been inscribed on the emerald tablets of Hermes Trismegistus, who is also thought by some authorities to be one and the same magical, mystical being as Melchizedek, the immortal priest-king who met Abraham. Whether as Thoth, Hermes Trismegistus, or Melchizedek, the Greco-Egyptian deity was a god of writing, of magic, and of wisdom. The secret knowledge he controlled, according to his followers, included the magic of numbers (numerology), astrology, and alchemy.

Hermes Trismegistus was also a psychopomp: a powerful paranormal entity with the responsibility of leading a dead person's soul up to Heaven. Seshat, goddess of numbers and wisdom, is also referred to as the lady who opens Heaven's door.

A study of the Egyptian myths makes it abundantly clear that number was vitally important to the thought processes of ancient Egypt. There are 8 gods involved in their creation stories. "Eight" is highly significant to numerologists and symbolizes practical, constructive work and the quest for power. There were Nu and Nut, deities of the sky and the rain that fell from it; Hehu and Hehut were gods of fire; Kekui and Kekuit were gods of darkness and deep, still waters; and Kerh and Kerhet were the deities of chaos — the benign gods set out to destroy an evil entity known as Apepi.

One creation myth tells how Ra took another entity, Khepera, the creator, into himself and in this dual identity he made the Heavens and the Earth. In other ancient Egyptian creation myths there are 9 gods rather than 8. "Nine" is also very important to numerologists. It symbolizes creative expression, selfless giving, and a sense of obligation — as if the gods of Egypt had felt duty-bound to create the universe.

Another intriguing part of ancient Egyptian mythology concerns the goddess Seshat, who is also referred to as Seshata and Safkhet. Like Hermes Trismegistus and Thoth, she is a deity of wisdom and sacred record-keeping. Seshat is also the deity responsible for numerology, designing, planning, astrology, architecture, mathematics, and building. One of Seshat's additional titles is "lady of the library." Wep-em-Nephret, a fourth dynasty prince, held the title of overseer of the royal scribes and he was a priest of Seshat.

Seshat was also described as the goddess of history, and was depicted with a 7-pointed emblem. Representing understanding, analysis, knowledge, awareness, and meditation, the "7" is extremely important to numerologists and is particularly appropriate for a goddess of wisdom like Seshat. The pharaoh Thutmosis III (1479–1425 BC) described Seshat as Sefket-Abwy, meaning "the lady of 7 points."

Seshat is often depicted in ancient Egyptian art as holding a notched palm stem. The notches have a numerical significance most frequently associated with time and more specifically believed to be the years allotted to a pharaoh. In other representations of her, Seshat is holding tools and instruments associated with building and architecture. Knotted cords were used when land was being surveyed and measured in ancient Egypt, and Seshat is often shown holding these as though in the act of measuring.

Another part of Seshat's divine work was to guide and help the pharaoh when he laid out the foundations of a new temple. She also surveyed the land after the annual Nile flood, when boundaries were in dispute. Among her additional titles, Seshat was known as the lady of the builders and as the enumerator, or goddess of number.

The priestess of Seshat who carried out this work was highly skilled in mathematics and especially sacred geometry. Only the highest-ranking priests and professionals — architects and surveyors — were entrusted with this numerical wisdom. When Thoth became more prominent than Seshat, she was regarded first as his daughter and later as his wife.

The Rhind Mathematical Papyrus, dating from *circa* 1650 BC, contains some very strange and mysterious numerological ideas. It refers to the writer going 3 times into a bushel and adding a seventh part to his mass. He is then declared to be fully satisfied. Yet again, the numerologically significant "3" and "7" are represented.

The ancient Egyptian mathematicians had the deepest respect and veneration for the famous "3, 4, 5" of the Pythagorean right-angled triangle — something that they were apparently well aware of long before Pythagoras himself came on the scene. "Three" symbolizes joy, contentment, and the pleasure of being alive; "4" is order and steady progress; "5" is adventure and the best use of freedom. Orderliness, joy, and freedom are very satisfactory symbols for the good life. It can also be argued that "3" represents the triangle; "4," the square; and "5," the pentagon. The early Egyptian followers of the sacred geometry would have argued that all other figures and 3-dimensional solids could be constructed from this "3, 4, 5" basis.

It was also an essential feature of ancient Egyptian numerology to recognize that everything was in constant movement. The very act of counting and measuring moved on from number to number as life moved on from season to season and from year to year. Making wine and measuring the amount produced was also very important to the ancient Egyptians.

A detailed study of the Great Pyramid of Giza, apparently built around 2560 BC, reveals a host of mysteries. It has fairly been described as the most remarkable structure on Earth, and its measurements provide numerologists with highly significant data. The first of its mysteries is the precision with which its mighty stones, some weighing 70 tonnes, were put together. There is considerable justification for the argument that ancient human history may well need to be rewritten when the real truth about the Great Pyramid's construction and purpose is known. The geometric relationships within it are so strangely exact that they raise very deep and penetrating questions about its planners and builders.

It is estimated that there are 2,300,000 stone blocks in the Great Pyramid. The number "23" is of great significance to numerologists. It is also of importance to followers of the philosophy known as Discordia, in which almost everything is dependent upon the number "23." The ancient Greek goddess Eris, also known as Discordia, is the goddess of chaos, and her followers practise what can be referred to as chaos magic. Robert Shea and Robert Anton Wilson, who are acknowledged experts in metaphysics, have written a number of books about the number "23." They conclude that there are major shifts in human collective consciousness in 23-year cycles. One strange fact about "23" is that it is the lowest prime number comprised of 2 consecutive primes.

Toth, alias Hermes Trismegistus

Twenty-three is also significant because the "2" was thought to be feminine and the "3" masculine. By putting them together, as in the number "23," mating and offspring were symbolized. This could be thought to tie in very strangely with the 23 chromosomes in each human sperm and ova.

In some other ancient versions of numerology, "23" stands for judgement and severe punishment.

Another strange fact about the Great Pyramid is its temperature. This is a constant 68 degrees Fahrenheit or 20 degrees Celsius. By adding the "6" and "8" of 68 together to get 14, and the "1" and "4" together to get 5, the numerological symbolism of these 2 temperatures reflects adventure and the constructive use of freedom. Who were having an adventure in ancient Egypt in 2560 BC? Who were using their freedom constructively then? Is it remotely possible that it was the Atlanteans, or extraterrestrial aliens? The Great Pyramid is so strange and mysterious that it might have been the work of someone or *something* other than the ancient Egyptians.

The base of the pyramid covers an area of 55,000m². Take the symbolism of the "5"s once more: visionary adventure and the constructive use of freedom. Consider reducing 55 (5+5) to reach 10, which is further reduced to 1. This "1" symbolizes initiation, pioneering, starting something, and attaining something. The 55,000m² can be translated as 592,000ft². The "5," once again, represents adventure and freedom. The "9" represents unselfish giving and creative expression. Was someone or *something* alien and mysterious giving something to humanity? The "2" symbolizes cooperation and partnership. Who were humanity's unknown partners when the Great Pyramid was being constructed nearly 5,000 years ago? Adding the digits of 592 (5+9+2) produces 16. Reduce 16 by adding "1" and "6" together to get 7. The symbolism of the "7" is powerful. It gives understanding, knowledge, and analysis. The outer casing of the Great Pyramid once had 144,000 casing stones. The "1" and the "4"s symbolize initiating action and foundation, order, and steady growth. What better way to describe the construction process of the Great Pyramid? Adding the digits of 144 together (1+4+4) equals 9, and "9" symbolizes unselfish giving and creation. These highly-polished casing stones weighed approximately 15 tonnes each. "One" is the symbol of starting, of initiation. "Five" represents visionary adventure and the constructive use of freedom. Adding the "1" and "5" together gives us 6, which evokes the numerical symbol of responsibility and protection. What else does a pyramid do other than *protect* its contents?

When its polished mantle was originally in place, the Great Pyramid would have been clearly visible from space. Does that say anything significant about its builders and their real purposes?

The relationship between π and ɸ, which was explained in Chapter 4, can be observed in the fundamental proportions of the Great Pyramid. The numbers of π and ɸ are around 1.61803 and 3.14159, respectively. Their appearance among the Great Pyramid's dimensions increases their amazing significance further still.

From corner to corner of the base in a straight line measures 9,131 pyramid inches. There is some controversy over the idea of the pyramid inch, but those who support the theory of it maintain that it is exactly 1/25 of a sacred pyramid cubit. This would make the pyramid inch 1.00106 contemporary imperial inches long. It could also be calibrated as 2.5426924 centimetres. Where does the measurement of 9,131 pyramid inches lead us numerologically? The "9" stands for unselfish giving and creativity; the repeated "1"s initiate pioneering activity. The "3" represents happiness and the arts at their highest level. All of these interpretations fit in well with the idea of the Great Pyramid as a special kind of gift from someone with abilities over and above the normal human range. If the "9," "1," "3," and "1" are added together, they come to 14, which, reduced (1+4), comes to a total of 5. The "5" carries the meaning of visionary adventure and freedom, all of which makes the Great Pyramid more and more mysterious. These 9,131 pyramid inches become 365.24 pyramid cubits — 1 for every day of the year, even down to the decimal fraction of a day.

When the height of the Great Pyramid is used as the radius of a circle, its circumference is the same as the perimeter of the square base. Someone, nearly 5,000 years ago, appears to have mastered the supposed mathematical "impossibility" of squaring the circle!

Another very strange mathematical issue with the Great Pyramid is the diagonal of the base. The diagonal of a square can be found quickly by multiplying the side by the square root of 2, which comes to 1.414214. By multiplying 9,131 pyramid inches by the square root of 2 gives the diagonal of the Great Pyramid's base as 12,913 to the nearest pyramid inch.

This converts to an approximate diagonal of just over 300 metres. Half the diagonal is therefore 150 metres, and that half-diagonal multiplied by a million gives the estimated distance from the Earth to the sun, which varies between 147 million kilometres and 152 million kilometres. Did *someone* who built the Great Pyramid have a rather unusual knowledge of astronomy, or an unusual sense of humour, or both? Another strange little mathematical fact about the Great Pyramid is that its height multiplied by a billion equals the average radius of the Earth's orbit around the sun. Also, just as we can use the square root of 2 multiplied by a side for finding the diagonal of a square, we can also use the square root of 3 (1.7320508) multiplied by the side of a cube to get its diagonal.

There is a shaft in the southern side of the King's Chamber within the Great Pyramid that pointed to the star known as Al Nitak or Zeta Orionis approximately around the time when the pyramid was built. The constellation of Orion was associated with the Egyptian god Osiris. The northern shaft in that same royal chamber pointed to Alpha Draconis during this same epoch. As if these alignments were not sufficiently significant, there were also shafts in the Queen's Chamber of the Great Pyramid that were uncannily accurate. At the time when the pyramid was constructed, the northern shaft in the Queen's Chamber pointed unerringly at Ursa Minor. The southern shaft in her chamber pointed to Sirius. Sirius was associated with the Egyptian legends of Isis, and is central to the strange mystery of the Dogon people of Africa. Although there is some anthropological controversy about the matter, there is interesting and challenging evidence to the effect that the Dogon people had a knowledge of astronomy many years before it became known to Western astronomers. Could that Dogon mystery somehow be linked to the shafts in the royal chambers of the Great Pyramid?

The ancient Egyptian numerologists were extremely interested in the mysteries of the "3, 4, 5" triangle and endowed it with mythological properties. The upright was Osiris, the horizontal was Isis, and the powerful hypotenuse was their son Horus. There were also other types of symbolism in the sacred triangle. Ancient Egyptian alchemists and numerologists regarded the whole of the sacred "3, 4, 5" figure as representing the first matter — the original substance from which all else had come. The vertical side was 3 basic chemicals: mercury, salt, and sulphur. The horizontal female side became the 4 fundamental elements of alchemy: earth, air, fire, and water. Horus, the hypotenuse, became the 5 stages of life starting with minerals, then plants, then animals, and human beings were fourth. The fifth stage was enlightened human beings, those with divine wisdom and knowledge. Other ancient Egyptian numerologists and alchemists described the 3 sides of the sacred triangle as doors, or mystical portals, leading from the physical realm to spirit worlds.

The myths and folktales that were such a major part of ancient Egyptian life and belief systems often included numbers. This can be observed in their use of canopic jars to hold the viscera of the dead as part of the mummification process. There were 4 jars, each of which was dedicated to a particular deity. These were the 4 sons of Horus, who were also responsible for guarding the 4 points of the compass: north, south, east, and west. The first jar was used to hold the corpse's stomach and large intestines. This jar bore the image of man-headed Mesti, also referred to as Amset. The second jar was decorated with the image of ape-headed Hapi and held the smaller intestines. The third jar held the heart and lungs and was protected by the jackal-headed image of Tuamutef. The fourth and final jar was used to contain the liver and gall bladder and carried the falcon image of Qebehsenuef. The numerological significance of these 4 deities and the 4 points of the compass that they guarded is the idea of foundation and order; service; struggle against all limits, including death; and steady growth and progress. The Egyptian army was also subject to numerical arrangements.

The number "3" represented all kinds of plurality to the old Egyptian numerologists. They also liked to arrange their gods in "3"s: Atum, for example, was 1 and became 3 — which is strangely similar to the Christian concept of the Holy Trinity. Atum's companions were Shu and Tefnut. Horus, Isis, and Osiris were another well-known trinity of gods. Ra, the sun god, was represented in 3 ways: as dawn, midday, and sunset. Thoth, alias Hermes Trismegistus, is thrice-blessed and regarded as thrice-great.

Furthermore, Sekhmet, the dangerously fierce lion goddess, was tricked by alcohol that soaked into the ground to 3-hands-depth; an Egyptian wise man used a spell to enter the land of the dead, which involved throwing enchanted powder into a sacred fire 3 times; and the land of the dead had various divisions within it, the third of which was regarded as the most important.

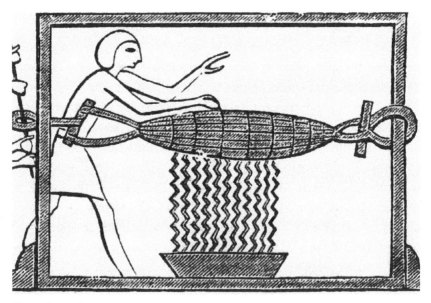

Egyptian wine press

"Five" also had special numerological significance for the ancient Egyptians. Thoth increased the length of the year by 5 days when he won light from the moon as they played a gambling game together. A boastful Egyptian magician claimed that he could take Pharaoh to Ethiopia and back in 5 hours. Another of the highly competitive ancient magicians claimed that he could read all 500 lines of a sealed letter. This event is recorded in the Bible (Exodus, chapter 7, verse 22) where Moses and Aaron are in competition with the magicians before the Exodus takes place.

The Egyptian infantry

The number "7" was also very important to ancient Egyptian numerologists. Seven thousand barrels of alcohol were used to make the dangerous lion goddess Sekhmet drunk and incapable of further slaughter. The Nile flood amounted to 7 cubits at one point and 28 (4×7) at another: the symbol for water was 7 wavy lines. The Egyptian symbol for gold has 7 lines below it.

In addition to the significant third stage in the land of the dead, other legends tell of the 7 halls in Sekhet Aaru — a kind of paradise of islands among the reeds, where Osiris reigned and gave pleasure to all who reached it. Each of the halls in Sekhet Aaru were in the care of 3 gods, and each had a different function. One served as the doorkeeper, another was on lookout duties, and the third interrogated those who arrived. Knowing the names of the 3 gods was a condition of entry and further progress.

In so many ways, the ancient Egyptians laid a significant foundation for numerology. After all, it was their mastery of the sacred "3, 4, 5" triangle that paved the way for Pythagoras and the Pythagoreans, who are the subjects of the next chapter.

9
PYTHAGORAS AND GREEK NUMEROLOGY

P ythagoras the Samian, or Pythagoras of Samos, as he was also
known, lived from 570–495 BC. Best known as a pioneering mathematician, he was also an Ionian Greek philosopher, mystical thinker,
and founder of a religious secret society — the Pythagoreans. He
travelled extensively, studying as he went and acquiring a great
deal of knowledge from ancient Egypt. He also studied in Arabia,
Phoenicia, Judea, Babylon, and India, and learned advanced theories of ethics under the guidance of Themistocles. *Circa* 530 BC,
Pythagoras moved to Croton, which was then a Greek settlement in
the south of Italy. It was here that his mysterious Pythagorean sect
was established. Eventually their presence created political and social
problems, and their enemies burnt their headquarters. Pythagoras
himself fled from Croton and went to Metapontum, an important city of what was then known as Magna Graecia on the Gulf of
Tarentum, not far from modern Basento. During the time of Marcus
Tullius Cicero (106–43 BC) the tomb of Pythagoras was known to be
at Metapontum.

Strange myths and legends accumulated around Pythagoras. Some said that he was a demigod, the son of Apollo. He was also supposed to glow in the dark — perhaps some kind of radioactivity. It was also rumoured that one of his legs was gold. Abaris, the semi-legendary magician and healer from Hyperborea, who allegedly flew with the aid of a golden arrow, came to visit Pythagoras and debate philosophy and mathematics with him. Abaris is credited with many good and helpful works, including the purification of both Sparta and Knossos. He and Pythagoras together argued with the Sicilian tyrant Phalaris (610–554 BC) and tried to persuade him to mend his ways.

Much that is known or speculated about concerning Pythagoras and his life came from Assyrian philosopher Iamblichus Chalcidensis (245–325 AD). One of the strangest myths attached to Pythagoras was that he was capable of being seen in several places at the same time. Leaving aside the legend that Pythagoras was the son of the god Apollo, his real father seems to have been Mnesarchus. According to legend, he and his wife, Parthenis, were visiting Delphi to consult the famous oracle. The oracle told them that Parthenis was pregnant with a son who would grow up to surpass all others in wisdom and would be a great benefactor to humanity for many centuries to come. Pythagoras is said to have learnt geometry in Egypt, arithmetic in Phoenicia, and astronomy in Chaldea. Pherecydes (600–550 BC), a firm believer in reincarnation and the immortality of the soul, was one of his Greek teachers. It is recorded that Pythagoras himself believed in reincarnation and thought he remembered being a soldier in the Trojan War in a previous life, recalling that he had served in that war as Euphorbus, the son of Panthus. Pythagoras was particularly interested in secrets relating to the mystical cults attached to the Greek and Egyptian deities. He was also thought to be knowledgeable about the mysteries of Crete and the fabled Cretan labyrinth.

Plutarch records that Pythagoras studied under the guidance of a very old and learned Egyptian priest named Oenuphis of Heliopolis. There are suggestions from some researchers that there was a mysterious connection between this Oenuphis of Heliopolis and the

Priest of Sais, who supposedly told Solon (638–558 BC) about the history of Atlantis and its inundation more than 9,000 years earlier. Plato (424–348 BC) also wrote of the Atlantean mystery. How much did Pythagoras know about Atlantis, and how many of his amazing mathematical discoveries might have had Atlantean origins? From the writings of Xenophanes (570–475 BC) it is clear that Pythagoras's belief in reincarnation was a central part of his thought and behaviour. On one occasion it is recorded that Pythagoras intervened when a dog was being beaten and was crying pathetically. Pythagoras maintained that in the dog's cries he recognized a reincarnated friend.

As well as all the mathematical and scientific discoveries that were attributed to him, Pythagoras made great advances in medicine and astronomy. A lesser known fact is that he was an expert in music, and linked it with mathematics. He was also revered for his religious teaching, and was renowned for his prophecies and religious divination. He taught vegetarianism as part of his social and religious ethics.

In some accounts of his life Pythagoras married Theano, a Croton girl, and they had 3 daughters, Damo, Arignote, and Myia. They also had a son, Telauges.

The Cretan Labyrinth

Pythagorean and Greek mathematics associated numbers very closely with shape and space. For instance, "1" was associated with a point, "2" with a line, and "3" with a triangle — the first plane figure. Next in their reasoning came the number "4," which was linked to the tetra-hedron — a triangular-based pyramid and the first solid figure. For the Pythagoreans, these 4 numbers were capable of encompassing the whole of space. They put the shapes into a symmetrical format and venerated it as the *tetractys*. In their words, it was "the fountain spring of eternal nature." In Pythagorean thought, creation consisted of the separation of primordial unity into discrete sections. Each number had a particular meaning attached to it — this was pure numerology. Numbers, for them, existed as 10 pairs of opposites. For example, there were: odds versus evens, finite versus infinite, right versus left, and male versus female. The number "4" was of particular significance to Pythagoreans as it had 2 clearly opposed meanings. The good, positive aspect of "4" consisted of the ability of 4 points to create a solid tetrahedron. Conversely, however, because "4" was made up of 2 pairs of "2"s acting differently (2+2 or 2×2), it was also considered to be the symbol of evil and misfortune.

When numbers are allocated to the Greek alphabet in the old numerological tradition, Pythagoras's name appears as Πυθαγόρας — *pi, upsilon, theta, alpha, gamma, omicron, rho,* and *sigma.* In the Greek alphabet these carry the following number values:

Pi=16
Upsilon=20
Theta=8
Alpha=1
Gamma=3
Omicron=15
Rho=17
Sigma=18

Totalling the numbers numerologically (1+6+2+0+8+1+3+1+5+ 1+7+1+8) brings us to a sum of 44, and "44," when reduced, becomes 8 (4+4). Numerologists associate the number "8" with power-seeking, being status-oriented, aiming at high goals, and practical endeavours.

That would certainly seem to apply to a man like Pythagoras, who sought the power that comes from the mastery of numbers. In the eyes of his disciples he occupied a very high, almost divine status. He aimed at the highest possible goals materially, intellectually, and spiritually.

Greek myths and legends are filled with significant numbers that were very meaningful to the numerologists of the time. For instance, the single eye of the Cyclops was numerologically significant. Although by no means a pleasant or friendly entity, the Cyclops initiated action and was an independent, pioneering individual. The union of Aphrodite, the alluring sex goddess, and Ares, the powerful and dominant war god, produced 2 frightening sons whose names were Terror and Fear: τρόμος (*Tromos*) and φόβος (*Phobos*). The numerological "2" in their case refers to cooperation and partnership. These awesome sons of Ares and Aphrodite worked *together* to defeat any enemy and to overwhelm any fortification.

The number "3" was also highly significant to the ancient Greeks. At one point, Zeus was married to Themis, the Titan, who personified righteousness and goodness. She gave birth to 3 daughters: Eirene, the bringer of peace; Eunomia, the creator of order; and Dike, the giver of justice. Her next 3 daughters were the 3 Fates: Clotho, Lachesis, and Atros. Their role was to spin out human life and decide when it was to end. They also apportioned fortune and misfortune as life proceeded. The "3"s in each case are associated with the joy of living — even though the 3 Fates brought bad and unwelcome experiences as well as good and happy ones. Two "3"s together make the numerologically significant "6," which signifies responsibility, community, balance, sympathy, and protection. These qualities were certainly within the province of Eirene, Eunomia, and Dike, but related to the Fates only when they bestowed what was good.

Cerberus, the canine guardian of the land of the dead, possessed 3 heads, which were no part of the traditional numerological "3" that was usually associated with the joys of living. Overcoming Cerberus was the twelfth and most difficult labour of Heracles, and he accomplished it by doping the fearsome dog with a cake soaked with opium.

After Cerberus awoke, Heracles put 3 collars around his 3 necks, patted his 3 great heads affectionately, and took him for a walk to the world above. Cerberus greatly enjoyed this excursion, so perhaps the "3" as a sign of the joy of living did have a role in the relationship of Heracles and the fearsome dog after all!

The number "4" was also very important to Greek thought. The 4 Anemoi were the wind gods, who were of great significance to a maritime nation. Hesiod the poet (*circa* 650–560 BC) wrote that Aeolus, the storm god, was the father of the 4 Anemoi, and the beautiful Eos, goddess of the dawn, was their mother. They were sometimes represented as men with wings, rather like the concept of angels. At other times they were shown as fleet horses. Boreas, who became Aquilon in Latin, was the north wind; Euros the east wind; Notus the south; and Zephyrus the west. Each had different characteristics: Boreas brought the cold; Euros was temperate weather; Notus conveyed summer storms; and Zephyrus was the most welcome and friendly of the 4, bringing warm, gentle, refreshing breezes with him. Numerologically, "4" carries the idea of a struggle against limits followed by steady growth. It applies appropriately enough to the 4 winds and their struggle through the air, as well as the idea of steady growth from a gentle, barely perceptible breeze to a storm-force gale carrying all that lies before it.

"Five" had the special numerological significance of the 5 ages that Hesiod wrote about. The Golden Age came first: a time of ease and contentment. This was followed by the Silver Age, when Zeus introduced the 4 seasons and it became necessary for humanity to work to produce food. The people of the Silver Age were less attractive and healthy than their Golden Age predecessors, but children could still enjoy a century of carefree play before they grew up.

The third of the 5 mythological ages was the Age of Bronze. Zeus manufactured the men and women of this era from the wood of ash trees. The Bronze Age warriors were strong and aggressive. Many ancient myths and legends have tales of a flood, like the Biblical version that involved Noah and the Babylonian hero Utnapishtim. The Bronze Age ended with a great, destructive flood.

The fourth age was referred to as the Heroic Age. The outstanding leaders of this period were the Henitheoi. They were braver and stronger than any who had gone before them, and according to Hesiod, none who came after would ever be greater. They were demigods who faced danger and death without hesitation or fear, and they went on to the Isles of the Blessed when their earthly lives ended.

The fifth period, according to Hesiod, was his current age — extending as far as our current age — which he referred to as the Iron Age. All manner of dangerous and unpleasant things made it difficult and hazardous, according to him. Goodness left the Earth. Piety evaporated. The Olympian gods and demigods who had been on Earth all left. Hesiod's pessimism decreed that Zeus would destroy the Iron Age sooner or later.

The numerological "5" carries the context of expansiveness, adventure, and the constructive use of freedom. This was certainly true of the Heroic Age, although the "adventure" element of the current Iron Age is not a positive or optimistic one.

Greek legends involve the numerologically important "6" in the story of Persephone and the pomegranate seeds. She was kidnapped by Hades, god of the underworld, and kept there as his wife. Her mother, Demeter, the nature goddess in charge of harvests, eventually persuaded Zeus to order Hades to let Persephone go. However, because Persephone had eaten 6 pomegranate seeds, she was compelled to spend 6 months every year with her husband in the Land of the Dead, and was able to spend the other 6 months on Earth with Demeter. Numerologically, the "6" is very appropriate in this particular myth as it stands for balance. The two 6-month periods were balanced: the bleak winter season weighed against the fertile warmth of spring and summer. There is also a sense of nurturing and protection attached to the number "6" and Demeter displayed great powers of nurturing and protection over Persephone.

"Seven" is numerologically significant, one of the most powerful and interesting numbers in the numerological scale. It stands for analytical knowledge, meditation, understanding, and awareness. "Seven" is found in several important places in Greek mythology. The 7 Pleiades were the daughters of Atlas and Pleione. Their names were: Maia, Taygete, Electra, Alcyone, Celoeno, Sterope, and Merope. The first 3 became the lovers of Zeus, himself. Poseidon took Alcyone and Celoeno. Ares, despite being the husband of the beautiful Aphrodite, became the lover of Sterope. Merope, unlike her sisters, became the lover of Sisyphus, who was only human and not a god like the consorts of her sisters. The astrologers taught that it was because of this that her star in the Pleiades constellation was dimmer than the other 6.

Another significant numerological "7" occurs in the wanderings of Ulysses, or Odysseus. He lands on the island of the beautiful nymph, Calypso, who entertains him luxuriously and erotically for the next 7 years. At last, after this time has passed, his conscience stirs and he sets off for Ithaca and his family once more.

"Eight" refers numerologically to power and status, and in the minds of the early Greeks there was no status higher than that of their gods — though the gods themselves existed in a hierarchical order and could be divided into categories, or classes. First came what were called the Protogenoi. These were linked to creation and the first-born entities, and they represented the various parts of the universe itself, materially as well as spiritually. Gaia — as later celebrated in Lovelock's famous Gaia Hypothesis — was the Earth. Pontos was the sea, and Ouranos (spellings vary) was the sky, or the celestial dome. These early creation entities could also acquire human form when they chose.

The entities of the 8 groups were known both as Daimones and Nymphai. Their function was to support and reinforce life in all of its forms. The Naiades were water nymphs, and part of their duties consisted of caring for fish and amphibians. The Dryades looked after forests, woods, and trees of all kinds. The Satyrs also belonged to this second group. They were associated with music, especially playing on pipes like the god Pan. Satyrs also played the bagpipes and cymbals. Their chief, Silenus, was associated with eroticism and fertility. They tended to be comical and mischievous and some of the great tragic Greek plays ended with a light-hearted Satyr story as relief from the tragedy of the main piece. Satyrs were servants of Dionysus, and as such were associated with all kinds of pleasure-seeking, wine-drinking, and womanizing. The Tritons also belong in this second group. The original Triton was the son of Poseidon and Amphitrite, and serves as a herald to his father. According to Ovid's description, Tritons as a group have fish tails and human upper bodies. Tritons also have conch shells, which they blow in different ways to raise the sea to fury or to calm it.

The third category of the 8 consisted of various entities that had the power to influence and control human feelings, emotions, and stages of life. These spirit-beings included Hypnos, who had the power of causing sleep; Eros, who initiated love; Euphrosyne, the giver of ecstatic pleasure and joy; Eris, who stimulated hatred and loathing; Phobos, who created fear and terror; Thanatos, who initiated death; and Geras, the cause of old age, bodily decay, and senility.

The fourth category of the 8 contained the Theoi — those gods who had power over the forces of nature, and gave art, music, culture, wisdom, and knowledge to humanity. These included Helios, the sun-god, and the 4 wind gods.

Category 5 of the 8 held the 12 Olympian gods. They were regarded as the rulers of the universe and had power over all the other gods and paranormal entities. These top 12 were: Zeus, Hera, Poseidon, Demeter, Artemis, Apollo, Ares, Athena, Aphrodite, Hephaestus, Hermes, Dionysus, and Hestia.

The sixth group of the 8 consisted of the divine entities that occupied the stellar constellations. These deities included Sagittarius the centaur and the Gemini twins. They circled the night sky and included all the characters of the astrologers' Zodiac.

The seventh group of the 8 contained what might be loosely categorized as giants and monsters of various types. This group includes Cerberus, the 3-headed dog that guards the land of the dead, as well as creatures like the Sphinx and the Griffin. The beautiful but murderous Sirens also fall into this category.

The eighth and final group consists of the semi-divine heroes and demigods. These include Alkmene, the mother of Hercules, and Baubo, the goddess of laughter, who was able to restore Demeter's spirits after the abduction of Persephone. Theseus and Perseus are also found in this eighth category of divine and semi-divine entities.

Numerologically, "9" is associated with the concepts of unselfish obligation to others and innovative creativity. Both of these apply fittingly to the manner in which Hercules killed the monstrous 9-headed Hydra, which had slaughtered so many of the people of Lerna when they went to draw water from a well on the far side of the pool, where it lived. Hercules displayed his unselfish courage by tackling the monster on behalf of the citizens of Lerna, and ingenuity was displayed by his young charioteer, Iolaus, who brought flaming torches with which to burn the severed necks of the Hydra as Hercules lopped off its multitudinous heads. Before Iolaus's intervention with the torches, 2 heads had grown for every 1 that Hercules cut away.

In Greek numerology, and to the Pythagoreans, the number "10" stood for completeness and perfection. It is probable — almost a certainty — that this veneration for the number "10" was related to the number of human fingers and toes.

The ancient Greeks were very numerate and knowledgeable, and their views on the special significance of particular numbers is worthy of careful investigation and analysis. The uniquely powerful mind of Socrates, the great philosopher, epitomized the best and highest in Greek culture and learning.

The Babylonians were also extremely intelligent people with long traditions of wisdom, and their contribution to numerology is explored in the next chapter.

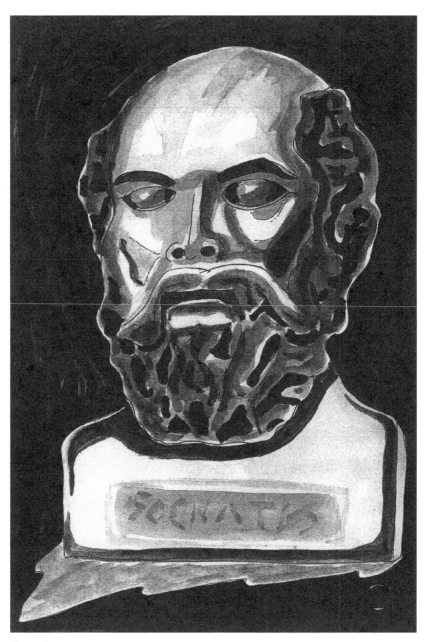

Socrates

10
BABYLONIAN NUMEROLOGY

In Assyro-Babylonian mythology, the story of creation was written on 7 tablets that were found in the library of Ashurbanipal in Nineveh. These date back as far as 1000 BC, but would seem to be based on far older creation mythology. The existence of 7 tablets brings up the numerological "7" and its significance as the number that represents analysis, knowledge and understanding, and awareness and study. These 7 tablets are an attempt to analyze and explain what brought the Earth into being. This creation mythology is based on water as the origin of all things, which is not too far removed from the idea in Genesis, chapter 1, verse 2: "And the Earth was without form and void; and darkness was upon the face of the deep. And the Spirit of God moved upon the face of the waters." In the Assyro-Babylonian account, the fresh water, which they called *apsu*, blended with salt water, which they referred to as *tiamat*. It was from their union that everything else was created, and the first parts of creation were their gods. There is a remarkable resemblance here to the Greek creation myth involving the River Oceanus, which Homer called the "father of all things." Tiamat was seen as the feminine element in creation and it was she who gave birth to the world. She also represented primitive chaos, again like the Genesis story where the Earth was "without form and void."

The two earliest Assyro-Babylonian gods were Lakhmu and Lakhamu, who are not as easy to define. The earliest surviving records are a little uncertain as to the nature of these first deities, and they were probably represented as gigantic snakes because of this uncertainty — the characteristic writhing movements of a serpent make it difficult to define its shape or position accurately. The fact that the numerological "2" comes into the creation myth again is interesting. "Two" signifies adaptability, cooperation, and partnership. The cooperation of Lakhmu and Lakhamu led to the birth of Anshar, the personification of masculinity, and Kishar, the personification of femininity. Some experts in Assyro-Babylonian mythology regard Anshar as the male sky god and Kishar as the earth goddess. Marduk also features prominently in the Assyro-Babylonian creation story as the entity that organized and arranged the universe. Anshar and Kishar were the parents of Anu, the mighty, and Ea, the great thinker: once again, a significant numerological "2."

There were 3 important gods concerned with celestial objects: Sin, god of the moon, was their father and leader; Shamash was the sun god; and Ishtar was the planet Venus. These 3 celestial beings were associated with the arts and the joys and delights of simply being alive. The numerological significance of "3" was appropriate for them.

There were 4 interestingly balanced Sumerian gods and goddesses, including the mother-goddess, Ninhursag: the sky god, An, who is occasionally represented as a jackal; Enlil, a subordinate god of the air; and his half-brother, Enki, a subsidiary god of earth and water. Enki's mother was Antu and Enlil's mother was Ki. Sadly, the 2 half-brothers were not friendly towards each other. The most relevant numerological significance of the number "4" in the case of Ninhursag, An, Enki, and Enlil would seem to be the concept of a struggle against limits.

The Sumerians also believed in 50 of what they termed "great gods," which included An's children and were known both as the *Annuna* and the *Annunaki*. In the traditional numerological working, the reduction of 50 (5+0) becomes 5, and the numerological association with "5" is the constructive use of freedom. The Annunaki exercized their divine freedom to work in various ways to control the environment and the forces within it, and so, rightfully, the Sumerians believed that it was vitally important to retain their favour with worship, prayers, ceremonies, and sacrifices. It is also numerologically interesting in the case of the number "5" to note that Gilgamesh — the protagonist of the famous epic — was the fifth king of Uruk after the deluge. He was undeniably an expansive, visionary adventurer, and those are the numerological characteristics associated with "5."

The various Assyro-Babylonian accounts of the Deluge — their version of Noah's flood story from Genesis, chapter 6 — refer to their flood as lasting for 6 days and 6 nights. Their hero, Utnapishtim, certainly displayed the numerological characteristics of "6" through his sense of responsibility, protection, and nurturing.

Traditionally, there were 7 sages who brought culture and wisdom to the 7 oldest cities in Mesopotamia, and numerologically "7" is associated with analysis, understanding, and knowledge as well as awareness and meditation: ideal characteristics for sages.

The Sumerian city of Lagash, similar in socio-political organization to one of the well-known Greek city-states, was known to have had 62 priests at the head of things. The "6" has the numerological significance of responsibility, protection, and nurturing. These were essential parts of the integral role of priests. The "2" stood for consideration of others and mediation: again, parts of any worthwhile priestly role. Adding the "6" and "2" together to get 8 creates the numerological significance of practical endeavours and a sense of status, which are relevant associations with the concept of "8." The 62 governing priests of Lagash had a great many practical things to sort out in addition to their spiritual functions, and they must certainly have enjoyed a sense of status. There were 180 instrumentalists and singers who also participated in the religious ceremonies of Lagash. The "1" of 180 has the significance of initiating action and leading, and the instrumentalists and singers led the ceremonial music on feast days and during festivals. The "8" of 180 represented their practical musical endeavours. When the "18" of 180 is reduced through the equation 1+8, it becomes 9. The number "9" is numerologically associated with the concept of creative expression, and music comes clearly into this category.

Babylonian civilization lasted for some 12 centuries — from 1800 BC–600 BC. It was largely a city-based civilization, but it depended heavily upon its fertile rural areas, as Babylon was not industrialized. There were numerous hamlets, settlements, and villages that augmented the cities. The rulers were very close to being absolute monarchs, as their powers extended over executive affairs, legislative matters, and control of the judiciary. Babylonian records were preserved using their cuneiform writing.

Babylonian cuneiform

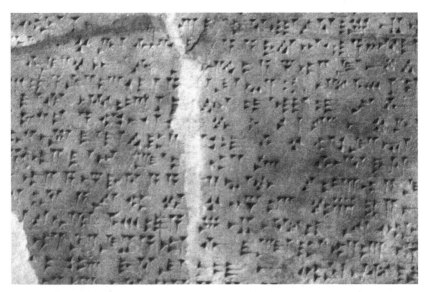

Engraved cuneiform

The monarch was assisted by city leaders — rather similar to modern mayors in the United States and Western Europe. There were also numerous elders and general administrators. The name *Babylonia* originally meant "the portal of God," and referred to Mesopotamia, the area between the Tigris and Euphrates rivers. Herodotus (484–425 BC) deserved his title as "The Father of History." In some of his outstanding chronicles he mentions that he intends to write a history of Babylonia, but he did not appear to carry out that work, or, if he did, it has been lost. Hecataeus of Miletus (550–476 BC) tended to write Babylonian myths and legends rather than a serious and factual history of Babylonia. Ctesias, who lived in the fifth century BC, was a Greek physician who served King Artaxerxes Mnemon. Ctesias had access to ancient Babylonian records via the Persian royal archives and his historical writings may well be accurate and trustworthy. Berosus was a Chaldean priest who lived and wrote in the third century BC. He was into numerology and astrology, as well as his historical studies. When Alexander the Great conquered Babylon, Berosus went to live near Rhodes on the island of Cos. Berosus covered dynasties of many thousands of years going back before the flood, during which Utnapishtim was the saving hero. There were then accounts of post-diluvian dynasties that had also lasted for millennia, and which brought the histories up to the reign of Nabonassar in the year 747 BC. The great Greek astronomer, numerologist, and astrologer, Claudius Ptolemaeus, calculated an era — the beginning of a particular period of time — from the first year of the reign of Nabonassar. Wednesday, February 26 in 747 BC was regarded as the first day of the Egyptian calendar. Being an astronomer, along with his many other talents and prodigious wisdom, Ptolemaeus was able to pin that particular starting-point year to some astronomical observations he had made. Other astronomers also used these, but ironically the Babylonians did not.

One strange and unusual aspect of Babylonian culture and social organization was the appointment of an official referred to as a *limu*. This royal officer gave his name to the year so that chroniclers would be able to date an event by stating "It was in the year of…" The king gave his name to the first year of his reign; the next year was named after his *turtan*, the commander-in-chief of the Babylonian army. The *grand vizier* came next, then such officers as the chief musician and various city governors. Records of each limu were carefully preserved and these records have proved extremely valuable to historians. After the actual name of the limu, some especially noteworthy event that had taken place during his year would be added to the records. A clear and useful example of the value of this record-keeping system was that there was a solar eclipse during the limu of Pur-Sagali, which took place during the reign of Ashurdan III, who reigned from 773–755 BC. This effective combination of the limu system and the astronomical and astrological records date the solar eclipse as taking place on June 15 in 763 BC.

The work of King Nabuna'id, who was himself something of an early archaeologist, unearthed a foundation stone while searching the ruins of the sun temple at Sippar. This ancient stone had been laid approximately 3,000 years earlier by Naram Sin, the Akkadian ruler under whom the Akkadian Empire flourished. Nabuna'id discovered Naram Sin's stone about 550 BC, which helps to fix the reign of Naram Sin *circa* 3,500 BC.

These dating methods enable the serious historians of Assyria, Babylon, Persia, and that area of the Middle East to establish a broad timeline. The earliest period of the first Mesopotamian numerologists

Assyrian deportation

was the era during which the city-states grew and developed until they were united into the super city-state of Babylon itself. In these very early days, numerous rival groups fought one another for supremacy in the Tigris-Euphrates area. These numerous battles frequently led to the deportation of prisoners and livestock.

By around 2000 BC, the area of Babylonia was more or less unified under the rulers of Babylon City. Peace was disturbed when Kassites arrived from the east, and, after a number of invasive battles, began a Kassite dynasty in Babylonia. This lasted for some 6 centuries. However, the Kassite dynasty roused the opposition of an older community with its heartlands at Assur on the River Tigris. This group eventually developed into Assyria, and under the great leadership of Tiglathpileser I, overcame the Babylonian Kassites. This period ended around 1000 BC. The next major socio-military event affecting Mesopotamia was the arrival of vast numbers of Arameans from the Arabian Steppes. Rulers like Ashurnacirpal, Shalmaneser II, and Tiglathpileser III were great generals as well as highly effective administrators and organizers. They created an empire that controlled everything from the Persian Gulf to the Egyptian border.

Although like most areas of numerology, from all ages of history, there is considerable controversy over what the Chaldeans and Babylonians actually *thought* about numbers and their mystical meanings. It has been suggested by some expert historical numerologists that the Chaldeans attached the following values to their alphabet. Using the English letter equivalents, the Mesopotamian system seemed to number their letter equivalents as:

A, I, J, Q, Y=1
B, K, R=2
C, G, L, S=3
D, M, T=4
E, H, N, X=5
U, V, W=6
O, Z=7
F, P=8

If we select the name of the famous Naram Sin and subject it to this Babylonian/Chaldean/Mesopotamian system, an interesting result ensues.

N=5

A=1

R=2

A=1

M=4

S=3

I=1

N=5

This gives a total of 22, which reduces to 4 (2+2). The number "4" is associated with laying a foundation, creating law and order, struggling against limits, and growing steadily. For a ruler of Naram Sin's vast ability and success, the "4" seems highly appropriate.

Eventually, a new Babylonian Empire emerged under the guidance of Nebuchadrezzar II (also known as Nebuchadnezzar II). Applying the Chaldean numerology system to his name gives us the following results:

N=5

E=5

B=2

U=6

C=3

H=5

A=1

D=4

R=2

E=5

Z=7

Z=7

A=1

R=2

These all add to 55. The reduction of 55 (5+5) gives us 10, which, when further reduced, equals 1. For an emperor like Nebuchadrezzar II, the "1" is an ideal number to portray his character and ability. The "1" stands for a pioneering spirit, one who loves to initiate action, a leader, and an independent individual who uses all his power and energy to attain things.

Historical circumstances changed again in 538 BC, resulting in Cyrus the Persian as the dominant ruler. Again, the application of Chaldean numerology produces a very interesting result:

C=3

Y=1

R=2

U=6

S=3

These numerological equivalents add to 15, which, reduced, becomes 6 (1+5). In the Chaldean system, "6" is associated with responsibility, protecting others, nurturing those in need, a strong sense of community, and a balanced and sympathetic outlook on life. Cyrus the Great, as he was justifiably known, was one of the kindest and most enlightened rulers in history. He treated his subjects with fairness and there was justice for all under his rule. No matter what controversies surround the Chaldean numerological system, it certainly seems to have worked remarkably well in the cases of Naram Sin, Nebuchadrezzar, and Cyrus!

The location of the Babylonian Plain had a profound influence on the history and development of the area. It is easily accessible, and many different cultures and ethnic groups settled within it. As wave upon wave of new conquerors came and brought their culture with them, so the varied cultures mixed. As communication along the great rivers was easy, as it was by land routes, Sumerian, Akkadian, and Babylonian ideas spread all over the ancient world and, not surprisingly, their ideas about numerology spread alongside their culture. Merchants and scholars came and went, as did armies; literature and religious observation were established, and so was Mesopotamian numerology.

One of the most interesting questions concerning Assyro-Babylonia and the other ancient lands of the area is the mystery of Oannes. He was a strange entity who came up from the water near Eridu, where there was a temple to Ea, god of the waters. Sumerian accounts of what sounds very much like an amphibian-humanoid give rise to speculations about Oannes being an extraterrestrial, or a survivor of the lost civilization of Atlantis.

In the old Sumerian accounts, Oannes was completely benign and taught such vital cultural skills as language and mathematics. To what extent — if he was a real being and not merely a myth or legend — did he contribute to the ancient numerological traditions of Sumer and the surrounding areas? Suppose that he was a highly intelligent, technologically advanced being from elsewhere who knew far more about the mysterious power and influence of numbers than human beings had yet discovered in Sumer. What if part of Oannes's teachings covered the unsuspected *command* that numerologists believe numbers can exert in unidentified ways over people and their environment? Suppose that part of Oannes's highly advanced culture — terrestrial or extraterrestrial — was knowledge of secret numerological influences as yet unknown to the Sumerians and their contemporaries? Was it Oannes who taught the associations between numbers and their various powers and influences? Did he reveal to humanity some 5,000 years ago that "1" stood for pioneering action and independence? Did he show his worshippers that "2" meant adaptability and cooperation? Was it Oannes who gave the earliest Sumerian numerologists the idea that "3" signified the joy of living and the arts? Did he teach his contemporaries that "4" signified a strong and secure foundation and the triumph of order over chaos? Was it from Oannes the wise that the early Sumerian numerologists learnt to associate "5" with visionary adventure? Had Oannes himself experienced a strange adventure that had led to his arrival on Earth? Had he survived a journey of many light years from some distant planet such as Kepler 22b? Or, had he miraculously survived the inundation of a high-tech society that had once lived on Atlantis? Was it from Oannes that the early Sumerian numerologists learnt that the mystical significance of "6" was responsibility for others, protection of those in need, and sympathy? Did he in his own great wisdom teach them that the number "7" had the numer-ological significance of analysis and understanding, of true wisdom and profound knowledge? Was it from Oannes the wise that the early Sumerian numerologists learnt the practical endeavours and goals that were associated with the number "8"? Did he teach them the mystical implications and the powers that could stem numerologi-cally from the all-important number "9"? Did he show them that "9" was the ultimate humanitarian number, that it taught unselfishness, creativity, and generosity?

The very strange-looking *lamassu* were portal guardians. They, too, looked as if they might have come from somewhere very strange and dis-tant. In Mesopotamian religion, the lamassu were thought of as benign entities who acted as guardians and protectors of human beings. They were often represented as part-bull, part-man, and in some representa-tions they also had wings. Their statues were frequently placed alongside doorways and gates. In some ancient accounts, the name *alad* or *shedu* is used instead of *lamassu* for the benign, winged bull-man. As well as being placed beside portals, they were sometimes modelled in clay and buried under the thresholds of houses to protect the occupants.

Another impressive and interesting feature of the ancient Mesopotamian civilizations were the titles that some of their rulers used. Often they were referred to as "King of the Four Regions," or even as "King of the World." This title of superior, all-encompassing authority is numerologically significant yet again. The "4" symbolizes a firm foundation, good order and discipline, steady growth, and a battle to extend the boundaries of the empire. Another title, which was used to indicate a ruler's power, was "King of the Totality." This specifically takes a numerologist back to the power of "1." Such an Assyro-Babylonian monarch regarded himself as a pioneer, an inde-pendent individual, one who set out to initiate action and to attain all his political and military goals.

An outstanding ruler named Enshagsagana ruled the kingdom of Kengi in southwestern Babylonia, *circa* 4500 BC. Analyzing his name using the numerological system gives an interesting result.

Lamassu portal guardian from Nimrud City

E=5
N=5
S=3
H=5
A=1
G=3
S=3
A=1
G=3
A=1
N=5
A=1

The numerological sum of Enshagsagana is therefore 36, which, when reduced, becomes 9. The significance of "9" suggests that Enshagsagana was unusually humanitarian and generous for a ruler of that distant period.

In a variety of ways, therefore, Babylonian numerology may claim to be one of the oldest forms of numerological analysis. Babylonian travel and trading over ancient Mesopotamia and far further afield very likely carried their numerological system extensively — to Greece, Egypt, Rome, and North Africa. Was that system based on the strange, alien wisdom of Oannes, and were some amazing numerological facts buried in his teachings?

Impressive as the Mesopotamian system of numerology may have been, the ancient Indian system, the subject of the next chapter, could justifiably claim to be its equal.

11
INDIAN NUMEROLOGY

Tracing the earliest evidence of human beings in ancient India finds recognizable human ancestors in the form of *Homo sapiens* from more than 70,000 years ago. Earlier species such as *Homo erectus* in India go back half a million years. Civilization was dawning in the Indus Valley over 5,000 years ago. India experienced Bronze Age and Iron Age developments. What was known as the Harappan period lasted from 2600–1900 BC. Over 1,000 years later the Maurya Empire held sway, and for the next 1,500 years it was believed that the Indian economy was among the largest in the world. This was the case until the end of the seventeenth century. As far as the spread of knowledge and culture, including Indian numerology, were concerned, from the end of the first century AD the southern Indian state of Kerala had commercial links with the Roman Empire and Indian numerology travelled with its culture and commerce.

Ancient Indian numerology can be detected in Indian religious mythology. There are many important myths within the pages of the *Rigveda*, which translates as "verses of praise and knowledge/wisdom."

This ancient Indian collection of Vedic Sanskrit hymns was almost certainly composed in the northwestern area of the Indian subcontinent well over 4,000 years ago. As well as accounts of creation, the Rigveda is full of prayers to the Hindu gods, as well as supplications for the health and prosperity of their worshippers.

A Rigvedic Shakha is a branch, or recension, of the main work. A holy, academic hermit named Sakalya gives his name to such a recension. His version contains 1,017 hymns, which is very significant numerologically. Taken individually, the numbers give the meaning of "1" as pioneering action and attainment. The holy hermit Sakalya undertook pioneering action in creating and recording his branch, or recension, of the Rigveda. Academically, as the number "11" indicates, he was a leader. The "7," which signifies responsibility and concern for the community that looked to him for leadership, is also applicable to Sakalya. There is also significance in the numerological calculation of his number of hymns (1+0+1+7), which comes to the sum of 9. The "9" suggests that Sakalya's collection of 1,017 Vedic hymns were numerological indicators of his unselfishness, generous and giving nature, his creativeness, and the love he had for his fellow beings. In addition to the 1,017 regular hymns in Sakalya's Shakha, there are 11 *valakhilya* hymns. The valakhilya are very tiny paranormal entities who, among their other duties, surround the sun's chariot. These 11 hymns carry the numerological significance of intuition, sensitivity, and spirituality. Numerologically, "11" refers to idealism, patience, and honesty — all qualities that are associated with the holy hermit Sakalya. When reduced, "11" can also translate into the number "2," which represents duality in the best sense of cooperation, mediation, and partnership. "Eleven" is also referred to, numerologically, as the "Bearer of Light" or "The Bearer of Illumination." It is the bringer of peace, sensitivity, gentleness, and the deepest possible insight. The colours associated with "11" also have mystical meanings. These colours are gold, deep purple, gentle orange, white, and black.

When the 11 hymns in the appendix are added to the main contents of 1,017, the grand total in the Sakalya Shakha rises to 1,028. When added numerologically (1+0+2+8) we once again reach the highly significant sum of 11, and again, through reduction, the numeral 2. All the hymns together in the Sakalya Shakha serve to emphasize the messages related to the numbers "2" and "11."

Another wise compiler of a Rigvedic Shakha was named Baskala, and his compilation differed in minor details from the work of the holy hermit Sakalya. Baskala included only 8 of the 11 valakhilya hymns, which Sakalya had included in the appendix to his work. This made a total of 1,025 in Sakalya's collection. The meanings of the numbers "1" and "2" have already been expanded above, but what of the "5" that Baskala included? It is the numerological indicator of visionary adventure and the constructive use of freedom. Adding the digits of 1,025 in the numerological style gives us the sum of 8. When this fact is combined with the 8 valakhilya hymns used by Baskala, the importance of the numerological meaning of "8" is reinforced. The Shakha, as compiled by Baskala, relates to practical endeavours, power-seeking, and high material goals. It is here that his work differs from that of the holy hermit-scholar Sakalya. Another significant numerological difference between the 2 recensions is that Baskala's version has its own distinct appendix containing 98 hymns, referred to as the Khilani. When these 98 are added to the main body of 1,025 it gives a total of 1,123. Numerologically, this adds to a total of 7. The numerological association with "7" is knowledge, understanding, awareness, analysis, and meditation. This, again, is very appropriate for Baskala's work. It is also interesting to note that the total can be viewed as an 11, followed by a 23.

The numerological significance of "11" has already been commented on in depth in an earlier part of the chapter. It refers to honesty, patience, and idealism. It is also known as the bearer of illumination both literally and metaphorically. "Eleven" is the bringer of peace and insight. Very different from "11" is the strange number "23." Associated outside of India with Eris, the Greek goddess of chaos and disorder, it is also linked to the religion of Discordia in which Eris is worshipped in rituals referred to as "chaos magic."

There is further significance when reducing the 98 hymns of the Khilani (9+8) to make a total of 17, which in turn is reduced to 8. The "8" is there again to indicate practical endeavours, power-seeking, and high material goals.

As centuries passed, Britain became the dominant power in India, which changed dramatically in 1947. Numerology is as interested in significant dates — under whatever dating system is used — as well as in name numbers and totals such as those found in the various recensions. What is to be made of the year 1947, numerologically? It adds to 21, which in turn reduces to 3, and "3" is one of the most significant of all numerological associations. The number "3" represents free expression, the arts and sciences, and, above all, the sheer joy of living. What could be more appropriate than a numerological "3" for the year in which India regained its freedom?

Another numerologically interesting Indian association with "3" is the reference in the Brahma Purana to the 12 "gods" who are actually 12 different names for Surya, covering 12 different aspects of him, as well as his general role as the sun god. Adding together the digits "1" and "2" of 12 gives Brahma Purana his all-important "3," signifying expression and the joy of living. The warmth and light of the sun enhances life and the sun's brightness is very expressive. According to expert numerologists, "12" has special cosmic significance — an ideal number for Surya, the sun god. Life, in association with the number "12," is harmonious, just as a calm, bright, warm summer day is harmonious. The perspective of the numerological "12" is from above — just as the sun appears to be above the Earth. There are echoes of this in the positioning of the number "12" at the highest point on the dial of a clock. Expert numerologists also see "12" as a problem-solving number. The influence of "12" makes things better, repairs and restores things, and brings new health and energy to the sick. There is clearly a sense in which sunlight and gentle warmth, the gifts of Surya, do make things better and have an uplifting psychological effect. Numerologically, "12" is also associated with arts and music. Technically there are 12 major half-tones in music. "Twelve" also fits with the signs of the Zodiac, and the 12 astrological houses. Numerologists would also consider that "12" is divisible by 2, 3, 4, and 6. It can, therefore, be argued, numerologically, that the powers of these 4 numbers can be united in "12."

The first of the 12 aspects of the sun is Indra, captain of the gods and demolisher of their enemies. Numerologically, Indra calculates as follows:

I=1

N=5

D=4

R=2

A=1

Added together, this comes to a total of 13. Among its numerous meanings, "13" stands for change — radical change and vast improvement. This meaning connects strongly to the power of Indra to bring about such changes for his disciples and worshippers. Further reducing 13 to "4" (1+3) signifies a strong foundation, good order, progress, and growth: all of which are encouraged by Indra.

The second of Surya's 12 names, or 12 aspects, is Dhata, the creator god. Numerologically, Dhata translates as follows:

D=4

H=5

A=1

T=4

A=1

This gives Dhata a numerological total of 15. Numerologically, "15" is a very fortuitous number. It is associated with harmony and happiness. It combines physical and spiritual pleasure and welfare. Numerologists would say that "15" brims with life: an ideal number to associate with Dhata, the creator god.

The third of the 12 aspects of Surya is Parjanya, the benign sender of rain from the clouds. The numerological translation of Parjanya is:

P=8

A=1

R=2

J=1
A=1
N=5
Y=1
A=1

Added together, this comes to a total of 20. The numerological characteristics associated with "20" are generous giving and being of service to those in need. This is very appropriate for Parjanya, the rain giver. There is also an element of wise decision-making in the number "20," the ability to wait until the time is ripe. It is as if the rain god Parjanya knew better than the farmers who were waiting hopefully for the rain to fall when their crops were in need. Because rain can do good *or* cause damage such as flooding if circumstances are wrong, the number "20" carries within it the idea of judicious choice. Parjanya has the power to distinguish between good and evil and sends the rain or withholds it as he thinks best. Numerologically, "20" also refers to the optimal use of time, and it seems relevant to have a time element with Parjanya: gentle rain on the vitally important crops has to come at the right time. Reducing the numerological total of 20 to "2" makes Parjanya cooperative and considerate.

The fourth manifestation of Surya is Tvashta. This is that aspect of divinity that occupies all matter. One classical definition records that Tvashta "lives in all corporal forms." Translating Tvashta numerologically, we get:

T=4
V=6
A=1
S=3
H=5
T=4
A=1

This makes a total of 24 for Tvashta. Some expert numerologists would regard "24" as indicative of creativity. The presence of the god Tvashta in all material things may be thought to represent creativity, in so far as his followers may think that the spiritual and the divine permeate physical objects and, in that sense, enable a carving of something beautiful to be made from wood or stone, or a beautiful tapestry to be made from coloured threads and fabric. The potential beauty, like the divine Tvashta, is somehow encapsulated within the object. The "2" of his 24 represents adaptability — the plain, raw material being adapted into something good, attractive, and worthwhile. The "4" of his 24 represents the god Tvashta within simple, basic, physical objects, giving them order and making them the foundations of more elaborate things. Because of these connections with turning simple physical matter into the divinely beautiful, Tvashta is worshipped by Hindu blacksmiths and carpenters.

The fifth aspect of Surya is known as Puchan the provider. It is he who supplies food for living beings. Numerologically, Puchan translates as follows:

P=8

U=6

C=3

H=5

A=1

N=5

His numerological total is 28. Puchan is also referred to in the mythology as the god of meeting. He is a good and wise leader and the guardian of cattle and sheep, who retrieves lost animals and restores them to their rightful owners. He is also a god of marriage, and blesses newly married couples as they set out in life together. The 28 days of the lunar month are very significant. If we add the "2" and "8" of 28 together to get 10, further reduced to 1, we find that "1" is also numerologically significant in connection with Puchan the provider. He initiates action, he helps his worshippers to attain things they need, and he is a pioneering god who leads his followers in good and desirable ways.

The sixth aspect of Surya is known as Aryana. She is the goddess who brings sacrifices to fruition. She sees that good is rewarded. If we translate Aryana numerologically, we get:

149

A=1
R= 2
Y=1
A=1
N=5
A=1

Her numerological total of "11" carries with it the concepts of honesty, patience, and the highest ideals. When the two "1"s are added numerologically to produce "2," the concepts evoked are mediation, partnership, and cooperation. "Eleven" brings illumination in both the literal and metaphorical senses. With her highly positive "11," the goddess Aryana is thought of as gentle, sensitive, and peaceful.

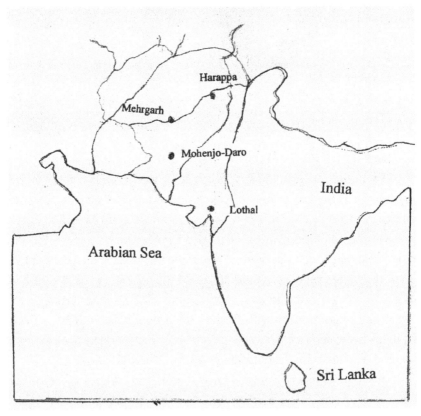

Ancient Indus Valley civilization

Surya's seventh aspect is that of the god who bestows generous gifts on beggars.

The eighth aspect is named Vivasvan, and is a god of health and happiness who helps his worshippers maintain good digestion. Translated numerologically, Vivasvan becomes:

V=6

I=1

V=6

A=1

S=3

V=6

A=1

N=5

Vivasvan numerologically totals 29. "Twenty-nine" is a special numerological symbol for completeness, success, and achievement. It also suggests fulfilment. The "2" of 29 stands for cooperation and adaptability. These concepts can rationally refer to food and digestion, as the body takes in nutritious food and uses it to produce energy and to repair itself and grow. The "9" has other good and relevant connotations with food. An expert cook or chef can use food creatively and there is an element of creativity in the numerological "9." Adding the "2" and "9" together to get 11 evokes all the positive associations that go with "11": gentleness, sensitivity, and peace. When food is easily digestible it gives the alimentary canal a feeling of peace, which makes the "11" appropriate for Vivasvan — the god who brings the blessing of good, healthy digestion.

The ninth aspect of Surya is Vishnu, who, like Indra, is a defender and guardian of the other gods. Numerologically, Vishnu equates to:

V=6

I=1

S=3

H=5

N=5

U=6

Vishnu's numerological score is 26. The "2" in his case shows consideration of the other gods that he defends fearlessly. The "6" clearly denotes protection and responsibility. Some expert numerologists have suggested that, when taken together as "26," the number is traditionally associated with fearless warriors. When added numerologically (2+6), this comes to "8," which has the connotations of practical endeavours; there are few more practical things Vishnu undertook than the protection of his fellow gods.

The tenth aspect of Surya is Ansuman, another god of good health. Where Vivasvan is primarily the guardian of good digestion, Ansuman has responsibility for all the bodily organs and their functions. Translated numerologically, Ansuman becomes:

A=1
N=5
S=3
U=6
M=4
A=1
N=5

Ansuman's numerological total is 25. This is associated with deep, careful, objective thought: exactly what is needed for the kind of health supervision that falls to Ansuman. Observed separately, the "2" is associated with consideration for others, and in Ansuman's case, it is consideration and concern for the health of his worshippers. The "5" reflects the visionary nature of Ansuman's work, in which the vision extends to the perfect health of his followers. There is also a sense in which the "5" refers to the constructive use of freedom, and while guarding and caring for the health of his devotees, Ansuman allows them to be free. He is a god of encouragement rather than a god of control.

The eleventh of the 12 aspects of Surya is known as Varuna, a water god, who symbolically gives the water of life to the entire universe. Just as Tvashta is thought of as dwelling in solid matter, so Varuna is conceived of as dwelling in the heart of the purest and deepest waters. We can examine this further through Varuna's numerological translation:

V=6
A=1
R=2
U=6
N=5
A=1

Varuna has a numerological total of 21, which signifies great vitality and fluidity: totally appropriate for a water god. The number "21" can also evoke restlessness. Taken separately, the "2" in this case emphasizes adaptability. Water adapts to the shape of its container, whether ocean, sea, lake, or river. The number "1" leads and initiates action. The power of the water god leads the way. Water can also initiate action, especially in such examples as the use of the watermill. When we add the numerals of 21 together to get 3, we find a number associated with the joy of living. Fresh mountain streams bound over the rocks like happy children at play.

The twelfth and final aspect of Surya is referred to as Mitra, associated with the moon. Mitra is generally regarded as a benign god who works for the welfare and freedom of his followers. Looking at Mitra numerologically, we find:

M=4
I=1
T=4
R=2
A=1

Appropriately for the twelfth god, Mitra has a numerological score of 12. Mitra can be thought of as a god who aids human recovery and supplies new energy to the exhausted. Mitra gives vitality when it is most needed, and there is also a sense in which Mitra enables his followers to relax and enjoy life when their duties have been well fulfilled. Expert numerologists would suggest that the doubly emphasized "12," as outlined earlier, has a special cosmic significance. Just as with Surya the sun god, so Mitra and his association with the moon have an overhead perspective on the world and the life upon it. Again, as noted earlier, "12" is at the top of the clock dial. "Twelve" is also considered to be a problem-solving number, which is quite appropriate for Mitra's divine role as a welfare god. When we reduce 12 to the separate digits "1" and "2," and examine this aspect of Mitra's numerology, we find that "1" is the factor that initiates the benign actions that Mitra undertakes for his worshippers' welfare, and "2" is his benign consideration for his followers and their welfare. The sum of the digits 1 and 2 is 3. The number "3," again, symbolizes the joy of living in a numerological connotation, and Mitra is seen by his followers as a caring deity who wants them all to enjoy life.

There are some expert Indian numerologists who have interesting theories about the *shapes* of numbers and the significance of these shapes. According to them, the "0" is all-encompassing; it encircles important characters, objects, and events. It can be protective or it can be imprisoning. The figure "1" is straight, simple, and direct; it points to things and undertakes tasks with swift ease. The figure "2" is regarded as a part-circle; it can encompass and encapsulate things, but there is always an escape route. The circle is not complete. It can be thought of as a shield. The figure "3" can be regarded as the wings of a bird. It represents flight to a destination or flight away from difficulties and dangers. It can be an escape from unpleasant or hazardous situations. The figure "4" represents relationships. The upright line and the cross-bar can represent loving partners or parent and child, brother and sister, reliable friends, or trustworthy business associates. The dark side of the "4" can be a triangular relationship, infidelity, betrayal, or jealousy.

The figure "5" is similar in many ways to the "2." It symbolizes a partial shield — a limited area of protection. It can also represent the tools or instruments of a trade or craft, such as a plough or a scythe in agriculture. It could, in modern times, represent a computer, or an advanced computer program for carrying out a particular process. The "6" offers complete protection, a perfect shield — or, at its darkest, a complete incarceration. The tail leading into the circle suggests a pathway to protection or a route to imprisonment. The figure "7" offers direction and guidance; it points the way. It can also represent reconciliation — a place where 2 conflicting paths meet and unite. It could be the end of a feud or quarrel. It could mean an armistice after a war. The figure "8" represents infinity, or eternity — a path that goes on forever. It is the sign of permanence in a relationship. It can also represent a double shield — perhaps the protection and care offered by a devoted, loving partner, and protection from financial risks, or health risks. With both meanings taken together, the "8" can signify an enduring relationship that offers protection on multiple levels. The "9" has much the same meaning as the "6," although it is far less likely to have a dark side. The tail of the "9" is a path that leads upwards towards protection and security.

If this scheme is applied, for example, to Mitra, whose score came to 12, working on the number-shape-meaning concepts listed above, the "1" undertakes tasks with simple directness and the "2" encircles and encapsulates things, rather like a shield. Mitra's characteristics can then have these 2 number-shape concepts added to them.

Vardhamana lived from 599–527 BC and was the founder of the Jains in India. Experts in the history of Jainism believe that he, himself, learned its excellent philosophical principles from what Parshwa (877–777 BC) had set down over a century earlier. Jainism is a good and worthwhile system based on logic, rational thought, and objective, scientific observation of the environment. Philosophically, it understands the very important argument that when a subject is approached from different intellectual directions, different conclusions may well be reached. Jainism embraces the concept of Karma, as do many other Indian systems of thought. In other words, they believe that a person's actions affect his or her life for better or worse.

If we examine Vardhamana numerologically, we get the following:

V=6

A=1

R=2

D=4

H=5

A=1

M=4
A=1
N=5
A=1

This adds to a total of 30. The "3" of 30 stands for the joy of living, and the religious system that he helped to originate is one that brings joy to its adherents. When the "3" is examined for its shape it is thought to signify a bird in flight and to represent flight from danger to safety, or from an unsatisfactory life to a better and happier existence. Taking the number-shape connotations along with the traditional numerological associations, the founder of Jainism offers escape into a better life in which the joy of living dominates. Numerologically, the number "30" indicates a fine intellect and persuasive speaking ability. That certainly applies to Vardhamana. "Thirty" indicates charisma, genuine friend-liness, and the ability to love: Vardhamana was genuinely fond of his disciples and adherents. It also has connotations of harmony.

Parshwa, from whose writings Vardhamana learnt his philos-ophy, is also numerologically interesting. He was known by the title *purisadaniya*, meaning "beloved of the people," which is a significant indicator of his lifestyle and personality. Examined numerologically, Parshwa translates to:

P=8
A=1
R=2
S=3
H=5
W=6
A=1

Parshwa's numerological total comes to 26. As shown earlier for Vishnu, "2" shows consideration for others and "6" denotes responsi-bility and protection. "Twenty-six" is also associated with fearlessness, and Parshwa was a fearless missionary and teacher of Jainism. After "2" and "6" are added together, their sum "8" is associated with practical endeavours. Parshwa's missionary work was certainly practical.

When the letter shapes are studied and added to the general numerological meanings for Parshwa, the suggestion is that the "2" is a part-circle encompassing Parshwa's intellectual thought and his spirituality. The pathway out — the escape route — could be said to represent his open-minded, objective, rational thought, or the escape route from traditionalist fundamentalism and religious authority. The shape of the "6" symbolizes the pathway to the encircling protection of the new Jainist religion. The "8" relates to the enduring character of the new religion, which Parshwa was instrumental in establishing.

Indian numerology, Indian gods, Indian religious leaders, and profound Indian thinkers have all made their contribution to the development and uses of numerology in the subcontinent itself and the rest of the world. The next chapter looks into the mysteries of Norse mythology and its close relationship with Norse numerology.

12
NORSE NUMEROLOGY

Ancient Norse culture, religion, and mythology were deeply inter-twined with early numerology. The Norse people were particularly concerned with the number "9," and "3" was a close second to it. They were also especially observant of "27," as it was the product of 3 and 9.

Norse mythology recognizes 3 separate types of giants who were the enemies of the Norse gods. These were the fire giants, the frost giants, and the mountain giants. "Three" also has great significance right at the very beginning of Norse mythology. Audhumla the cow sustained herself by licking the salty ice that was there before cre-ation. She in turn provided milk to sustain Ymir, the first giant. Then Buri emerged after she had licked the ice of Ginnungagap for 3 days to release him. Ginnungagap was otherwise known as "The Yawning Void" and was there before creation. To the north of it lay the deadly cold of Niflheim. To the south was the equally fatal heat of Muspelheim. Buri became the grandfather of Odin, and was thus the first god. The great nineteenth-century Swedish academic Viktor Rydberg found an interesting parallel between the early Norse myths and the Zoroastrian creation stories. What he commented on in particular was that a giant ox or cow features in both sets of stories, and that the numerological "3" also recurs in both.

The highly significant numerological "3" appears again when Ymir has 3 children: a boy and a girl grew from under his arms and a son who possessed 6 heads came from his legs and feet.

Buri, whom Audhumla the cow had released from the primordial ice, became the father of Borr, who in turn had 3 sons. These were the brothers Vili, Ve, and Odin, who was destined to become the chief of the gods in due time. These 3 brothers killed Ymir, whose blood destroyed the other giants except for Bergelmir and his wife, who hid in a huge hollow tree. He became the ancestor of a new race of giants. Numerologically, Borr's 3 sons are, again, significant.

After killing Ymir, the brothers used his vast body to create the universe. Yet again, "3" features in the mythology. There were also 3 generations of giants before Ymir was killed.

The giant Hrungnir, who was later slain by Thor, had a triangular stone heart — "3" yet again!

Eric the Red's Viking runes

There are also 3 Norns in Norse mythology. Their names are Uror, Verdandi, and Skuld, and they serve much the same function as the Fates of Greco-Roman mythology. They live in a hall near the Well of Uror (the "Well of Destiny," or "Well of Fate"), from which they draw water to sustain Yggdrasil, the world tree upon which the 9 worlds of Norse cosmology depend. The gods of Norse mythology hold a daily court meeting beside Yggdrasil. The 3 Norns are maiden giantesses, referred to as Jotuns. Yggdrasil has 3 roots and serves 9 worlds.

When Odin, ruler of the gods, was hunting for the vitally important runes that feature in Norse mythology, he suffered 3 things on Yggdrasil: he was suspended there; wounded with a spear, and endured thirst and hunger.

Loki, the cruel, sinister, and irresponsible god, produced 3 evil offspring when he mated with the giantess Angrboda. The first was Fenrir, the monstrous wolf; the second was Jormungandr, the Midgard Serpent; and the third was Hel. She is the entity who presides over the kingdom of Helheim, where she receives the dead. In the mythology she was involved in the attempt to resurrect the god Baldur. Her realm of Helheim contains vast palaces and mansions and she has large retinues of servants. Its entrance is guarded by the dangerous hound Garmr.

Fenrir the Wolf

In Norse mythology, *Ragnarok* is a final terrible battle in which many of the gods are slain, but there is then a deluge and a rebirth of better things for both gods and human beings. Before Ragnarok, which is also referred to as the "twilight of the gods," there will be 3 exceptionally hard and severe winters with no summers between them. This period is referred to in Norse mythology as the *Fimbulwinter*. Another prelude to Ragnarok is the sinister crowing of 3 cockerels: Fjalar crows for the giants; Gullinkambi crows for Odin and the gods; a third cockerel crows for the dead.

The number "3" comes up again very significantly in the stories of the chaining of Fenrir, the great wolf. The 3 fetters were Loeding, Dromi, and Gleipnir. Only Gleipnir held him.

In the Norse poem "Voluspa," Garmr, the giant hound that guards the gates of Helheim near the Gnipa cave, makes his terrible howling noise 3 times.

The mysterious character Gullveig is speared and then burnt 3 times, yet she is magically resurrected each time. The Rainbow Bridge has only 3 colours instead of the 7 in the full spectrum: red, orange, yellow, green, blue, indigo, and violet. It also has 3 names: Bifrost, Asbru, and Bilrost. Heimdall, who guards the bridge, has 3 special super attributes that make him an effective guardian: he needs little or no sleep; he can see in the dark for over 500 miles; and his hearing is so acute that he can hear plants growing. The 3 handmaidens of Frigga, the goddesses, are named Fulla, Gna, and Hlin. Odin has 3 priceless treasures: his horse Sleipnir, which has 8 legs; his spear Gungnir; and his gold ring, called Draupnir. There are other strange numerological features associated with Draupnir. Every ninth night, the magic ring gives out 8 golden drops — each of which then becomes yet another ring — making up the magical set of 9. The 8 drops represent power-seeking and material objectives, and gold is certainly among the most sought-after of all material objectives.

Three gifts were asked in return for building the walls of Asgard: the moon, the sun, and the goddess Freyja as a bride. Freyja also has

3 priceless treasures: her necklace, Brisingamen; her chariot drawn by 2 great cats; and a magic cloak that enables her to fly as swiftly and gracefully as a falcon. Freyja numerologically becomes:

F=8

R=2

E=5

Y=1

J=1

A=1

This gives a total of 18, which, reduced, becomes 9. As the square of 3, "9" is of great significance in Norse numerology.

In a fruitless attempt to frighten the mighty hammer god Thor, the giants built a clay giant — shades of the Hebrew concept of a golem — that was 3 leagues wide. Needless to say, it was the clay model named Mokkurkalfi who was frightened of the heroic Thor! The numerological "3" is found again in Thor's 3 weapons: Mjolnir, his hammer; the metal gauntlets that he wears when he uses it; and the magic belt that doubles his strength when he puts it on.

"Nine," as noted earlier, is also of special importance in Norse numerology. "Nine" signifies unselfishness and obligation to others. Odin's ordeal on Yggdrasil lasted for 9 days and nights. The great tree itself supports the 9 worlds of Norse mythology. The giant Thrivaldi has 9 heads.

There are also 9 heavenly realms: Vindblain, Andlang, Vidblain, Vidfedmir, Hrjod, Hlyrnir, Gimir, Vet-Mimir, and Skatyrnir.

There are 9 points, each forming an angle of 60 degrees, on what is known today as the valknut symbol made from 3 interlocking triangles. It was called the "knot of the slain," or "Hrungnir's heart," in earlier times. Experts in Norse mythology and religion have suggested that it may also refer to reincarnation.

A Norse witch named Groa has a son named Svipdag and gives him 9 magical gifts. In the same saga there are 9 girls who attend to Menglod, the imprisoned princess whom the hero Svipdag eventually succeeds in rescuing.

The blot was a special form of Norse sacrifice, which involved using a religious fire that had to be kindled from 9 different types of wood. It was customary to sacrifice animals during the blot festivities: pigs and horses were the usual choices. The meat was boiled after the animals had been slaughtered, and the blood was sprinkled on the statues of the Norse gods and their worshippers. The blood was believed to give strength and courage to the people it was sprinkled on. There was an extra special Blot festival held at Uppsala every ninth year and the festival lasted for 9 days.

The persistence of the Norse numerological "9" even insinuates itself into a domestic disagreement between 2 divinities: the god, Njord, and Skadi, his wife. In one version of the tale, Njord wanted to live in Noatun and Skadi preferred Thrymheim. As a compromise it was decided that they would spend 9 nights at a time in each location. Njord's son, Freyr, also had relationship problems when he wanted to marry the beautiful Gerd, who was a giantess. After a great many problems and difficulties, his wily servant, Skirnir, arranged things for him — but in one version of the story Freyr had to wait 9 days before the wedding took place.

Aegir and Ran both represent the sea in Norse mythology. They have 9 daughters, all of whom represent different aspects of the ocean. Himinglaeva means that water is transparent. Dufa signifies the pitching movement of the waves. Blodughadda symbolizes the colours of the foam. Hefring suggests that the sea rises. Udr indicates frothing waves. Hronn means waves that are welling up. Bylgja signifies billowing waves. Drofn indicates foam-flecked waves, sometimes referred to as combers by seafarers. Kolga suggests wintry waves when the water is especially cold.

Having examined the special numerological importance of "3" and "9" in so many aspects of Norse mythology, the names of the various gods can be examined in detail and compared numerologically with what is known of them from the stories about them.

Telly is regarded in some versions of Norse mythology as the supreme and ultimate god. He was the creator of Audhumla, the primordial cow. Telly is omnipotent, omniscient, and omnipresent — very like the One God of the Abrahamic faiths. Nothing can injure him in any way and he waits patiently inside Yggdrasil until Ragnarok is over. He then emerges from Yggdrasil and rules the 9 worlds and their inhabitants with eternal peace, happiness, and love. Numerologically, Telly becomes:

T=4
E=5
L=3
L=3
Y=1

This adds to 16, which in turn adds to 7. The numerological "7" indicates understanding, knowledge, and awareness. In the case of Telly, those qualities are at their ultimate. His understanding, knowledge, and awareness are infinite.

Baldr is the god of beauty, peace, rebirth, and innocence. Numerologically, Baldr translates to:

B=2
A=1
L=3
D=4
R=2

The numerological total for Baldr is 12, which reduces further to 3 — the Norse "3" appears yet again. Baldr's mother is the chief goddess, Frigga, wife of Odin. Numerologically, Frigga becomes:

F=8
R=2
I=1
G=3
G=3
A=1

This gives her a numerological total of 18, reduced further to 9.

Thor, the god of war, the mighty hammer-wielder, becomes:

T=4
H=5

O=7

R=2

Thor's total is 18. Reduced further, the sum of 18 becomes 9, and once again the Norse predilection for "9" is evident.

Freyr is associated with the weather and farming. He is also a god of fertility. He has a wonderful ship called *Skiobladnir*, which is always propelled by a favourable wind and can be folded away into a pouch and carried when not needed on the ocean. Numerologically, Freyr becomes:

F=8

R=2

E=5

Y=1

R=2

This gives him a total of 18, reduced, once again, to "9" — exactly as in the case of Frigga and Thor, who is Frigga's stepson. The "9"s and "3"s persist.

Loki, the god of mischief, selfishness, chaos, and evil translates to:

L=3

O=7

K=2

I=1

This gives him a numerological total of 13. Where "13" is regarded as a number of ill-luck, misfortune, disaster, hardship, trouble, and adversity, it is totally appropriate for Loki. When reduced numerologically (1+3), we get the sum of 4, which signifies a struggle against limits. Loki's main motive is his over-reaching, unscrupulous ambition. He struggles all the time against the other gods because he wants to be their supreme ruler in place of Odin.

The exact role of the Norse god Heimdallr — also known as Heimdall — is not easy to define. He sits at the heavenly end of the Rainbow Bridge and drinks vast quantities of delicious mead of the highest quality. His eyesight and hearing are incredibly sensitive and acute and he keeps vigil for the start of Ragnarok. He is associated with the ram as his sacred animal.

Numerologically, Heimdallr translates to:

H=5

E=5

I=1

M=4

D=4

A=1

L=3

L=3

R=2

Adding all of the letters' numerical equivalents together gives us a numerological total of 28. The sum of "28" further resolves to 10 (2+8), and again further to 1 (1+0). The numerological sense here is that "1" is an indicator of difference or independence, and Heimdallr is different and independent. When the "1" is associated with attainment, Heimdallr has attained exceptional sight and hearing. "One" is also the

Co-author Patricia with Aries the Ram

number that initiates action, and Heimdallr watches, listens, and waits for Ragnarok. It is his early warning that will initiate the actions of all the other gods.

Vor is an interesting goddess associated with wisdom. Her name, numerologically, becomes:

V=6
O=7
R=2

When added together, the numerical equivalent of Vor results in a total of 15, which becomes 6 when reduced (1+5). As a goddess of wisdom, Vor is, in extension, also a goddess of responsibility, sympathy, balance, and protection. There is also a numerological sense of community attached to the number "6," and the wisdom of Vor is for the benefit of the whole community — the kind of wisdom that includes education and a sharing of knowledge.

An interesting minor deity in the Norse pantheon is known as Andhrimnir. In some versions of the mythology he is listed as the cook who provides meals for the other gods. Numerologically, his name works out as:

A=1
N=5
D=4
H=5
R=2
I=1
M=4
N=5
I=1
R=2

This produces a numerological total of 30, which, when reduced becomes 3. Andhrimnir, therefore, maintains the continual Norse involvement with "3."

The Norse god of poetry is Bragi. Numerologically, his name works out as:

B=2
R=2
A=1
G=3
I=1

This gives him a total of 9, which is just as important to Norse numerologists as their favoured "3." Indeed, so many of the Norse sagas were written in the form of poetry that their god of poetry was very important. There was almost a sense in which Bragi, as the inspirer of verse, was the medium through which the great Norse tales of courage and adventure were told. His consort was the bewitchingly beautiful Idunn, the exquisite goddess of youth and energy, hope, and inspiration. Her gifts were well matched with Bragi's gift of poetry. It was Idunn who inspired the poets to write; it was Bragi who provided their medium. Numerologically, Idunn translates to:

I=1
D=4
U=6
N=5
N=5

Her total is 21, further reduced to 3. Yet again, the persistent Norse "3" is revealed in the name of the glorious goddess of youth, energy, and optimism.

Eir is another very welcome member of the Norse pantheon: she is the goddess of healing. Numerologically, she amounts to:

E=5
I=1
R=2

Her total is 8, which is associated with high material goals and practical endeavours. Healing was vitally important to the Norsemen, who spent so much of their lives in battle. Axes and swords created massive wounds, and prayers to Eir, the benign goddess of healing, were an integral part of the life of a Norse warrior.

Forseti was the god of truth, justice, and peace. He was the son of Baldr and Nanna. Numerologically, Forseti becomes:

F=8

O=7

R=2

S=3

E=5

T=4

I=1

Forseti's total is 30. Reduced further, this becomes 3 — and once again the Norse "3" returns.

Sjofn is the goddess of love, marriage, and affectionate relationships. Numerologically, her name works out as:

S=3

J=1

O=7

F=8

N=5

This produces a total of 24, reduced, numerologically, to 6. The number "6" is associated with ideas of protection and balance, which are essential ingredients of a stable, loving relationship. Her opposite is Weth, the goddess of anger, hostility, rage, and fury. Numerologically, Weth translates as:

W=6

E=5

T=4

H=5

This totals 20, reduced further to 2. "Two" is a benign number signifying cooperation and consideration. It does not apply in any way to Weth. In order to investigate the mysteries and secrets of numerology in an objective and balanced way, it is essential to examine cases where the numerological concepts associated with a name do not reconcile at all with the characteristics of the entity being examined. In the great majority of examples examined in this chapter, the names

of the gods have broken down numerologically into the characteristics associated with them. However, Weth, goddess of anger, does
not fit the idea of cooperative adaptability, partnership, mediation,
and consideration for others. However, the number "20" — before
being reduced numerologically to its single figure "2" — was disliked
intensely by the mystical theologian Jakob Bohme (1575–1624), who
said it was the devil's number. The scholarly Saint Jerome (347–420)
also considered the number "20" to be ominous and threatening. So
"20" has a connection with Weth, the goddess of anger, even though
"2" doesn't.

Norse numerology has provided many interesting and intriguing
examples of the association of the Norse gods' characters with their
numerological numbers, and the Norse obsession with "3"s and "9"s
is also fascinating. In the next chapter, numerology is examined where
it occurs in the Kabbalah — the rich and ancient compendium of
Hebrew wisdom.

13
NUMEROLOGY IN THE KABBALAH

The term *Kabbalah* can be broadly translated from the ancient Hebrew as meaning "the process of receiving," and it is used in the sense of receiving secret knowledge and hidden wisdom. It is especially interesting to investigators of strange, mysterious, and anomalous phenomena because of its connections with the Hachmei Province of southern France — not far from Rennes-le-Château and all the mysteries there centring on the puzzling treasure allegedly discovered by Father Bérenger Saunière. This leads one to wonder: did the mysterious Priory of Sion, who allegedly operated in the Rennes area, have any access to the secrets of the Kabbalah?

The mysteries of the Kabbalah were organized and systematized in that area of France and just across the border into Spain during the eleventh and thirteenth centuries. Those dates in themselves are numerologically significant. The eleventh century was numerologically associated with intuition, sensitivity, and spirituality. The number "11" is thought of as an idealistic number. Although "13" does have some dark associations in many numerological interpretations, it can also stand for enlightenment and can be associated with the enlightenment within the Kabbalah during the thirteenth century.

The innermost teachings of the Kabbalah explain the nexus between the immortal and all-powerful spiritual Creator of the universe and the physical universe itself, which He has made. Some denominations use the Kabbalah extensively and depend upon its teachings, but this can be confusing to general observers of its usage: the Kabbalah is not a denomination — it is ancient, secret wisdom on which some denominations depend. It is not actually part of the traditional Jewish scriptures. Kabbalah can, perhaps, be understood from some perspectives as a sublime dictionary that defines the universe and the place of human beings within it, as well as setting out to explain the reason for human existence. There are experts who define the Kabbalah as an encyclopedia of ontology. But what do they mean by "ontology"? Originating in classical Greek, ontology can be explained as "that which is." It asks the big questions about what exists, and about the nature of reality. It puts existence into categories, looks at what entities may occupy those categories, and examines the hierarchies of such entities. All of these questions are targeted in the Kabbalah.

Church of St Mary Magdalene at Rennes

One important foundation text for the Kabbalah is known as the *Zohar*, which teaches that studies of the Torah can be undertaken at 4 levels. The "4" is numerologically significant here, as it indicates order and a foundation, as well as steady growth and a struggle against limitations. The Torah corresponds approximately to the first 5 books of the Christian Bible: Genesis, Exodus, Leviticus, Numbers, and Deuteronomy. These are known in Judaism as *Torah Shebichtav*, meaning "The Torah that is written." Over and above these 5 written books there is also *Torah Shebe'al Peh* meaning "The Torah that is spoken."

The numerology of the Kabbalah may be said to begin with the 5 books of the written Torah. The "5" represents visionary adventure, the best use of freedom — physical and intellectual — and expansiveness. All of these qualities can be found in the written Torah.

The 4 levels of studying the Torah referred to in the Zohar are first, the simple, direct level — taking everything literally and at direct face value. The second level, known as *Remez*, looks for the metaphorical, allegorical meanings. The third level, *Derash*, aims to find enlightening comparisons between particularly significant words and verses, and to enhance meaning and understanding by studying those comparisons in depth. The fourth and highest level is concerned with mysteries and secrets concealed within the Torah. Serious students of the Kabbalah and its secret mysteries believe that it is essential to approach the Torah at this level.

There are experts in the study of the Kabbalah who believe that many of its deep secrets were understood by a brilliant Jewish philosopher named Solomon ibn Gabirol (1021–1058). Subjecting his name to numerological analysis is very interesting:

S=3

O=7

L=3

O=7

M=4

O=7

N=5

MYSTERIES AND SECRETS OF NUMEROLOGY

I=1
B=2
N=5

G=3
A=1
B=2
I=1
R=2
O=7
L=3

Numerologically, this adds to 63, which reduces further to 9. This is highly significant for a religious philosopher of the stature of Solomon ibn Gabirol. The "9" shows his humanitarian nature, his generosity, his unselfishness, and his creative powers. All of these characteristics are totally appropriate.

Another significant early Kabbalist was Bahya ben Asher (*circa* 1260–1340) and his name can be analyzed numerologically as:

B=2
A=1
H=5
Y=1
A=1

B=2
E=5
N=5

A=1
S=3
H=5
E=5
R=2

This leads to the numerological total of 38, reduced to 11 (3+8), and once again to 2 (1+1). Expert numerologists regard "11" as indicating intuition, idealism, sensitivity, and spirituality: ideal qualities for a religious philosopher like Bahya ben Asher. The "2" indicates his consideration of others, his cooperation, and his adaptability.

Other major contributions to Kabbalistic thought and scholarship were made by Isaac ben Solomon Luria Ashkenazi (1534–1572). Numerologically, his names becomes:

I=1
S=3
A=1
A=1
C=3

B=2
E=5
N=5

S=3
O=7
L=3
O=7
M=4
O=7
N=5

L=3
U=6
R=2
I=1
A=1

A=1
S=3

H=5
K=2
E=5
N=5
A=1
Z=7
I=1

This adds to a total sum of 100, which, when reduced, becomes 1. Isaac ben Solomon Luria Ashkenazi has the numerological characteristics of leadership, a man who initiates action, and a pioneering individual who is noted for his attainments. This is totally appropriate for him.

Ashkenazi, who was nicknamed "The Lion," worked as one of the leading rabbis in the Jewish community at Safed in Galilee. His talents included poetry and he was a great and respected leader among his people. One of his important teachings concerned *tzimtzum*. By this, Luria meant an elemental act of God that in some way beyond human comprehension drew in and constricted God's infinite light, power, and energy in order to make room for creation to take place, to make an emptiness that the universe could subsequently fill. *Tzimtzum* is a very interesting word numerologically:

T=4
Z=7
I=1
M=4
T=4
Z=7
U=6
M=4

This totals 37. The reduction of 37 comes to 10, further reduced to 1. Numerologically, "1" initiates action and tzimtzum was the action that initiated God's creation of the universe.

Maimonides (1135–1204) was a leading Jewish rabbi, philosopher, and expert on the Kabbalah. He was also an outstanding physician. Numerologically his name can be calculated as:

M=4

A=1

I=1

M=4

O=7

N=5

I=1

D=4

E=5

S=3

This comes to 35, which reduces to 8. Numerologically, "8" indicates high material goals, power-seeking, a status-oriented person, and one with practical endeavours. As a very successful physician, Maimonides was concerned with the immediate physical objectives of curing his patients. As a leading rabbi and religious philosopher, he was status-oriented and battled for power against rival thinkers. Maimonides was philosophically interested in the true nature of power when he thought his way through the relationship of the all-powerful Creator and his creation. In his own words, Maimonides summed it up like this: "The foundation of foundations and the pillar of pillars of true wisdom is knowing that God exists and brought into being all existence. The heavens, and the earth, and what is in them and all that lies between them came into existence from God's being." In Kabbalistic thinking, God is neither spirit nor matter, but something entirely different from which both were created. This again points to the mysterious numerological "3": God, spirit, and matter. Kabbalists also invoke the mysterious numerology of "2." They believe that there are 2 aspects of God. They think first of God himself who is beyond all human thought and knowledge and is completely unknowable. Their second envisioning of God is as the revealed God, creator and sustainer of the cosmos, and the aspect of God that cares for human beings. This brings in the numerological "2," referring to the 2 aspects of God. The numerological thoughts associated with "2" are consideration, cooperation, mediation, and adaptability. Just as with the mystery of the Christian theology of the Trinity, consisting of God the Father, Son, and Holy Spirit, so there is a mystery of the Holy Duality of the Kabbalah: God the Unrevealed and God the Revealed.

The Biblical vision of Ezekiel (Ezekiel, chapter 1, verses 4–28) is of particular interest to followers of the Kabbalah. The prophet's name works out numerologically as:

E=5

Z=7

E=5

K=2

I=1

E=5

L=3

This produces a total of 28, which can be reduced to 10, then further reduced to 1. This is totally suitable for the prophet Ezekiel, as "1" carries the numerological significance of initiating action, leading, pioneering, and showing independence. All of these qualities apply to Ezekiel.

A wise medieval Kabbalah teacher

Another central thought in philosophical and theological Kabbalah teachings was that light energy was the connection between God and the universe that he had created, and which was sustained by his power. Light formed the links that held the chain of being together.

Another great thinker, writer, and religious teacher who contributed to later developments of the Kabbalah was Rabbi Shneur Zalman (1745–1812). Numerologically, his name becomes:

S=3
H=5
N=5
E=5
U=6
R=2

Z=7
A=1
L=3
M=4
A=1
N=5

This gives a numerological total of 47, which reduces to 11, followed by 2. "Eleven," as stated earlier, is regarded as an idealistic number, and Shneur was an idealist. The number "2" stands for cooperation, adaptability, consideration for others, and mediating. All of these are ideal qualities for a leading rabbi and Kabbalah expert such as Shneur Zalman.

Another theological numerological mystery is to be found in the Sefirot. These are the 10 so-called emanations of God. The word *Sefirot* itself can be calculated as:

S=3
E=5
F=8
I=1
R=2

O=7

T=4

Numerologically, this totals 30. The number 30 can be further reduced to 3 (3+0). This "3" symbolizes the sheer joy of living. The Sefirot's 10 reduces to 1, which symbolizes the initiation of action, leading, and attaining. The "3" and the "1" are therefore totally appropriate for God as understood in the Kabbalah, and there is the additional mystery of the Trinity here as understood in Christian theology: 3 in 1 and 1 in 3.

The numerological mysteries of the Kabbalah continue with the references to the *Shechina*, understood to be the feminine divine presence. Genesis, chapter 1, verse 27 reads: "So God created man in his own image, in the image of God created he him; male and female created he them." The final Sefirah of the 10 Sefirot is regarded as the Shechina — the feminine aspect of God. When Shechina is analyzed numerologically, it becomes:

S=3

H=5

E=5

C=3

H=5

I=1

N=5

A=1

This produces a total of 28. The sum "28" can be reduced to 10, which is then further reduced to 1. The number "1" takes us back to the concept of God as the Initiator of all things.

The Kabbalah teaches the 10 Sefirot, and the feminine Shechina, as well as what it refers to as the 4 worlds through which the power of God flows and radiates like light. These worlds are known within the Kabbalah as Atziluth, Beriah, Yetzirah, and Assiah. They are very interesting numerologically. Atziluth becomes:

A=1

T=4

Z=7
I=1
L=3
U=6
T=4
H=5

This gives a total of 31, which in turn becomes 4. Numerologically, the "4" suggests a firm foundation and steady growth. Beriah becomes:

B=2
E=5
R=2
I=1
A=1
H=5

This gives a numerological total of 16, further reduced to 7. Numerologically, "7" is associated with understanding, knowledge, and meditation.

Translated numerologically, Yetzirah becomes:

Y=1
E=5
T=4
Z=7
I=1
R=2
A=1
H=5

This totals 26, which in turn reduces to 8. The "8" suggests power-seeking and high material goals, practical endeavours, and a concern with hierarchical status. The "2" of 26, on the other hand, is cooperation, adaptability, and consideration of others. The "6" of 26 represents responsibility, protection, nurturing, and a strong sense of community. Taken individually, therefore, the "2" and "6" of 26 are appropriate for one of the 4 worlds into which God's divine light and energy flows. The fourth world is Assiah and this can be calculated as:

A=1
S=3
S=3
I=1
A=1
H=5

This produces a total of 14, which can then be reduced to 5. "Five" is associated numerologically with expansiveness, visionary adventure, and the constructive use of freedom. All of these qualities are compatible with one of the 4 worlds into which God pours light and energy.

An allied area of mystical Kabbalah teaching suggests that within the Sefirah named Chessed, the predominant influence is loving kindness. Numerologically, Chessed translates to:

C=3
H=5
E=5
S=3
S=3
E=5
D=4

This comes to a total of 28, which, when reduced, becomes 10 and then 1. The number "1" initiates action, leads, and attains. It reinforces the idea that Chessed is the Sefirah of loving kindness, which is infinitely the best and most effective way of initiating action, leading, and attaining.

The Sefirah known as Gevurah is morality, ethics, and justice. Numerologically, Gevurah becomes:

G=3
E=5
V=6
U=6
R=2
A=1
H=5

This comes to a total of 28. Adding the "2" and the "8" of 28 brings us to 10, which further reduces to 1. The number "1" initiates the action of justice and the fair and balanced independence of divine morality. Mercy works with justice, and the Sefirah of mercy is Rachamim. This works out numerologically as:

R=2
A=1
C=3
H=5
A=1
M=4
I=1
M=4

Numerologically, this comes to a total of 21. If we reduce 21 further, we get 3. The number "3" relates to social expression and the joy of living in a world where mercy is shown. The Sefirah of attractiveness, beautiful robes, jewels, and other adornments is called Tiferet. Numerologically, this can be worked out as:

T=4
I=1
F=8
E=5
R=2
E=5
T=4

This gives a total of 29, reduced to 11, and even further to 2. "Eleven," as noted earlier, indicates spirituality, and "2," when taken in association with adornment, shows awareness of others and consideration of them, which is a prime reason for personal adornment.

Moses ben Jacob Cordovero (1522–1570) was a vital contributor to the Kabbalah and leader of a school of mystics. His powerful book, *Tomer Devorah*, which translates as "Deborah's Palm Tree," is filled with clear ethical doctrines. Moses ben Jacob Cordovero is very interesting numerologically:

M=4
O=7
S=3
E= 5
S=3

B=2
E=5
N=5

J=1
A=1
C=3
O=7
B=2

C=3
O=7
R=2
D=4
O=7
V=6
E=5
R=2
O=7

This gives a numerological total of 91. "Ninety-one" reduces to 10, and then further to 1. The number "1" has the numerological association of initiating action, pioneering, leadership, independence, and individuality. All of these excellent qualities applied to Moses ben Jacob Cordovero and his style of Kabbalah leadership.

Another great Kabbalah thinker was Abraham Abulafia (1240–1295). He founded the school of "Prophetic Kabbalah" and taught that there were 3 aspects of the human soul — the numerological "3" is clearly in evidence here again. The first part of the soul resides in every human being and is called the *nefesh*. The next 2 parts of the soul are called the *ruach* and the *neshamah*. These have to be developed, and do not exist until a person has made the most of his or her innate spirituality. Abraham Abulafia can be worked out numerologically as:

A=1
B=2
R=2
A=1
H=5
A=1
M=4

A=1
B=2
U=6
L=3
A=1
F=8
I=1
A=1

This equals a numerological total of 39, which reduces to 12 and then 3. This number is most appropriate for a leader like Abraham Abulafia. It shows expression, verbalization, and the arts. It also reveals the sheer joy of living, which he experienced through leading his Kabbalah School.

It is also numerologically interesting to analyze the 3 names of the different parts of the soul as taught in the Kabbalah. Nefesh works out as:

N=5
E=5
F=8
E=5
S=3
H=5

This totals 31, which then becomes 4. "Four" is the foundation, the basic soul, the one that struggles against limits. This is appropriate for nefesh. The second, or central, soul is ruach.

Ruach translates numerological as:

R=3

U=6

A=1

C=3

H=5

Altogether this totals 18, which can be further reduced to 9. "Nine" is an excellent number. It reflects humanitarianism, generous, unselfish giving, creativity, and a keen sense of obligation. This is precisely the nature of ruach, which is morally and ethically virtuous, and distinguishes clearly between good and evil. The third and highest soul is neshamah. Sometimes referred to as the super soul, it is the one that qualifies human beings as candidates for immortality.

Neshamah translates to:

N=5

E=5

S=3

H=5

A=1

M=4

A=1

H=5

When added together, this totals 29, which further reduces to 11. "Eleven" indicates a very high level of spirituality, which is totally consistent with neshamah. When 11 is reduced further to 2 in numerology, it is also associated with cooperation, adaptability, and consideration of others: all of these excellent qualities are compatible with neshamah, the highest of the 3 souls.

In addition to the 3 souls that actually occupy the body, there are 2 others that do not. These are known as *chayyah* and *yehidah*. According to the eminent philosopher and historian Gershom Scholem

(1897–1982), a leading student of the Kabbalah and a professor of Jewish mysticism at the Hebrew University of Jerusalem, these 2 external souls were the highest level of intuitive cognition. Analyzed numerologically, chayyah becomes:

C=3
H=5
A=1
Y=1
Y=1
A=1
H=5

This comes to a total of 17, which reduces further to 8. "Eight," numerologically, stands for status, and here it is one of the highest statuses that a human being can aspire to. Chayyah is that part of the human soul that enables the individual to experience the divine life force.

When analyzed numerologically, yehidah becomes:

Y=1
E=5
H=5
I=1
D=4
A=1
H=5

This adds to a total of 22. Each "2" separately stands for cooperation, adaptability, and consideration of others, which is totally compatible with the working of yehidah. When we reduce 22 to 4, we find that "4" is associated with a sound foundation, good order, willingness to serve, and steady growth. These admirable numerological qualities are in harmony with the overall concept of yehidah as union with God.

The Kabbalah incorporates the belief that all Hebrew letters, words, accents, and numbers are part of hidden codes and ciphers, and the Kabbalah shows those who study it in-depth how these secret meanings can be found. The system, which is known as gematria, or gimatria, assigns numerical values to words and phrases and teaches that those words and phrases, which have the same or very close totals, must also be connected in meaning. This theory comes close to some modern numerological teachings.

Another basic Kabbalah belief is that numbers revealed as significant by the above methods may refer to the age of a person at which certain events in the gematria code may occur. The numbers revealed by gematria may also reveal a date on which the events in the coded message will take place. The word *gematria* is interesting in terms of its possible derivation. Did it come from *gamma*, the third letter of the Greek alphabet, and therefore have the important significance of the numerological 3? Might it have been derived from the Greek *geometria*, meaning geometry? Pythagorean geometry is of massive significance to numerologists.

Giovanni Pico della Mirandola (1463–1494) was a brilliant Renaissance philosopher, theologian, and magician whose lasting work *Oration on the Dignity of Man* has been thought of as the manifesto of the Renaissance itself. His name, analyzed numerologically, becomes:

G=3
I=1
O=7
V=6
A=1
N=5
N=5
I=1

P=8
I=1
C=3
O=7

D=4
E=5

L=3
L=3
A=1

M=4
I=1
R=2
A=1
N=5
D=4
O=7
L=3
A=1

This makes a total of 92. The sum "92" further reduces to 11, which finally becomes 2. The "11" indicates spirituality and the "2" stands for cooperation, adaptability to new circumstances (as with the Renaissance), consideration of others, partnership, and mediation. All of these numerological factors fit well with Giovanni.

Taken together, the essential concepts of the Kabbalah are numerologically very significant, and the later chapter dealing in depth with isopsephy and gematria, as such, will take it down to finer detail. What the Kabbalah reveals clearly is that there was a profound belief in the numerological aspects of the Kabbalah mysteries. Words and numbers worked together to associate different concepts, and to suggest ages and dates on which particular events would occur. The major problems here — as with all techniques of foretelling the future — are that it is difficult theologically and philosophically to conceive of the future as being cut and dried. If everything is predestined and inescapable, ethics and morality are excluded. If the holiest, kindest, gentlest, and most generous of saints and the vilest and cruellest serial killers are simply *programmed* by fate to carry out their deeds, then Jack the Ripper and Francis of Assisi are neither morally better nor worse than the other. Perhaps all that numerological calculations can predict — if they do predict anything at all — is a series of likelihoods and possibilities. Choice remains the responsibility of every individual human being.

Following on from these profound Hebrew mysteries of the Kabbalah, the next chapter looks at the numerological enigmas of the Bible.

14
BIBLICAL NUMEROLOGY

The division of the Bible into the Old and New Testaments, books, chapters, and verses, is itself an indication of the importance of numbers within it. But other interesting numerological aspects can also be found. "Forty," which sometimes carries the general meaning of "many" or "several," occurs with reference to the wanderings in the wilderness during the Exodus. Jesus was in the wilderness for 40 days during the period referred to as "the temptations." During the account of the flood in Genesis, chapter 7, verse 12, it rained for 40 days and 40 nights. Still with the story of the deluge, in Genesis, chapter 8, verse 6, Noah waited 40 days before opening a window in the ark. In Genesis, chapter 50, verse 3, after his death, Jacob was embalmed by Egyptian experts on the orders of his son, Joseph. The process took 40 days. In Exodus, chapter 24, verse 18, Moses was on the holy mountain with God for a period of 40 days.

The spies who were sent to investigate the Promised Land and brought back fine specimens of figs, pomegranates, and grapes from Eschol took 40 days to complete their explorations, as recorded in

Numbers, chapter 13, verse 25. The first book of Samuel, chapter 17, verse 16 tells how the giant, Goliath of Gath, paraded challengingly in front of the Israeli army for 40 days before David dealt with him. The prophet Elijah travelled for 40 days until he reached Mount Horeb, known as the Mount of God. This is recorded in the first book of Kings, chapter 19, verse 8. In the book of Jonah, chapter 3, verses 4 and 10 tell how the prophet warned the city of Nineveh that they had only 40 days to repent before God destroyed the city. The Ninevites duly repented in time. Jesus appeared to the disciples during a period of 40 days after his resurrection. The account is given in Acts, chapter 1, verse 3.

Biblical numerology also has a set of meanings and values for the different numbers. "One" is said to indicate unity. The Holy Trinity is 1 in 3. God the Father is 1, so is God the Son, and God the Holy Spirit — yet all 3 persons are unified. Deuteronomy, chapter 6, verse 4 emphasizes the *oneness* of God. "Hear, O Israel, the Lord our God is *One* Lord." St Paul's letter to the Ephesians also emphasizes unity. In chapter 4, verses 5 and 6, he writes: "*One* Lord, *one* faith, *one* baptism, *one* God and Father of all …"

Moses

In contrast to the unifying aspects of "1," the number "2" is seen as representing division, separateness, and categorization. God the Son has 2 natures: divine and human. Matthew, chapter 12, verse 32 refers to 2 worlds — this present earthly world and the world to come. Matthew, chapter 13, verse 49 contains eschatological references to separating the wicked from the just. Romans, chapter 9, verse 21 refers to the potter making 2 kinds of vessels.

Biblical numerologists tend to view the number "3" as something very special: first because of the Holy Trinity, then because they regard the universe itself as consisting of 3 discrete parts: time, matter, and space. Each of these, in turn, may be conceived of as possessing 3 ingredients. Time can be split into past, present, and future. Matter can be thought of simplistically as existing in 3 forms: vapour, fluid, or solid. Space, in the sense of volume, has 3 dimensions all at right angles to one another: length, width, and height. A case can be argued for saying that human beings have 3 separate parts: mind, body, and spirit. It may also be argued that human expression comes into 3 categories: thought, word, and deed.

"Four" is significant because of the 4 gospels: Matthew, Mark, Luke, and John. In Revelation, chapter 7, verse 1, there are 4 angels who stand on the 4 corners of the Earth holding the 4 winds under their control.

"Five" can be linked to David's victory over the giant Goliath of Gath. The first book of Samuel, chapter 17, verse 40 tells how David selected 5 smooth stones from the brook. When directions for making holy anointing oil are given in Exodus, chapter 30, verses 23–25, there are 5 sacred ingredients: myrrh, cinnamon, calamus, cassia, and olive oil.

In the creation story, Genesis, chapter 1, verse 27, human beings were created on the sixth day. There were 6 days of labour, followed by rest. Significantly, there were 6 steps that led up to the throne of King Solomon the Wise, as recorded in the first book of Kings, chapter 10, verse 19.

Genesis, chapter 2, verse 3 records how God blessed the seventh day and sanctified it. In Revelation, chapter 16, verse 17 the seventh angel pours out his vial into the air and a voice from Heaven declares: "It is done." Genesis, chapter 7, verse 2 tells how Noah took the "clean" animals into the ark 7 at a time. In Leviticus, chapter 8, verse 35, Aaron and his sons stay in the tabernacle for 7 days as part of their priestly confirmation. In Leviticus, chapter 16, verse 14, the sacred blood of the sacrifice has to be sprinkled 7 times on the mercy seat. Another example is the 7 years that Solomon took to finish building the Temple, as recorded in the first book of Kings, chapter 6, verse 38. The Hebrew phrase "70 times 7," which means an infinite or unlimited number of times, is used by Jesus in Matthew, chapter 18, verse 22, in connection with forgiveness.

"Eight" in the Bible is associated with new beginnings. There were 8 people on the Ark in the flood story: Noah and his wife, their sons Ham, Shem, and Japheth, and their 3 wives. The full account is given in the book of Genesis, chapters 6–9. "Eight" also has important significance in the resurrection appearances of Jesus. When Thomas told the other disciples that he could not believe in the resurrection unless he saw Jesus for himself, a period of 8 days elapsed before they were together again and Jesus appeared to them. The account is given in John, chapter 20, verse 26.

"Nine" is associated with the 9 gifts of the spirit as delineated in the first book of Corinthians, chapter 12, verses 8–10. These 9 gifts are: wisdom, knowledge, faith, healing, miracles, prophecy, discerning spirits, speaking in tongues, and interpreting tongues.

A vineyard

"Ten" is associated with the famous 10 commandments in Exodus, chapter 20, and again with the 10 plagues of Egypt before Pharaoh released the Israelites. The account of the 10 plagues can be found in Exodus, chapter 7, verse 14 onwards.

"Eleven" is found in the parable of the workmen in the vineyard, when those who were hired at the eleventh hour received the same pay as those who had worked all day. The parable is located in Matthew, chapter 20, verse 1 onwards.

"Twelve" is highly significant Biblically. There were 12 tribes, and there were 12 disciples.

"Thirteen" is mentioned in Genesis, chapter 14, verse 4, where the reference is to a rebellion: "Twelve years they served Chedorlaomer, and the thirteenth year they rebelled." When the numerological reduction technique is applied to "13," we get the sum of 4. The association with "4" is a struggle against limits, hence a rebellion.

In the fourteenth year, Chedorlaomer and his allies and vassals return in power and reverse the situation. Lot, who is Abraham's nephew, is taken prisoner, and Abraham sets out to recover him. He is blessed and supported by the mighty and inexplicable Melchizedek, the Priest-King of Salem. There are fascinating theories to the effect that the mysterious Melchizedek is one and the same person as Hermes Trismegistus and Thoth, scribe to the Egyptian gods and master of the emerald tablets. Abraham rescues Lot and all his possessions. The "14" here is a particularly powerful and blessed number. In the first chapter of Matthew's Gospel, verse 17, there are precise references to the 14 generations from Abraham to King David, another 14 from David's reign to the captivity in Babylon, and a final 14 generations from the captivity to the appearance of Jesus.

Two interesting Biblical references are associated with "15." The first is from Genesis 7, verse 20, where Noah's ark floats 15 cubits above the submerged land. The second is from John's Gospel, chapter 11, verse 18, where the distance between Jerusalem and Bethany is given as 15 furlongs. When reduced, 15 becomes 6, and "6" has the significance of protection, just as the ark protected Noah and his family from the flood water. In much the same way, Bethany was a place of protection and rest for Jesus and the disciples after their strenuous and demanding public work.

There are 16 prophets in the Old Testament, and 16 apostles and evangelists in the New Testament. When reduced, 16 becomes 7, which is associated with knowledge, understanding, awareness, analysis, and meditation. These are all totally relevant for the work of prophets, apostles, and evangelists.

"Seventeen" is found in Revelation, chapter 13, verse 1. The beast that rises from the sea has 7 heads and 10 horns, totalling 17. When reduced, 17 becomes 8. The number "8" is numerogically associated with being status-oriented and power-seeking. The fantastic beast is said by some theologians to be an image of ruthless, secular, political power. In Revelation, chapter 13, verse 18, the beast is given a mysterious number "six hundred, three score and six."

There are, however, a number of interesting variations of interpretation. In some early texts the number of the beast is given as "616" instead of "666." There are earlier references to 666 in the first book of Kings, chapter 10, verse 14, and in the second book of Chronicles, chapter 9, verse 13. In these references to "666," it is referring to the number of talents of gold that Solomon received each year. But what was a Biblical gold talent worth? Greeks, Romans, Egyptians, and Babylonians all had rather different ideas about the size and value of a talent. A talent of water was the amount of water that would fill an amphora. A talent of silver, however, in the old Greek system, was approximately 30 kilograms. Another rendering of the Greek (or Attic) talent of silver was 26 kilograms. Rome looked for 32.3 kilograms as a talent. The ancient Hebrews used the Babylonian talent measure of 30.3 kilograms, although by New Testament times there were Hebrew heavy talents amounting to 58.9 kilograms. To the nearest kilogram, even using the Babylonian standard, Solomon reportedly received 20,179.8 kilograms of gold every year. This comes to some 20 tonnes of gold annually. At 2011 prices of £30 per gram, 1 kilogram of gold is worth £30,000. A tonne of gold is worth £30 million. Solomon's annual income in gold was approximately £20 billion.

A number of expert Bible scholars and theologians go along with the theory that "666" was the encoded number for Nero Caesar, whose cruel persecutions of the early church certainly merited his description as the Great Beast.

The number "18" in the Bible is generally thought to represent bondage, slavery, and captivity. For example, in the book of Judges, chapter 3, verse 14 there is an account of a Jewish captivity: "So the children of Israel served Eglon king of Moab 18 years."

For a New Testament reference to the number "18," there is again an association with bondage or imprisonment, but this reference in Luke, chapter 13, verses 10–13 is to the bondage of illness or infirmity.

> "Now He was teaching in one of the synagogues on the Sabbath. And behold, there was a woman who had a spirit of infirmity eighteen years, and was bent over and could in no way raise herself up. But when Jesus saw her, He called her to Him and said to her, 'Woman, you are loosed from your infirmity.' And He laid His hands on her, and immediately she was made straight, and glorified God."

The numerological reduction of 19 produces 1, which has strong associations with independent, pioneering individuals who initiate action. In the New Testament example, Christ's loving, caring action of healing and extraordinary leadership of his people are appropriate for "1."

"Nineteen," using a Hebrew form of the gematria, works for the names of Eve and Job. Theologically, both characters and the things that happen to them represent attempts to solve the age-old problem of theodicy. When God is infinitely good, kind, and loving, as well as infinitely powerful, why do good and innocent people suffer? In the story of Eve, her suffering is attributed to the serpent's temptation of her. In the story of Job, the suffering is again attributed to a personified force of evil. But a closer inspection of the story of Job suggests that the Satan who appears in the book of Job is not so much a force of evil but a questioning, testing entity, a sort of spiritual version of the counsel for the prosecution. Numerologically, 19 calculates to 10, which then becomes 1, so Eve and Job are seen as initiating action, independent, pioneering individuals. In Eve's case, the action she initiated was not the right response to the serpent's temptation, but she made the choice. She took and ate the forbidden fruit. Job's steadfast refusal to listen to his so-called friends and to blame God for his misfortunes was also a course of pioneering, independent action — but in Job's case, his choices were right.

"Twenty" is a number that seems to suggest a protracted waiting period, a long delay. Jacob waited for 20 years in Laban's service before taking his wives and his livestock. This is recorded in Genesis, chapter 31, verses 38 and 41. In the book of Judges, chapter 4, verse 3 there is an account of the sufferings of the Israelites under Jabin, King of Canaan. These lasted for 20 years. In the first book of Samuel, chapter 7, verse 2, the Ark of the Covenant waited at Kirjath-jearim. It took Solomon 20 years to complete the Temple and his grand palace, as is recorded in the first book of Kings, chapter 9, verse 10.

When the sum of 20 years is numerologically reduced to 2, the ideas associated with "2" are cooperation, adaptability, partnering, and mediating. This seems appropriate for coping with long periods of waiting.

The major significance of the number "21" is that it is the product of 3 and 7. "Three" owes its importance to the Holy Trinity and the 3 parts of the universe: time, space, and matter. Time has 3 aspects: past, present, and future. Matter exists as solid, liquid, and gas. Space has 3 dimensions, all at 90 degrees to one another. Human beings are mind, spirit, and body, and can express themselves in thought, word, and deed. God blessed the seventh day. Noah took 7 of each "clean" animal into the ark. Solomon needed 7 years to complete the Temple. Numerologically, the argument for "21" is that all these significant "3"s and "7"s are empowered and amplified when they are multiplied together. Numerologically, reducing 21 to 3, as outlined above, is extremely powerful and significant. It is also associated with the joy of living.

When the Bible is analyzed by academic theologians, it is often divided into 6 major categories. There are books of history such as Kings and Chronicles; books of prophecy such as Isaiah and Jeremiah; books of the law such as Leviticus; poetry and inspired ethical writings such as Psalms and Proverbs; the Gospels focused on the life and person of Jesus and the epistles of Paul. The 6 divisions carry associated ideas of responsibility, protection, balance, and sympathy: these are all appropriate.

The Old Testament consists of 39 books. Numerologically, these can be reduced to 12, and then further to 3. Once again, the highly significant "3" is prominent. When "3" is multiplied by 9, the product is 27, which is also the number of books in the New Testament. Reducing 27 numerologically gives the sum of 9, with the associations of creative expression. The entire Bible contains 66 books and numerologically this becomes 12, followed by 3 yet again!

Solomon's Temple

Having examined some of the numerological aspects of the Bible, it is logical to proceed to explore the connections between numerology and Gnosticism in the next chapter.

15
GNOSTICISM AND NUMEROLOGY

Gnosticism can be described as a group of religious beliefs based on the Greek word meaning "knowledge." Aspects of it occur in the early church, the Graeco-Roman mystery religions, Zoroastrianism, and Neoplatonism. It can also be found in some varieties of Hellenistic Judaism. Gnostics believe that the material world is not a pleasant or happy place. They wish to leave it by reaching what they refer to as *gnosis*.

Irenaeus (130–202) was one of the Church Fathers and a powerful attacker of all heresies. It was he who coined the term *Gnosticism*. Irenaeus, when analyzed numerologically, becomes:

I=1
R=2
E=5
N=5
A=1
E=5
U=6
S=3

This totals 28. When reduced, 28 becomes 10, which then reduces further to 1. The numerological associations with "1" include: initiating action, pioneering, independence, and leadership. Irenaeus certainly had all of these qualities.

The numerology of the term *gnosis* is interesting.

G=3
N=5
O=7
S=3
I=1
S=3

This produces a numerological total of 22, which in turn becomes 4. The numerological significance of "4" is steady growth during a struggle against limits. It is also associated with the concept of foundation and order. Zoroaster is also significant numerologically:

Z=7
O=7
R=2
O=7
A=1
S=3
T=4
E=5
R=2

This provides a numerological total of 38, which in turn yields 11, followed by 2. The number "2" is associated with cooperation, adaptability, consideration of others, partnering, and mediating. These are all suitable associations for Zoroastrianism.

Gnostics believe that the physical world was not directly created by the entirely spiritual God, but by what they refer to as "the demiurge." In some branches of Gnosticism, this demiurge is regarded as evil. In other interpretations, the demiurge is merely imperfect, and has made serious errors in the physical universe. It is sometimes referred to as Ahriman, as Satan, or as Samael, and it has several other names.

Numerologically, Ahriman produces:

A=1
H=5
R=2
I=1
M=4
A=1
N=5

This produces a numerological total of 19, which reduces to 10, and then to 1. The numerological concepts here include initiating action, leading, and being independent. If Ahriman is considered to be a type of Gnostic demiurge, rather than an evil entity, then the numerological associations are relatively appropriate. Examining Samael numerologically produces:

S=3
A=1
M=4
A=1
E=5
L=3

This comes to a total of 17. When reduced, 17 becomes 8, and "8" has the significance of being status-oriented and power-seeking. In the Talmud, Samael has an ethically mixed character. He can be an accuser, a seducer, or a destroyer. In some traditions he was the guardian angel of Esau, twin brother of Jacob. He was also seen as a patron angel of the Roman Empire at its zenith. In some accounts, legends make him the angel of death. Other legends make him the serpent in Eden who tempted and then seduced Eve, making her pregnant with Cain. Some accounts place Samael in Genesis, chapter 32, verse 25 as the angel who wrestled with Jacob. In some creation legends, Adam's first wife was Lilith, who fled from him. She was later taken as a wife by Samael.

Texts found in the Nag Hammadi Library maintain that Samael is one of the names used for the Gnostic demiurge. The Nag Hammadi

Library itself is a collection of early Christian Gnostic texts that were discovered near the Egyptian town of Nag Hammadi in 1945. The library consisted of 12 leather-bound papyrus codices sealed in a jar. They were found by a local man named Mohammed Ali Samman. The Nag Hammadi texts also gave other names for the demiurge. These included Yaldabaoth and Saklas. Samael is also referred to in these Nag Hammadi texts as Ariael. Ariael numerologically becomes:

A=1
R=2
I=1
A=1
E=5
L=3

This totals 13, then further reduces to 4. The significance of "4" is steady growth and a struggle against limits. These are appropriate for the demiurge.

Yaldabaoth becomes:

Y=1
A=1
L=3
D=4
A=1
B=2
A=1
O=7
T=4
H=5

This totals 29. The number 29 reduces to 11, which then becomes 2. The number "2" is associated with cooperation and adaptability. Saklas becomes:

S=3
A=1
K=2
L=3

A=1

S=3

This gives a total of 13, which translates further to 4. "Four" is associated with steady growth and a struggle against limits.

Samael is also well-known to anthroposophists as one of the 7 archangels. With their headquarters in the Goetheanum in Dornach in Switzerland, anthroposophists work in many socially beneficial areas, including ethical banking, agriculture, medicine, and special education. Founded by Rudolph Steiner, anthroposophy believes in the existence of an accessible spiritual world. Saint Gregory the Great (540–604) named the 7 archangels as Anael, Gabriel, Michael, Oriphiel, Raphael, Samael, and Zachariel. All of these are very interesting numerologically. Anael becomes:

A=1

N=5

A=1

E=5

L=3

Numerologically, this totals 15, then further reduces to 6. "Six" is associated with responsibility, protection, and sympathy. Gabriel becomes:

G=3

A=1

B=2

R=2

I=1

E=5

L=3

This makes numerological total of 17, which reduces to 8. "Eight" is associated with practical endeavours.

Michael translates numerologically to:

M=4

I=1

C=3

H=5

A=1
E=5
L=3

This adds to 22, which then becomes 4. "Four" is associated numerologically with a strong foundation, good order, willingness to serve, and steady growth.

Numerologically, Oriphiel becomes:

O=7
R=2
I=1
P=8
H=5
I=1
E=5
L=3

This totals 32. The sum 32 further reduces to 5, and "5" is associated with expansiveness, visionary adventure, and the constructive use of freedom. All of these qualities seem highly appropriate for a benign archangel.

Raphael works out numerologically as:

R=2
A=1
P=8
H=5
A=1
E=5
L=3

This gives a total of 25, which reduces further to 7. "Seven" is associated with knowledge, understanding, and awareness — all excellent qualities for an archangel.

Zachariel works out as:

Z=7
A=1
C=3

H=5
A=1
R=2
I=1
E=5
L=3

This totals 28, which reduces to 10, then 1. "One" is associated numerologically with the initiation of action, with pioneering, and with attainment.

Some Gnostic groups have explained Jesus as a physical embodiment of the supreme spiritual God, who became incarnate in order to bring gnosis into the physical world. Other Gnostic groups regard it as impossible that the supreme spiritual being could become flesh. In their opinion, Jesus was a very spiritual human being who reached divinity by acquiring gnosis and then taught his followers how to do the same. In some other Gnostic communities the saving heroes are identified as the 2 salvific figures Mani and Seth. The prophet Mani, who founded Manichaeism, lived from 216–276. Seth, the third son of Adam, was an ancestor of Noah.

The names of these Gnostic heroes, Mani and Seth, are both numerologically interesting. Seth works out as:

S=3
E=5
T=4
H=5

This totals 17, which then becomes 8. Seth, therefore, is associated with practical things and seeks high material goals.

Mani can be calculated numerologically as:

M=4
A=1
N=5
I=1

This totals 11, which then reduces to 2. "Two" is associated with cooperation, adaptability, consideration of others, and mediating.

Gnosticism was originally regarded as a branch of Christianity, but the *Jewish Encyclopedia* for 1911 suggested that much Gnostic terminology was Jewish. Gnosticism continued to spread and flourish in lands controlled by the Roman Empire and the Arian Goths. It also spread well through the Old Persian Empire. The arrival of Islam, and the Albigensian Crusade of the thirteenth century severely reduced the Gnostics.

The Cathars, also known as the Albigensians, were strongly established in the area around Rennes-le-Château in the southwest of France, and just across into Spain. This was the area where the later mystery of Bérenger Saunière's treasure still remains unsolved. One of the theories relating to that mystery concerns some unknown object of inestimable value, which may at one time have been in the keeping of the Cathars at Montsegur.

Co-author Patricia at Montsegur

One group of early Gnostics were known as the Paulicians. They had communities in Asia Minor, Bulgaria, and Armenia. There was evidence of them up until the eleventh century when they seemed to more or less disappear until the eighteenth. Clear evidence of them appeared in 1828 when they turned up in Russian Armenia with a book of teachings of unknown origin. They called this mysterious volume "The Key to the Truth," or "The Key of Truth."

Information about the Paulicians is mainly derived from the *Chronicon* of Georgios Monachus (*circa* 820–890), and from *Historia Manachorum*, written by Photius (820–891). He was the Patriarch of Constantinople, a brilliant and reliable academic whose work is still well worth reading. The Paulicians apparently regarded their founder as Paul of Samosata, the Patriarch of Antioch from 260–272.

Examined numerologically, Paul of Samosata becomes:

P=8

A=1

U=6

L=3

O=7

F=8

S=3

A=1

M=4

O=7

S=3

A=1

T=4

A=1

This totals 57. Adding the numerals 5 and 7 together brings us to 12, which then further reduces to 3. "Three" signifies expression, verbalization, the arts, and the joy of living.

Like the Adoptionists and Ebionites, Paul taught that Jesus of Nazareth became the Son of God by divine adoption, rather than being the pre-existent divine Logos of John's Gospel. The adoptionist heresy was compatible with Gnostic doctrine because it implied that Jesus had moved by divine intervention from the role of a normal human being to the Son of God by acquiring divine knowledge. It also implied that what he had done could be repeated by other normal human beings.

Other Gnostic Paulician teachings denied the existence of the Virgin Mary as a historical human being. They regarded her as a symbol of the Church, nurturing and protecting the Word of God. She was also thought of as a symbol of the Upper Jerusalem — a mysterious non-physical realm that Christ visited periodically. The Paulicians thought of the Eucharist as an allegory. They also despised crosses instead of venerating them, and, on occasion, actually destroyed them. That is significant in the light of later accusations levelled against the Templars and Cathars, who were accused of similar things.

Paulicians denied Peter's role as the rock on which the Church was founded. One of their strangest ideas was to regard traditional monks' habits as an invention of the devil! Prudently, and this may well have aided their survival in times of dangerous persecution of so-called heretics, they taught that it was perfectly all right to conform outwardly to the rules and regulations of whichever church was in power.

In the ninth century, the Paulicians retreated into the Balkan Peninsula, where they came under the influence of a new leader named Bogomil, which translates as "Beloved of God."

Examined numerologically, the name Bogomil works out as:

B=2

O=7

G=3

O=7

M=4

I=1

L=3

A Templar

This totals 27, which reduces to 9. The numerological associations with "9" are humanitarianism, a generous and giving nature, unselfishness, and creativity.

Under their new name of Bogomils, they established themselves in Bosnia and Serbia. Their teachings spread to Italy, and then to Toulouse and the Rennes-le-Château area. The Cathars, also called Albigensians, grew from the Paulicians and Bogomils. By 1167, the Cathars were so strong that the Bulgarian bishop Nicetas, also known as Nikita, convened a Council of Cathar Bishops and Priests at Saint Félix de Caraman, near Toulouse. No longer a mere heretical sect, the Cathars were now a powerful rival church.

Nicetas translates numerologically as:

N=5

I=1

C=3

E=5

T=4

A=1

S=3

This totals 22, which numerologically becomes 4. The "4" is associated with foundation, good order, service, a struggle against limits, and steady growth. All of these qualities are appropriate for Nicetas. What does his other name, Nikita, produce?

N=5

I=1

K=2

I=1

T=4

A=1

This totals 14, which then becomes 5. "Five" is associated with visionary adventure and the constructive use of freedom. Here again, the characteristics are most appropriate for the man and his religious work.

Their central creed was very similar to the teachings of the Manichaeans, Paulicians, and Bogomils. They combined Gnosticism with Hermeticism. Their God was not the omnipotent God of Judaism, Christianity, or Islam. To a Cathar, the physical universe — and his or her own physical body — was evil. It was the creation of the devil, or demiurge. However, God's help had been needed to *animate* these physical forms that the demiurge had made. According to Cathar beliefs, it was the good, spiritual God who had animated the lifeless clay forms created by the demiurge. In the form of Satan, the demiurge had then lured angels down from Heaven so that he could use their souls to fill the bodies of the progeny of his 2 original human beings.

Dr. Arthur Guirdham (1905–1992) was a great authority on the Cathars and reincarnation. A number of his patients reported that they had experienced very similar nightmares concerning arrest and persecution during their previous lives as Cathars. Guirdham's books on the subject, especially *The Cathars and Reincarnation*, published by Spearman of Saffron Walden in 1990, are outstandingly good. Co-author Lionel had the pleasure of interviewing Dr. Guirdham, and found him to be a very powerful thinker. Numerologically, Arthur Guirdham becomes:

A=1
R=2
T=4
H=5
U=6
R=2

G=3
U=6
I=1
R=2
D=4
H=5
A=1
M=4

This totals 46, which reduces to 10, and then 1. The numerological characteristics associated with "1" are individualism, initiating action, pioneering, leading, and independence. All of these apply markedly to Dr. Guirdham.

A number of religious groups in Europe and North America today have links with the old Gnostics, and may well be secret continuations of them.

There is a particularly interesting connection between the Gnostic beliefs in the spiritual and physical worlds and the numerological beliefs in the 2 distinct powers of numbers. What might be termed the *physical* use of numbers for measuring and calculating corresponds to the *material* world in Gnostic theory. Numbers used for weighing, for calculating volumes and areas, for working out costs and profits in business — all these are in what Gnostics would describe as the *physical* realm. The mysterious powers of numbers, their paranormal influence on events and environments, on people and their personalities, in terms of numerological beliefs, correspond to the invisible *spiritual* universe of Gnosticism. If a physical object measures 1 metre, by 2, by 4, that deals effectively with its material volume. If the abstract "1" is taken to indicate initiating action, the "2" signifies cooperation and adaptability, and the "4" represents a struggle against limits, then, numerologically, there is much more potential in the object than its mere physical volume of 8 cubic metres. These numerological associations are the equivalent of the spiritual realm of Gnosticism, just as the material volume of 1, by 2, by 4 can be seen as equivalent to the physical realm of Gnosticism.

In the next chapter, the numerology of names, places, and dates is examined and analyzed.

16
THE NUMEROLOGY OF NAMES, PLACES, AND DATES

From the earliest epics and sagas to the most modern media presentations, real life and fictional stories have 3 essential ingredients: the characters, the locations, and the events that make up the narrative. The characters are influenced by 2 aspects of the locations, or settings: *where* does it happen, and *when* does it happen? They are also influenced by their own innate personalities, and the personalities of the other characters with whom they interact. Personality has been defined psychologically as a style of response that recurs.

Numerology suggests that the mysterious psychic powers of numbers can exert their influence not only over the personalities of the characters by virtue of their names, but on their birth years and locations. As an analogy, this may, perhaps, be compared to the influence of radiation. It is invisible and there are 3 major types: alpha, beta, and gamma. Each penetrates to a different depth. If alpha is compared to the numerological influence of the character's name, then beta may be compared to the birth year, and gamma to the location where the individual was born.

Before beginning detailed analyses of several famous characters, locations, and dates, a quick example can be taken by looking at William Shakespeare (1564–1616) of Stratford-upon-Avon. If we examine his name numerologically, we find:

W=6
I=1
L=3
L=3
I=1
A=1
M=4

S=3
H=5
A=1
K=2
E=5
S=3
P=8
E=5
A=1
R=2
E=5

This totals 59, reduced to 14, and then 5. "Five" reveals a visionary character, an expansive adventurer who uses freedom constructively. When the year of Shakespeare's birth, 1564, is taken into account as well, it totals 16, which then reduces to 7. The "7" is particularly relevant for Shakespeare. It carries the meanings of understanding, knowledge, and awareness. All of these qualities are revealed consistently in Shakespeare's work. How does the location of his birth affect him numerologically?

S=3
T=4
R=2

A=1
T=4
F=8
O=7
R=2
D=4

U=6
P=8
O=7
N=5

A=1
V=6
O=7
N=5

This totals 80, further reduced to 8. The number "8" is associated with high endeavours, with someone who is status-oriented and power-seeking. The numerological "5," "7," and "8," taken from Shakespeare's name, date of birth, and place of birth can be added together to make 20, further reduced to 2, which relates to cooperation, adaptability, and consideration of others. This Shakespearean example demonstrates the ways in which names, birth years, and locations can be used numerologically, and then combined to produce one overarching total that encapsulates everything about the character.

Alexander Graham Bell (1847–1922) was born in Edinburgh. He moved to Canada in 1870. Numerologically, his name is:

A=1
L=3
E=5
X=5
A=1
N=5

219

D=4
E=5
R=2

G=3
R=2
A=1
H=5
A=1
M=4

B=2
E=5
L=3
L=3

This comes to a total of 60. If we reduce 60 to get 6, the numerological concepts associated with "6" are: responsibility, protection, nurturing, community, and sympathy. Bell's date of birth, 1847, totals 20, which further reduces to 2. Associated with "2" are the ideas of cooperation, adaptability, and consideration of others. Edinburgh, his birthplace, comes out as:

E=5
D=4
I=1
N=5
B=2
U=6
R=2
G=3
H=5

This totals 33, which then becomes 6. The numerological qualities of "6" are shown immediately above. Adding his name score of "6" to his birth year and location scores produces a total of 14, which reduces to 5. The numerological characteristics of "5" are expansiveness, visionary adventure, and the constructive use of free-dom. This would all seem highly relevant for a scientist and inventor of Bell's quality.

Andrew Bonar Law (1858–1923), the British prime minister from 1922–1923, was born in Rexton, which subsequently became part of Canada. Numerologically, his name works out as:

A=1
N=5
D=4
R=2
E=5
W=6

B=2
O=7
N=5
A=1
R=2

L=3
A=1
W=6

This totals 50, which becomes 5, and "5" is associated with expan-siveness, visionary adventure, and the constructive use of freedom. His birth year of 1858 comes to a numerological total of 22, which then becomes 4, and "4" carries the numerological qualities of an orderly foundation, service, and steady growth. His place of birth was Rexton, and numerologically that becomes:

R=2
E=5
X=5
T=4
O =7
N=5

This totals 28, which reduces to 10 and then 1. Numerologically, "1" signifies initiating action and an independent, pioneering spirit. Adding his scores for name, date, and place gives 10, further reduced to 1. Numerologically, the value of "1" is given immediately above.

Sir Frederick Grant Banting was born in Alliston, Ontario, in 1891, and died in a tragic plane crash in 1941. He was an exceptionally able doctor and medical scientist, winning the Nobel Prize in Medicine in 1923 for his work on insulin with his colleague Dr. Charles Best. Banting was knighted by King George V in 1934. Originally a student of theology, he transferred to medicine at the University of Toronto. Having taken his medical degree in 1916, he served with great gallantry in the First World War. Wounded at the Battle of Cambrai, he continued working to help other wounded soldiers for over 16 hours before another doctor compelled him to rest. He was awarded the Military Cross for heroism under fire for these efforts. Returning to Canada after the war, Banting worked with sick children and lectured in pharmacology. He began studying diabetes and the source of insulin together with details of the ways that the pancreas functioned. With his friend and colleague Dr. Best, who was then a medical student, Banting worked on the insulin problem at the University of Toronto.

His many other richly deserved honours included Fellowship of the Royal Society and the Reeve Prize from the University of Toronto. His hobbies and leisure interests included painting, and he participated in a painting expedition within the Arctic Circle. His interest in aviation medicine was the indirect cause of his premature death at only 49. He was flying to the United Kingdom to work on the Franks flying suit that had been developed by his colleague Wilbur Franks, when his plane crashed as it was flying over Newfoundland.

Frederick Grant Banting can be treated numerologically to produce:

F=8
R=2
E=5
D=4
E=5

R=2
I=1
C=3
K=2

G=3
R=2
A=1
N=5
T=4

B=2
A=1
N=5
T=4
I=1
N=5
G=3

This totals 68, which becomes 14 and then 5. The number "5" is associated numerologically with visionary adventure and the constructive use of freedom. These associations seem ideal for a genius like Banting.

His birth year of 1891 totals 19 numerologically, further reduced to 10 and then 1. The characteristics of "1" are for a man who initiates action, a pioneer, a leader and an independent individual. Banting was all of these.

His birthplace was Alliston, which numerologically yields:

A=1
L=3
L=3
I=1
S=3
T=4
O=7
N=5

This totals 27, which reduces to 9. The numerological characteristics of "9" are a generous, giving nature, humanitarianism, unselfishness, and creativity. This creativity fits well with Banting's love of painting. Adding Banting's name score to his year of birth and place of birth gives 15, which finally reduces to 6. The numerological characteristics of "6" are responsibility, protection, nurturing the community, and having great sympathy for all in need. These characteristics seem totally appropriate for Banting.

King Robert the Bruce was born in Turnberry in Scotland in 1274, and died in 1329. He seems to have inherited his great courage and determination from his mother, Marjorie, the Countess of Carrick. Legend has it that she was a very formidable lady who imprisoned his father, Robert, Sixth Lord of Annandale, until he accepted her proposal of marriage. Her son inherited the Gaelic Earldom of Carrick from her, and a royal lineage from his father. His mother's death in 1292, when Robert was just 18, gave him control of the Earldom of Carrick.

Robert reigned as King of the Scots from 1306–1329 and was noted as an outstanding hero of the Scottish War of Independence. He had sworn fealty to Edward I of England in 1296, but changed tactics and joined Wallace. In 1306, Robert quarrelled with John Comyn, one of his political competitors. Bruce stabbed Comyn to death and then, with his supporters around him, was crowned King at Scone. He had to escape to Ireland, but came back in 1307 and soundly defeated the English at Loudoun Hill. After the death of King Edward in 1307, the English were expelled from Scotland and all the castles that they had held were recovered by the Scots except for Sterling and Berwick. Then came the Battle of Bannockburn in 1314, where the English were very heavily defeated. Sporadic battles, however, continued until the Treaty of Northampton was signed in 1328. This treaty recognized Scotland as an independent kingdom along with Bruce's right to the throne.

Robert Bruce can be dealt with numerologically as:

R=2

O=7

B=2
E=5
R=2
T=4

B=2
R=2
U=6
C=3
E=5

This adds up to 40, which reduces to 4. The numerological associations with "4" include creating a foundation, the implementation of order, a struggle against limits, and then steady growth. In view of Bruce's military career, these associations seem highly appropriate.

His birth year, 1274, gives a numerological total of 14, which, when reduced, becomes 5. Numerologically, "5" is associated with expansiveness, visionary adventure, and the constructive use of freedom. Bruce's career was marked by all of these qualities.

He was born in Turnberry, and this becomes:
T=4
U=6
R=2
N=5
B=2
E=5
R=2
R=2
Y=1

This totals 29, which reduces to 11, and then 2. "Two" in numerology should stand for cooperation, adaptability, consideration of others, and mediating. Do any of those qualities apply to the fiercely strong and independent Robert the Bruce? Adding his totals together gives 11, further reduced to 2. The numerological associations with "2" are given just above. They do not seem to fit closely with the character of the strong, independent, militant, and fearless King Robert who fought so hard to regain Scotland, and then ruled it firmly and justly.

Queen Elizabeth I of England was born in Greenwich in 1533 and reigned from 1558 until her death in 1603 at the age of 69. She was the last of the Tudor Dynasty. Her father, Henry VIII, had her mother, Anne Boleyn, executed when Elizabeth was only 2 and a half

Francis Drake

years old. Elizabeth was then declared illegitimate. Her half-brother grew up to become Edward VI, and bequeathed the throne to the hapless Lady Jane Grey, who was executed. The Catholic Queen Mary I then took the throne until 1558. One of Elizabeth's first major acts as Queen was to establish the English Protestant Church of which she was Supreme Governor. This Church later evolved into the Church of England. The Pope spoke against her and encouraged various riots and rebellions against her, but her superb Secret Service dealt with them all very effectively.

When war against Spain became inevitable, the Spanish Armada was decisively defeated by Sir Francis Drake and his redoubtable English sailors.

Aside from her religious and military successes, Elizabeth reigned over a highly cultured society in which dramatists like Shakespeare and Christopher Marlowe flourished. Analyzed numerologically,

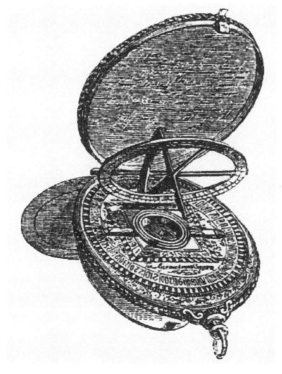

Drake's astrolabe

Elizabeth becomes:

E=5
L=3
I=1
Z=7
A=1
B=2
E=5
T=4
H=5

This totals 33, which then becomes 6. "Six" numerologically is associated with responsibility and protection for her people. Her birth year of 1533 becomes 12, then reduced to 3. Numerologically, "3" suggests the arts, which she greatly encouraged, and the sheer joy of living.

Elizabeth's birthplace of Greenwich becomes:

G=3
R=2
E=5
E=5
N=5
W=6
I=1
C=3
H=5

This totals 35, further reduced to 8. Numerologically, "8" is associated with status, power-seeking, practical endeavours, and high material goals. Adding her name, date, and place numbers together produces 17, further reduced to 8. The associations for "8" are shown immediately above. These all seem appropriate for Elizabeth I.

Sir Francis Drake, one of the greatest hero adventurers of Elizabeth's reign, was born in 1540 in Tavistock in Devon in England. He died of dysentery at Portobello in Panama in 1596 at the age of 55. Drake was officially a vice-admiral in the British Navy, but during his adventurous life was also a sea captain, a privateer, a slave-trader, a navigator, and a politician. He was knighted by Queen Elizabeth in 1581. As second-in-command of the English fleet, Drake was largely responsible for the defeat of the Spanish Armada. From 1577–1580 he carried out a circumnavigation of the world. A legendary hero to the British, especially among his Devonshire men, he was also known as *Franciscus Draco*, meaning "Francis the Dragon" to the Spaniards. King Philip II of Spain put a price of 20,000 ducats (about £5 million in modern money) on Drake's head.

Numerologically, his name calculates out as:

F=8
R=2
A=1
N=5
C=3
I=1
S=3

D=4
R=2
A=1
K=2
E=5

This brings Drake's numerological total to 37, which reduces to 10, and then further to 1. The numerological associations with "1" are pioneering and leading, and an independent character that attains things. All of these apply to Francis Drake. His year of birth was 1540, which adds up numerologically to 10, further reduced to 1, which invokes the same characteristics as his name. His birthplace of Tavistock in Devon works out numerologically as:

T=4
A=1
V=6
I=1
S=3
T=4

O=7

C=3

K=2

This totals 31, which reduces to 4. The numerological character-istics of "4" include a struggle against limits, and this certainly applies to Francis Drake.

Adding the scores for his name, year of birth, and place of birth gives a grand total of 6. The numerological characteristics of "6" are responsi-bility and protection. Drake was very well known for his excellent treat-ment of his crew, and, of course, for protecting England from the Spanish Armada. One of the most interesting speculations about him connects him to the mystery of the Money Pit on Oak Island in Mahone Bay, just off the coast of Nova Scotia. This totally inexplicable, deep shaft was almost certainly intended to contain treasure of some sort. Some theo-ries suggest that it was the work of pirates such as Captain Kidd — but that is unlikely. Pirates do not usually go in for elaborate workings such as the pit on Oak Island and the strange labyrinth at its base. Creating such a shaft and its flood tunnels would need a disciplined and well-organized force with mining experience. What if Drake and his men had captured one more Spanish galleon than they reported? What if the con-tents of that galleon went down into the depth of the Money Pit to serve as a "pension fund" for Drake and his Devonshire men when their pri-vateering days were over? Some expert Tudor historians have suggested that there is a period of several months in Drake's life that cannot be accu-rately accounted for. Was that the period during which he and his men were excavating the Money Pit and stowing their treasure away? It's only one of many possibilities concerning the Money Pit, but it is feasible.

Another major mystery in Drake's life is the romantic possibility connecting him to Queen Elizabeth I. Although he was a few years younger than Elizabeth, a secret romantic liaison between them is not impossible. One theory along those lines suggests that a child resulted from that romantic involvement, and was named Francis, after his adventurous young father. The Bacons were at the Court of Elizabeth at that time, and Lady Bacon, who always claimed to be the mother of

Francis, was utterly devoted to the queen she served. She would have literally done *anything* for Elizabeth. A scandal of that nature involving the so-called "Virgin Queen" would have toppled the throne. What if the loyal and totally trustworthy Lady Bacon had pretended to be pregnant, and then secretly smuggled Elizabeth's newborn son out of the palace and brought him up as her own? Another thread in that mysterious web of suppositions and speculations is that Francis Bacon owned land in Newfoundland. Had someone entrusted him in later life with the secret of his father's treasure on Oak Island?

Francis Bacon was the First Viscount St. Albans and a genuine polymath. Primarily a philosopher, Bacon was also a statesman, a legal expert, and a scientist. He wrote a great deal about the scientific method, which was then in its infancy. At one time he was the attorney general and then Lord Chancellor. The particular aspect of modern scientific method that is justifiably associated with Bacon is referred to as empiricism, and he argued strongly in favour of inductive methodology. The terms "Baconian method" and "scientific method" are virtually interchangeable. Tragically, it was an attempt at an empirical experiment involving the preservation of meat by freezing it that led to his catching the pneumonia that killed him.

What does numerology say about Francis Bacon?

F=8
R=2
A=1
N=5
C=3
I=1
S=3

B=2
A=1
C=3
O=7
N=5

This totals 41, which reduces to 5. The number "5" is associated with expansiveness, visionary adventure, and the constructive use of freedom. The year of Francis Bacon's birth was 1561, which adds to 13, and then reduces to 4. "Four" signifies an orderly foundation, a struggle against limits, and steady growth. Francis Bacon was a genius: one of the very first truly scientific thinkers and philosophers. The numerological "4" suits him particularly well. He was also born in London, which translates numerologically to:

L=3
O=7
N=5
D=4
O=7
N=5

This totals 31, which then reduces to 4 — the same number scored by his birth year. Adding his name score to his year of birth and place of birth scores gives us a total of 13. The 13 then becomes 4, and Francis Bacon is again shown to have the overall characteristics associated with the numerological "4."

Joan of Arc is surrounded by even more mysteries and anomalies than Francis Bacon. Most historians agree that her real name was Jehanne, not Joan, and that she preferred to call herself *Jehanne la Pucelle*, meaning "Jehanne the Maid." Born in Domremy in Lorraine in 1412, she led France against the English with great success, until being captured, falsely accused of witchcraft and heresy, and supposedly burnt at the stake in 1431. The most significant mystery attached to Joan's short but adventurous life was whether she really died in 1431. Over 20 years later, a woman in her mid-40s gave her name as Madame des Armoises, wife of Robert des Armoises. She was recognized as Joan of Arc by witnesses, including her brothers, who had known Joan as a young woman. The story of her survival developed until it became a romance between Robert and Joan in the days of the wars against England. Robert, a redoubtable soldier, had always ridden beside her and guarded her. In the battle that ended with her capture, Robert had been unhorsed and left for dead. When he finally recovered conscious-ness, it was too late.

A wealthy and resourceful man, as well as a loyal and dedicated lover, Robert devised a plan to rescue Joan at the last moment. In his retinue, Robert had 2 loyal and competent friends. One was an apoth-ecary and alchemist. The other was a blacksmith. Their plan was that the alchemist would throw powder on the execution fire so that it would create a dense pall of smoke. Camouflaged by that smoke, the blacksmith and Robert would deal swiftly with Joan's chains and sub-stitute the body of a beggar girl taken from the local mortuary. Still protected by the smoke, Joan and her rescuers would ride away. If that had been their plan, and if it had worked, the woman recognized as Joan 20-odd years later, and calling herself Madame Artoises, really was Joan.

Numerologically the name Jehanne turns into:

J=1
E=5
H=5
A=1
N=5
N=5
E=5

This totals 27, which reduces to 9. "Nine" has the numerological significance of unselfishness, a sense of obligation, a generous, giving nature, and humanitarianism. All of these fit well with the charac-ter of Joan of Arc. The year of her birth was 1412, which adds to 8. Numerologically, "8" stands for practical endeavours and power-seeking. Joan's battles against the English were very practical, and her quest for power was for France.

Her place of birth was Domremy in Lorraine. Numerologically, Domremy becomes:

D=4
O=7
M=4

233

R=2

E=5

M=4

Y=1

The total of 27 can be reduced to 9, yet again, verifying Joan's characteristics.

Adding her 3 numerological scores gives us 26. The digits of 26 add together to come to 8, which reinforces the numerological associations of Joan's birth year: practicality and power-seeking.

A fearless young Canadian heroine from Verchères named Madeleine Jarret was several years younger than Joan of Arc when all her skill and courage were needed to defend the family fortress against the Iroquois. Madeleine was born in Verchères in 1678. Her father, François, was a *seigneur*. Unfortunately, there had been hostilities between the French and the Iroquois in the late 1680s, which had arisen over fur-trading rivalries with the Algonquin. Because of these hostilities, and the likelihood that Verchères would be a target, the Jarrets had built a reliable fortification at Verchères. A raid came when Madeleine was only 12, and she learnt a great deal from her mother, who held off the attackers with only half a dozen helpers.

Two years later, in 1691, Madeleine's parents were away, and she was in charge of the fort with only a handful of helpers. The Iroquois duly attacked, but Madeleine inspired the others to put up a gallant and successful defence.

Numerologically, Madeleine works out as:

M=4

A=1

D=4

E=5

L=3

E=5

I=1

N=5

E=5

This totals 33, which then reduces to 6. The numerological characteristics of "6" are responsibility and protection. Madeleine was responsible for the others and protected them fearlessly. Her birth year was 1678 and this adds to 22, leading on to 4. The characteristics of "4" are a strong foundation and struggle; both are very appropriate. Verchères numerologically becomes:

V=6
E=5
R=2
C=3
H=5
E=5
R=2
E=5
S=3

This comes to a total of 36, which then reduces to 9. "Nine" numerologically is associated with unselfishness and a sense of obligation. Madeleine certainly had both of these in large measure. Taking her 3 totals — name, date, and place — comes to a total of 19, which finally reduces to 1. "One," numerologically, is associated with strength of character and leadership. Madeleine and her small band of helpers worked brilliantly under leadership to defend their fortress.

John Kenneth Galbraith (1908–2006) was a brilliant Canadian economist, who became an international mentor with a richly deserved global reputation. He was born in Iona Station, Ontario, and his parents were Scottish Canadians. As an outstanding economist, Galbraith was a Keynesian, and his books on the subject were justifiably bestsellers and very authoritative. He taught at Harvard University for many years, and worked for United States presidents Roosevelt, Truman, Kennedy, and Johnson. He also had the distinction of serving as the United States ambassador to India, and gave great support to Prime Minister Jawaharlal Nehru while he was there. In addition to all his academic success and the many excellent books he wrote on economics, he had even wider literary skill and edited a number of significant magazines.

Numerologically, his name translates as:

J=1
O=7
H=5
N=5

K=2
E=5
N=5
N=5
E=5
T=4
H=5

G=3
A=1
L=3
B=2
R=2
A=1
I=1
T=4
H=5

This totals 71, which adds numerologically to 8. "Eight" is associated with practical endeavours and high material goals. This is entirely appropriate for a man who rendered such excellent practical service in the world of economics. His birth year of 1908 adds to 18, and then reduces to 9. Numerologically, this suggests a humanitarian with a selfless, giving nature. This, again, is totally appropriate for Galbraith. His birthplace was Iona Station, and this gives:

I=1
O=7
N=5
A=1

S=3
T=4
A=1
T=4
I=1
O=7
N=5

This totals 39, which reduces to 12 and then 3. Numerologically, "3" suggests expression, verbalization, the arts, and the joy of living. All of these are applicable to Galbraith. Adding together the 3 scores for his name, his birth year, and his place of birth produces 20, which then reduces to 2. Numerologically, "2" is associated with cooperation, adaptability, consideration of others, and mediation. Again, all of these excellent qualities apply to John Kenneth Galbraith. As a side note, Galbraith much preferred to be called "Ken" rather than John, and in view of his preference, it is interesting to note the translation of Ken in numerology:

K=2
E=5
N=5

Added together, this gives us a total of 12, which again reduces to 3. This reinforces his sheer joy of living during a very long and highly successful life.

Guy Fawkes, also known as Guido Fawkes, was born in York in 1570 and ended his life on the gallows in 1606. His father died when Guy was only 8 years old, and his mother married again — this time to a recusant Catholic. Young Guy became a Catholic like his stepfather, and went to the continent as a soldier on the side of Catholic Spain against the Dutch Protestant reformers. This was part of what was known as the 80 Years' War. Later, Guy went to Spain to try to drum up support for a Catholic rebellion in England, but he met with little success. Shortly afterwards, Fawkes met Thomas Wintour and came back to England with him. Wintour introduced Fawkes to Robert Catesby, who was already planning to assassinate King James. The conspirators managed to rent an undercroft below the building in which the Lords met, and Fawkes was given charge of the gunpowder that they concealed there. An anonymous person tipped off the King's men that there was something sinister going on below the building and Fawkes was caught on November 5, 1605. Brave and determined — no matter how wrong he was — Fawkes threw himself off the scaffold and broke his neck in order to avoid the "quartering" that followed execution by hanging in those days.

Numerologically, Guy Fawkes can be analyzed as:

G=3
U=6
Y=1

F=8
A=1
W=6
K=2
E=5
S=3

This produces a total of 35, which then becomes 8. The association with a numerological "8" shows practical endeavour — explosives are undeniably a practical way of murdering enemies. Power-seeking could also be associated with a plot to kill the king. Guy's birth year was 1570, which adds to 13 and then reduces to 4. Numerologically, "4" is associated with a struggle against limits, and Guy and his fellow conspirators were struggling against James I and his followers. His birthplace of York is also numerologically interesting:

Y=1
O=7
R=2
K=2

This gives a total of 12, which in turn becomes 3. One important aspect of the numerological "3" is expression. Wrong as their motives were, Fawkes and his fellow conspirators were attempting to express their ideas with murderous violence. Adding the 3 scores together gives a total of 15, which in turn becomes 6. Numerologically, "6" should indicate responsibility, protection, nurturing, care for the community, and sympathy. "Six" is as far from the character and actions of Guy Fawkes and his fellow conspirators as it can possibly be!

William Wordsworth, the poet laureate, was born at Cockermouth in Cumberland, England, in 1770. He was the second of 5 children of John and Ann Wordsworth. His sister, Dorothy, was also a talented poet, and the 2 of them were baptized at the same time. They continued to have a great deal in common throughout their lives. William's elder brother Richard became a successful lawyer. Their younger brother, John, was a sea captain, and was drowned in 1805. The youngest of the 5 siblings, Christopher, went into the Church and ended up as Master of Trinity College in Cambridge. Their father, John, who died in 1783, had worked as a legal administrator for James Lowther, the First Earl of Lonsdale.

William's most memorable poetic achievements were to work with Samuel Taylor Coleridge as they launched what came to be known as the Romantic Age of English Literature. Their book *Lyrical Ballads* was published in 1798. Wordsworth's great work "The Prelude" was semi-autobiographical, but was not published until after his death in 1850. For the last 7 years of his life he was Poet Laureate. His great contribution to the understanding of the true meaning of poetry is his definition of it as "emotion recollected in tranquillity."

A deeply emotional man, Wordsworth fell in love with a French girl named Annette Vallon and had a daughter, Caroline, by her in 1792. Although they never married, Wordsworth did his best to support them both throughout his life, even after his marriage to Mary Hutchinson, a childhood friend, in 1802.

Numerologically, William Wordsworth can be calculated as:

W=6

I=1

L=3

L=3

I=1
A=1
M=4

W=6
O=7
R=2
D=4
S=3
W=6
O=7
T=4
H=5

This totals 65, which adds to 11 and then reduces to 2. Numerologi-cally, "2" is associated with cooperation — very relevant to his cooperation with Coleridge — adaptability, consideration of others, partnering, and mediating. All of these excellent qualities are very relevant for William Wordsworth. His birth year was 1770, which adds to 15 and then reduces to 6. The characteristics associated with "6" in numerology are responsi-bility, protection, nurturing, and sympathy. Again, these are very relevant for Wordsworth in view of his care and concern for Annette and their daughter. His birth at Cockermouth can be analyzed numerologically as:

C=3
O=7
C=3
K=2
E=5
R=2
M=4
O=7
U=6
T=4
H=5

This produces a total of 48, which becomes 12 and then 3. This is an ideal number for William Wordsworth as it is associated with expression, verbalization, socialization, the arts, and the joy of living. It fits the man 100 percent.

Adding Wordsworth's name score of "2" to his birth year score of "6" and his birthplace score of "3" produces 11, which then adds to 2. As shown above, the numerological associations with "2" are ideal for William Wordsworth.

Elizabeth Barrett Browning, the poet, was born in Kelloe in Durham, England, in 1806. She died at the age of 55 in 1861. The huge family fortune derived from Edward Barrett (1734–1798). He owned over 10,000 acres of estates, and other family wealth came from glass-works, sugar plantations, and mills. Elizabeth herself believed that the Jamaican side of her ancestry included African blood. There was a curious obsession with preserving the family name of Barrett, and it was frequently a condition of inheritance. Before her own marriage to Robert Browning, Elizabeth had called herself Elizabeth Barrett Moulton Barrett.

Elizabeth was educated at home and shared a tutor with one of her brothers. Brilliantly intelligent, Elizabeth was reading Latin and Greek while still only 10 years old. She also became enthusiastically religious, and attended a dissenting chapel with her family. Tragically, while still in her teens, Elizabeth began the lifelong battle with illness that eventually contributed to her early death. She took opiates continually to ward off the pain, and some literary critics have suggested that this contributed to the vivid imagery in her poems.

Politically, Elizabeth was a supporter of women's rights, and also opposed slavery. She married Robert Browning in 1846.

One of the writers who was very powerfully influenced by her poems was Edgar Allan Poe, and her "Lady Geraldine's Courtship" gave him the meter for his famous poem "The Raven." When Poe was writing as a reviewer for the *Broadway Journal*, he described Elizabeth's work by saying "...her poetic inspiration is the highest...." He dedicated his book *The Raven and Other Poems* to her.

Analyzing her name numerologically reveals:

E=5
L=3
I=1
Z=7
A=1
B=2
E=5
T=4
H=5

B=2
A=1
R=2
R=2
E=5
T=4
T=4

M=4
O=7
U=6
L=3
T=4
O=7
N=5

B=2
A=1
R=2
R=2
E=5
T=4
T=4

This totals 109, which becomes 10 and then 1. Numerologically, it suggests that Elizabeth was a woman who initiated action, as well as an independent, pioneering individual who was capable of attaining things. Her birth year of 1806 adds to 15 and then to 6. Numerologically, "6" indicates responsibility, protection, and nurturing. Elizabeth was certainly a very caring person, for example, in her feelings toward slavery that made her an abolitionist. The numerology associated with her birthplace of Kelloe is as follows:

K=2
E=5
L=3
L=3
O=7
E=5

This totals 25, which reduces to 7. "Seven" is associated with studiousness, understanding, knowledge, and awareness. The brilliantly academic Elizabeth had all of these qualities. Adding all 3 numerological totals together gives us 14, which then becomes 5. Numerologically, "5" is associated with visionary powers and the constructive use of freedom. These qualities are again very appropriate for Elizabeth Barrett Browning.

Co-author Lionel with ravens

Edgar Allan Poe, who was so strongly influenced by Elizabeth Barrett Browning, was a very complicated and chaotic character. There have been sinister suggestions about Poe and the real-life murder of 21-year-old Mary Cecilia Rogers in 1841. Poe's story "The Mystery of Marie Rogêt" was such a close parallel to the actual Rogers murder that some analysts have suspected that only the murderer could have known all the details. Poe was born in Boston, Massachusetts, in 1809. He died of unknown causes in 1849. Orphaned when very young, he was cared for by the Allan family, which gave rise to his second name. After a short period at the University of Virginia, Poe served with distinction in the army, rising to the highest non-commissioned rank, but he later failed to pass his officers' training course at West Point. He married his teenaged cousin Virginia Clemm in 1835, and was devastated by her death from tuberculosis in 1847. His "Raven" — inspired by Elizabeth Barrett Browning — was published with great success only 2 years before his beloved Virginia's death.

Numerologically, Edgar Allan Poe becomes:

E=5
D=4
G=3
A=1
R=2

A=1
L=3
L=3
A=1
N = 5

P=8
O=7
E=5

This totals 48, which reduces to 12 and then 3. The numerological characteristics of "3" include expression and verbalization, which are entirely appropriate for Poe as a writer.

The year of his birth was 1809, which totals 18 and then reduces to 9. Numerologically, "9" is associated with creative expression, which is again suitable for Poe as a poet and short story writer.

His birthplace of Boston, Massachusetts, becomes:

B=2
O=7
S=3
T=4
O=7
N=5

This gives a total of 28, which becomes 10 and then 1. Numerologically, "1" is associated with independence and attainment, pioneering, and initiating action. It is the score of the individual — and Poe was certainly individualistic to a marked degree. Adding his name number, which is "3," to his date number, which is "9," and his place of birth number, which is "1," produces a total of 13, further reduced to 4. The characteristics of "4" that apply best to Poe are a struggle against limits and the laying of a foundation. His life was a struggle and he certainly laid a literary foundation that is still remembered with awe today. One of many modern admirers of the poem, co-author Lionel has recorded "The Raven" on CD.

The boxer John Lawrence Sullivan, heavyweight champion of the world, was born in Roxbury, Massachusetts, in 1858 and died in 1918. Nicknamed the Boston Strong Boy, Sullivan won 38 out of his 41 fights, and 33 of those were won by a knockout. He reigned as champion from 1881 until 1892: a magnificent achievement. He is regarded as the first American sportsman to become an international celebrity, and the first to earn over $1 million.

Numerologically, John Lawrence Sullivan can be calculated as:

J=1
O=7
H=5
N=5

L=3
A=1
W=6
R=2
E=5
N=5
C=3
E=5

S=3
U=6
L=3
L=3
I=1
V=6
A=1
N=5

This produces a total of 76, which becomes 13, and then reduces to 4. The most appropriate numerological associations for "4," in Sullivan's case, are a struggle against limits and steady growth during his boxing career. His birth year of 1858 produces a numerological total of 22, which again becomes 4. His place of birth, Roxbury, Massachusetts, produces:

R=2
O=7
X=5
B=2
U=6
R=2,
Y=1

This totals 25, which becomes 7. "Seven," numerologically, suggests knowledge, awareness, and understanding. Sullivan was certainly a thinker and planner as well as an outstanding fighter. Adding his name score of "4" to his birth year score, which was another "4," to his location score of "7" yields a total of 15, which reduces to 6. This suggests responsibility, protection, and sympathy, and is not particularly relevant for a competitive sportsman like Sullivan. Sometimes the numerological characteristics are on target — at other times they are not!

Going from the unconquerable physicality of the great John Lawrence Sullivan to the uniquely powerful mind of Albert Einstein provides a powerful contrast of personalities and abilities. What differences do their numbers reveal?

Albert Einstein was born in Ulm in Germany in 1879 and died in 1955. His father was Hermann Einstein, a salesman and engineer. His mother was Pauline Einstein (née Koch). They moved to Munich in 1880, where his father and uncle founded Elektrotechnische Fabrik J. Einstein & Cie, making electrical equipment based on direct current.

Albert Einstein became an outstanding theoretical physicist who developed the theory of general relativity, which caused a revolution in physics as it had been understood up until then. He was awarded the Nobel Prize in Physics in 1921. This was described as being for "his services to theoretical physics and especially for his discovery of the law of the photoelectric effect." His discoveries made way for the development of quantum theory. What triggered his research in this area was his dissatisfaction with the interface between what is best described as classical mechanics and the problems associated with electromagnetic fields. His theories of relativity extended to gravitational fields, as well, and he was also responsible for particle theory and for investigating thermal properties of light, which opened the door to photon theory. He thought on the grand scale and applied his theories to the structure of the entire universe.

Einstein married Mileva Marić in 1903, but they were divorced in 1919. Einstein then married his cousin Elsa Löwenthal in 1919, having had a relationship with her for the previous 7 years. She died from heart and kidney problems in 1936.

Einstein's work at the Patent Office involved many questions about the transmission of electrical signals, and this led him to think deeply about the nature of light and the connection between space and time.

His academic career was strengthened by his Ph.D. from the University of Zurich, and he published outstanding papers on Brownian motion, the photoelectric effect, and relativity. His work on the equivalence of matter and energy was also outstanding.

Numerologically, Albert Einstein totals 46, which adds to 10 and then 1:

A=1
L=3
B=2
E=5
R=2
T=4

E=5
I=1
N=5
S=3
T=4
E=5
I=1
N=5

The characteristics associated with "1" are: an independent individual, a pioneer, a leader, a person who initiates action and who attains his or her objectives. This is particularly appropriate for Albert Einstein.

His birth year was 1879, which totals 25 and then 7. Numerologically, "7" is also totally appropriate for Einstein. It indicates an academic character with great knowledge, understanding, and awareness. His birthplace of Ulm scores:

U=6
L=3
M=4

This totals 13, and then reduces to 4. Numerologically, the "4" is also appropriate for Einstein. He laid the foundation of a whole new type of physics; his brilliant mathematical mind worked in an orderly way. He served science at a remarkable depth and kept up a steady growth of knowledge while struggling all the time against the limits of that knowledge. Adding his name to his year of birth and place of birth produces 12, which in turn becomes 3. Numerologically, this "3," in Einstein's case, refers to his amazing powers of expression. It also applies to his zest for living.

Moving on from Einstein's brilliant command of mathematics and physics, it is interesting to examine another mathematician, but one who is better known for his literary efforts and superb imagination.

Charles Lutwidge Dodgson wrote under the pen name of Lewis Carroll. He was born in 1832 in Daresbury near Halton in Cheshire, England, and died of pneumonia in 1898 following a bout of influenza. Under his pen name he was a highly successful children's fantasy writer, his most successful works being *Alice in Wonderland* and *Through the Looking Glass*. He was an outstanding mathematician, as well as photographer, Anglican clergyman, and an inventor. He is also remembered for 2 exceptional poems in the "nonsense" genre: "Jabberwocky" and "The Hunting of the Snark."

Charles was the third of the 11 children of his parents, Archdeacon Dodgson and his wife Frances Jane Lutwidge. Educated at Rugby, Charles was commented on by the maths teacher, R.B. Mayor, as the most promising boy he had taught since coming to Rugby. From Rugby, Charles went on to Christ Church, Oxford, but had been there only 2 days when his mother died at only 47. Charles persisted with his studies and was a very talented mathematician. He became the Maths Lecturer at Christ Church, and remained there for the next quarter-century. He was at Christ Church in a number of different capacities until he died. Physically, Charles was far from robust. Tall and slim, he walked rather awkwardly, was deaf in one ear, and stammered. He also had a weak chest.

The superb author George MacDonald was a friend of Charles, and encouraged him. MacDonald's own children greatly enjoyed the Alice stories, and George encouraged Charles to have it published. Among his other interests, Charles was a founding member of the Society for Psychical Research, of which co-author Lionel is also a member.

Looked at numerologically, Charles Lutwidge Dodgson can be calculated as:

C=3
H=5
A=1
R=2
L=3
E=5
S=3

L=3
U=6
T=4
W=6
I=1
D=4
G=3
E=5

D=4
O=7
D=4
G=3
S=3
O=7
N=5

This totals 87, which reduces to 15 and then 6. In numerology, "6" is associated with responsibility, protection, nurturing, and sympathy. Dodgson was extremely kind and understanding with children, and the caring aspect of "6" is appropriate for him.

His date of birth, 1832, adds to make 14, which then becomes 5. The numerological characteristics of "5" are the constructive use of freedom and visionary adventure. These qualities are both shown plainly in the Alice stories. Daresbury, his birthplace, can be analyzed as:

D=4
A=1
R=2
E=5
S=3
B=2
U=6
R=2
Y=1

This produces a total of 26, which becomes 8. Numerologically, "8" is associated with practical endeavours and with those who are status-oriented. Dodgson certainly made practical endeavours to get his books written and published, and he enjoyed his status as a university lecturer, author, and clergyman. Amalgamating his name score of "6," his birth year score of "5," and his location score of "8" produces a total of 19, which numerologically becomes 10, reduced further to 1. Numerologically, in Dodgson's case, "1" carries the association of independence and individuality. Both of these are applicable to Charles Lutwidge Dodgson.

As noted earlier, among Dodgson's influential friends was the great Christian writer George MacDonald, whose children had enjoyed the Alice stories and encouraged Dodgson to have them published. George MacDonald was born in 1824 in Huntly in Aberdeenshire, Scotland. He died in 1905. His father was a farmer that descended from the MacDonalds of Glencoe, who had been victims of an infamous 1692 massacre. Young George was raised in a Calvinistic Congregational Church, a denomination in which he later became a minister — although he had serious theological difficulties with the Calvinist doctrine. He took his degree at the University of Aberdeen, and then went on to Highbury in London to study for the congregational ministry. His brilliant fantasy novels and children's fairy tales inspired authors such as C.S. Lewis, W.H. Auden, and J.R.R. Tolkien of *The Lord of the Rings* fame. The great writer and thinker G.K. Chesterton once said that reading *The Princess and the*

Goblin — one of MacDonald's children's books — had made a differ-ence to his whole existence.

MacDonald's wife Louisa (née Powell) was 2 years older than George. Even after having their 11 children, she retained her trim, petite figure, and when they were on tour in the United States they often had to show their American friends family photographs of their 11 children to prove that such a tiny woman really had a family of that size.

Numerologically, George MacDonald can be calculated as:

G=3
E=5
O=7
R=2
G=3
E=5

M=4
A=1
C=3
D=4
O=7
N=5
A=1
L=3
D=4

This totals 57, further reduced to 12 and then 3. The number "3" is associated with expression, verbalization, socialization, artistic ability, and the sheer joy of living. MacDonald certainly had all of these qualities in abundance.

His year of birth, 1824, numerologically totals 15, which then reduces to 6. In numerology, "6" is associated with responsibility, pro-tection, nurturing, community life, balance, and sympathy. Here again, the numerological characteristics are very appropriate for the great and good George MacDonald. His birthplace, Huntly, calculates as:

H=5
U=6
N=5
T=4
L=3
Y=1

This totals 24, which then becomes 6. As described above, "6" is very appropriate for George MacDonald. Taking the scores for his name, his year of birth, and his place of birth gives a total of 15, further reduced to 6. George MacDonald's all-encapsulating score is "6," which is totally appropriate for him.

During George's American tour, he met Mark Twain, who became a close friend and admirer. Twain's real name was Samuel Langhorne Clemens. He was born in 1835 in Florida, Missouri, and died in 1910. Sam's father was John Marshall Clemens of Virginia, who was a judge, and his mother was Jane Lampton Clemens of Missouri. Sam, the sixth of 7 children, was born during a visit from Halley's comet, and was convinced that he would die when it returned. Remarkably, he died the day after the comet's approach in 1910. Sam grew up in Hannibal, Missouri — an area that provided the settings for *Huckleberry Finn* and *Tom Sawyer*. His first job was as an apprentice to a printer. He also wrote newspaper articles and worked as a typesetter. He then changed professions completely and worked as a riverboat pilot on the Mississippi — which is where he acquired his nickname, Mark Twain. He was a very successful writer and public speaker and was described as the father of American literature. His problem was money — no matter how much he earned, he had one financial disaster after another.

There were many tragedies in Sam's life. One of these occurred when he persuaded his younger brother Henry to work the Mississippi with him and Henry was killed when the steamship *Pennsylvania* blew up while he was working on it. Sam had seen the tragedy happen in a dream a month before it happened. He always held himself responsible for Henry's death. This experience prompted him to join the Society for Psychical Research just as Charles Lutwidge Dodgson had done.

Sam had another career change and became a silver miner. That, too, was a financial failure, so he went back to newspaper work.

In 1870, Sam married Olivia Langdon, and they were together until Olivia died in 1904. Tragedy struck their family when their son, Langdon, died of diphtheria before he was 2. Examining Mark Twain numerologically, under his real name of Samuel Langhorne Clemens, produces:

S=3
A=1
M=4
U=6
E=5
L=3

L=3
A=1
N=5
G=3
H=5
O=7
R=2
N=5
E=5

C=3
L=3
E=5
M=4
E=5
N=5
S=3

This totals 86, which becomes 14 and then 5. The numerological associations with "5" are expansiveness, visionary adventure, and the constructive use of freedom. All of these are quite relevant to Mark Twain. His birth year of 1835 adds up to 17, then reduces to 8. Numerologically, this "8" is associated with practical endeavours, orientation with status, power-seeking, and the quest of high material goals. Twain was always looking for material success and status, which was why he was frequently tempted into enterprises that promised vast profits but failed miserably. Florida, Missouri, can be calculated numerologically as:

F=8
L=3
O=7
R=2
I=1
D=4
A=1

This produces a total of 26, which then becomes 8, and reinforces the date score. The 3 scores, therefore, total 21, which can be further reduced to 3. "Three" is associated numerologically with expression, verbalization, socialization, and the arts. There was too much tragedy in Sam's life for him to experience much of the joy of living.

We now move on from the great American humorist Mark Twain to the equally great British humorist George Formby. George was born in Wigan in 1904, and died of a massive heart attack in 1961. His real name was George Hoy Booth, and his father, James Booth, was a talented music hall entertainer who used the stage name George Formby, after the town of Formby. In 1899, James had met and married Eliza Hoy, and George was one of their 12 children. At the age of 7, George was apprenticed as a jockey and rode in his first professional race at the age of 10, when he weighed less than 4 stone. After his father's death in 1921, George gave up his career as a jockey and went into show business. In 1924, he married dancer Beryl Ingham, who also became his manager until her death in 1960. George made many extremely humorous films, and was famous for playing the ukulele-banjo to accompany his numerous risqué songs, including "Leaning on a Lamp-post." He appeared in the Royal

Command Performance in 1937 and was awarded an OBE in 1946 in recognition of his work in entertaining the Allied forces during the Second World War. He was a keen motorcyclist and rode the famous Norton International, which also featured in his outstandingly good films. Analyzing him numerologically leads to:

G=3
E=5
O=7
R=2
G=3
E=5

H=5
O=7
Y=1

B=2
O=7
O=7
T=4
H=5

This totals 63, which in turn becomes 9. "Nine" is particularly appropriate for George, who was a good and kind man as well as a superb humorist. "Nine" signifies humanitarianism, a generous, giving nature, unselfishness, and a sense of obligation, as well as creative expression. His birth year of 1904 adds to 14 and then 5. "Five" is associated with visionary adventure, expansiveness, and the constructive use of freedom. His birthplace of Wigan can be analyzed numerologically as:

W=6
I=1
G=3
A=1
N=5

This adds up to 16, which then becomes 7. "Seven" is associated with powers of analysis and understanding, knowledge and awareness, studiousness and meditation.

Adding the 3 scores from his name, birth year, and birthplace produces a total of 21. Further reduced, 21 becomes 3. Numerologically, "3" suggests powers of expression, which George certainly had, as well as verbalization, socialization, and the joy of living. George's humorous songs accompanied by his banjo-ukulele differ dramatically from the serious and romantic songs of Elvis Aaron Presley (1935–1977). Elvis was born in Tupelo, Mississippi. His father was Vernon Elvis and his mother was Gladys Love Presley. Elvis was one of identical twin boys, but his brother, Jesse Garon Presley, was stillborn. Elvis grew up to become one of the greatest and deservedly most popular singers of the twentieth century. He was referred to as "The King of Rock and Roll" and as simply "The King." His superb song "Heartbreak Hotel," released in 1956, went to number one on the charts. He was conscripted into the army in 1958, but resumed his career in music and film once he had served his 2 years. On May 1, 1967, he married Priscilla Beaulieu. Their only child, Lisa Marie, was born a year later. His massive talent and brilliant showbiz career were cut tragically short by a heart attack when he was only 42.

Numerologically, Elvis Aaron Presley scores:

E=5
L=3
V=6
I=1
S=3

A=1
A=1
R=2
O=7
N=5

P=8
R=2
E=5
S=3
L=3
E=5
Y=1

This totals 61, which adds numerologically to 7. The characteristics of "7" are knowledge, understanding, and awareness. His year of birth, 1935, adds up to 18, which then reduces to 9. The numerological associations with "9" are: humanitarianism; a generous, giving nature; unselfishness; and creative expression. His place of birth, Tupelo, Mississippi, translates to:

T=4
U=6
P=8
E=5
L=3
O=7

This totals 33, which then becomes 6. Numerologically, "6" is associated with responsibility, protection, nurturing, care for the community, and sympathy. Adding all 3 scores for his name, his birth year, and his place of birth produces a total of 22, which reduces to 4. The numerological associations with "4" are a struggle against limits, and this seems appropriate for a great and talented man who nevertheless experienced many problems and struggles.

In this chapter, the 3 numerological influences of name, birth year, and birthplace have been examined and analyzed. In some examples they seem highly appropriate — in others they don't. This raises the question of the strength of will of the character concerned, and the extent to which he or she can contradict the numerological influences — *if indeed such influences really exist.*

In the next chapter, the influence of numerological forces on personality and the compatibility — or otherwise — of different personalities will be examined and analyzed.

17
NUMEROLOGY, PERSONALITY, AND COMPATIBILITY

There are aspects of numerology that suggest that numbers can exert an actual *influence* over people, locations, times, and objects — that the presence of certain numbers can *encourage* things to happen to a particular person in a particular place at a particular time. This aspect regards numbers as though they were magical ingredients in a spell, or the power words of a liturgy or incantation. The numbers are seen as the specific movements in a ritual or an elaborate enchantment. An alternative aspect of numerology regards numbers as indicators — clues that the numerologist detective can use to determine what is going on, or what is likely to happen. They can be regarded as omens or warnings, heralds of success and happiness, or their opposites. They affect nothing; they are merely signalling devices. They are the notices that say UNEXPLODED BOMB or DEEP WATER. They are not the bomb itself, nor the treacherous depths of the lake. They cannot influence a person to be either a saint or a serial killer, but, if this aspect of numerology is real, they can indicate which of the 2 options that person is. There is also the disturbing question of multiple personalities. Can numerology detect that and warn against it?

In earlier chapters, the 9 primary numerological associations have been considered in their benign and positive aspects. For example, "1" stands for leading, pioneering, and initiating action; "2" is cooperation, consideration of others, and mediation; and 3 is expression, socialization, verbalization, and the arts. There is, however, a range of equal and opposite negative qualities associated with each number. They may be thought of not so much as different qualities, but as the traditional good qualities taken to excess. "One" may be seen as rashness, impetuousness, ignoring all others as long as the individual can achieve what he or she wants, bull-headedness, and stubbornness. "Two" is a peace-at-any-price approach, an unhealthy compromise with wrongness, willingness to be an accomplice of evil, or to go into partnership with criminals to avoid trouble from them. "Three" is an excess of self-expression, an uncontrolled extroversion, far too much verbalization, which permits no one else to get a word in, weird extremes of art, and a chaotic series of celebrations of pleasure at the expense of others. The sadist who gets pleasure from causing pain and distress falls into this category. The negative side of "4" is repression, enforced conformity, the desire to regulate everyone and everything, a struggle against limits that boils over into revolution, and the establishment of a new, constricting regime. "Five" is a wild rebelliousness; anarchy; strange, sick visions of dystopias; and reckless adventures that endanger others. "Six" is similar in some ways to "4." The bad side of "6" is over-protective, nannying in the worst sense, and submerging the rights of the individual in the regulations aimed at protecting the community. "Seven" takes academia much too far. It studies and analyzes minute details and loses the real purpose of the investigation. It thinks about thought and the abstract nature of thought rather than the true purpose of thought, which is to solve problems. "Eight" is the most dangerous of all. It is the misuse of "8" that leads to tyrants and dictators — the insatiable desire for yet more and more wealth and power. "Nine," taken to its excess, destroys the personality. Just as a misused, negative "3" can produce sadism, so a misused "9" can produce masochism.

Multiple personalities

If numerology can warn what the dark side of numbers can indicate, it can also warn about compatibility and incompatibility. In an ideal situation, compatible people get together and enjoy living and working together. Incompatible people, when forced together, create hell for each other. But it is not only compatibility with other personalities that can be assessed numerologically; there is also compatibility and incompatibility between people and locations, especially work locations. A highly sensitive introvert, for example, would be incompatible with work as a market trader, a stage performer, or a teacher. A raucous extrovert would find little or no job satisfaction in being a lighthouse keeper or a member of a silent religious order.

Numerologically, various jobs and professions can be categorized according to their numbers.

Medicine becomes:

M=4
E=5
D=4
I=1
C=3
I=1
N=5
E=5

This totals 28, which becomes 10, followed by 1. This is the leading, pioneering category that initiates action.

Computer work becomes:

C=3
O=7
M=4
P=8
U=6
T=4
E=5
R=2

W=6
O=7
R=2
K=2

This totals 56, reduced to 11 and then 2. The characteristics of "2" are cooperation, adaptability, consideration, partnering, and mediating. Most computer workers will agree that to get the best out of their equipment they have to treat it as a partner and cooperate with it!

Flying can be calculated as:

F=8
L=3
Y=1
I=1
N=5
G=3

This scores 21, which becomes 3. The characteristics of "3" are: expression, the arts, and the sheer joy of living. Aviators who relish their work regard flying as an art, and take great pleasure from it. For them, flight is tantamount to the sheer joy of living.

The navy becomes:

N=5
A=1
V=6
Y=1

This comes to 13, which reduces to 4. The characteristics of "4" are good order, reliable service, steady growth, and fearless struggling against limits — which would be relevant for sailing through storms and dangerous waters.

Selling can be analyzed as:

S=3
E=5
L=3
L=3
I=1

N=5

G=3

This adds up to 23, which becomes 5. The characteristics of "5" are expansiveness and vision, along with the constructive use of freedom. The salesperson who works on advertising, sales displays and shop window displays, commercial websites, leaflets, and telephone sales would do well to have those characteristics associated with "5."

Farming translates as:

F=8

A=1

R=2

M=4

I=1

N=5

G=3

This adds to 24, which becomes 6. The characteristics of "6" are responsibility, protection, and nurturing, and every good farmer does this with his or her crops and livestock.

A teacher can be analyzed as:

T=4

E=5

A=1

C=3

H=5

E=5

R=2

This adds up to 25, and then reduces to 7. "Seven" is associated with analysis, understanding, knowledge, awareness, and studiousness.

Entertainments are expressed numerologically as:

E=5

N=5

T=4

E=5

R=2

T=4
A=1
I=1
N=5
M=4
E=5
N=5
T=4
S=3

This totals 53, which becomes 8. The number "8" carries the characteristics of practical endeavours and an interest in power and status.

A professional stage conjuror

Religion can be analyzed as:

R=2

E=5

L=3

I=1

G=3

I=1

O=7

N=5

This totals 27, which adds to 9. "Nine" carries the associations of humanitarianism, a giving, generous nature, unselfishness, and creative expression.

Having determined the numerological categories for a selection of professions, it is possible to look for notable members of those professions and see whether their numbers are compatible with the number relating to the profession. The numbers of the people will not necessarily be the same as the numbers of the sample professions, but should be compatible with them. That is, the characteristics of the profession and the person should be compatible.

Hippocrates (460–370 BC), the father of Western medicine, works out numerologically as:

H=5

I=1

P=8

P=8

O=7

C=3

R=2

A=1

T=4

E=5

S=3

This totals 47, which reduces to 11 and then 2. The characteristics of "2" are consideration of others, adaptability, and cooperation — all excellent qualities and fully compatible with medicine.

Steve Jobs, the brilliant computer expert, scores:

S=3
T=4
E=5
V=6
E=5

J=1
O=7
B=2
S=3

This totals 36, which then becomes 9. Numerologically, "9" is associated with creative expression, unselfishness, and humanitarianism. Steve displayed immense creativity with his many inventions.

Sir Douglas Bader (1910–1982) was one of the bravest and best aviators of the twentieth century. Numerologically, he scores:

D=4
O=7
U=6
G=3
L=3
A=1
S=3

B=2
A=1
D=4
E=5
R=2

This makes a total of 41, further reducing to 5. The numerological characteristics of "5" are adventure, a visionary outlook, and the constructive use of freedom. All of these qualities are compatible with any good aviator, but most especially with heroic Douglas Bader.

Horatio Nelson (1758–1805) was one of the greatest naval heroes of all time. His numerological score is:

H=5
O=7
R=2
A=1
T=4
I=1
O=7

N=5
E=5
L=3
S=3
O=7
N=5

This totals 55, which reduces to 10 and then 1. This is perfect for Nelson, as the characteristics of "1" are: a person who initiates action, a pioneer, a leader, a strongly independent individual.

One of the world's greatest salesmen and teachers of salesmanship was Heinz Goldmann (1919–2005). When co-author Lionel was chief training executive for the Phoenix Timber Group, he attended a course that Goldmann ran in London in June 1970. More than 40 years later, he still recalls Goldmann's amazing sales ability and charisma. Numerologically, Heinz Goldmann works out as:

H=5
E=5
I=1
N=5
Z=7

G=3
O=7
L=3

D=4
M=4
A=1
N=5
N=5

This totals 55, which becomes 10 and then 1. The numerological characteristics associated with "1" are initiating action, pioneering, independence, and attainment. All of these are highly relevant for Heinz Goldmann, and closely compatible with salesmanship.

One of the greatest farmers in history was Thomas William Coke (1752–1842), who became the Earl of Leicester of Holkham. He was the MP for northwest Norfolk from 1776–1833. His contributions to agriculture were enormous. He converted northwest Norfolk into a prolific wheat-growing district and greatly improved the breeds of farm animals there. Numerologically, he scores:

T=4
H=5
O=7
M=4
A=1
S=3

W=6
I=1
L=3
L=3
I=1
A=1
M=4

C=3
O=7
K=2
E=5

This totals 60, which becomes 6. The numerological characteristics associated with "6" are responsibility, protection, nurturing, and care for the community. As shown earlier, "6" is the number for farming as a profession, so "6" is ideal for a truly great farmer like Coke.

Dr. Thomas Arnold (1795–1842) was headmaster of Rugby School from 1828–1841. He was also an outstanding academic historian. Numerologically, his name scores:

T=4
H=5
O=7
M=4
A=1
S=3

A=1
R=2
N=5
O=7
L=3
D=4

This totals 46, which becomes 10 and then 1. The numerological characteristics of "1" are pioneering, leading, independence, initiating action, and individualism. Thomas Arnold had all of these qualities to a high degree, and was an ideal representative of the teaching profession.

Vesta Tilley (1864–1952) was one of the most successful and greatly loved music hall artists of the golden age of British theatre. She was an excellent singer of songs such as "Burlington Bertie" and "Angels without Wings." She was also a very entertaining male impersonator. Numerologically, her stage name scores:

V=6
E=5
S=3
T=4
A=1

T=4
I=1
L=3
L=3
E=5
Y=1

This totals 36, further reduced to 9. The characteristics of "9" are: a humanitarian, giving nature; unselfishness; and creative expression.

Thomas Becket (1118–1170) was born in Cheapside in London, son of Gilbert Becket and his wife Matilda. Both of them had originally come from France. Thomas was Archbishop of Canterbury and was martyred in 1170. Numerologically, he scores:

T=4
H=5
O=7
M=4
A=1
S=3

B=2
E=5
C=3
K=2
E=5
T=4

This totals 45, which can be reduced to 9, and "9" is totally compatible with religion as a profession. Thomas Becket had all the excellent qualities that the post required. He was unselfish and a humanitarian.

Having looked at these examples of good people who were compatible with their professions in numerological terms, it is interesting to consider some negative characters that were compatible with the negative aspects of their numerological scores.

Hawley Harvey Crippen (1862–1910) was hanged for the murder of his second wife, Cora Henrietta Crippen. Although referred to as Doctor Crippen, he was a homeopathic doctor whose American qualifications were not recognized for medical practice in the UK. His first wife, Charlotte, had died in 1892, ostensibly of a stroke. The second wife, whom he allegedly murdered and buried in the cellar at 39 Hilldrop Crescent, London, was born Kunigunde Mackamotski and had a German mother and a Polish-Russian father. She had aspirations to be a music hall singer under her stage name of Belle Elmore. The Crippens were on a very low income, and had to take in lodgers.

Hawley Harvey Crippen works out numerologically as:

H=5
A=1
W=6
L=3
E=5
Y=1

H=5
A=1
R=2
V=6
E=5
Y=1

C=3
R=2
I=1
P=8
P=8
E=5
N=5

This totals 73, further reduced to 10 and then 1. This is compatible for medicine as a profession, but the *dark* side of the numerological "1" is impetuosity and rashness, ignoring all others as long as the individual can get what he or she wants. Crippen wanted to be free of his wife so that he could continue his love affair with Ethel "Le Neve" Neave. She was born in Diss in Norfolk, England, in 1883, and was only 27 when Crippen was hanged in 1910. The dark side of his numerological "1" may have been what drove him to the rash and impetuous murder of Cora.

Without naming any individual computer hacker, hacking may be regarded as the dark side of the numerological "2." An ability to get into the workings of another human mind, or into the workings of a computer, and to use that ability to penetrate it in the wrong way lines up with the negative side of the numerological "2."

On May 11, 1945, Kiyoshi Ogawa (1922–1945), a kamikaze pilot, flew his plane into the USS *Bunker Hill*. Numerologically, his score is:

K=2
I=1
Y=1
O=7
S=3
H=5
I=1

O=7
G=3
A=1
W=6
A=1

This totals 38, which becomes 11, followed by 2. The negative side of the numerological "2" has been outlined above, but in the case of a kamikaze pilot, it may, perhaps, be thought to indicate that peace-at-any-price includes kamikaze attacks.

Just as Horatio Nelson was put forward as an example of an outstanding naval hero, so the pirate Edward Teach (1680–1718), known as Blackbeard, can be used as an example of marine crime.

He was finally brought to justice by Lieutenant Maynard. Numerologically, Edward Teach becomes:

E=5
D=4
W=6
A=1
R=2
D=4

T=4
E=5
A=1
C=3
H=5

This totals 40, which becomes 4, and is numerologically correct for a career at sea. The negative side of the numerological "4" is repression, enforced conformity, the desire to control and regulate everyone and everything, and a vicious struggle against limits. All of these characteristics would seem appropriate for piracy.

The numerological "5" is appropriate for top sales people like Heinz Goldmann, but the dark side of "5" is compatible with confidence tricksters such as Victor Lustig (1890–1947). Among his many memorable confidence tricks, he sold the Eiffel Tower to an unsuspecting scrap metal merchant!

Numerologically, his name translates to:
V=6
I=1
C=3
T=4
O=7
R=2

L=3
U=6
S=3
T=4

I=1

G=3

This totals 43, which adds to 7. Numerologically, the dark side of "7" is associated with too much attention to detail and an inability to use academic powers correctly. It could be argued that Lustig was an exceptionally able man, whose tragedy was a misuse of his formidable mental powers.

William Corder (1803–1828), a farmer from Polstead in Suffolk, England, murdered his girlfriend Maria Marten and was duly hanged for the crime. Numerologically, his name can be analyzed as:

W=6

I=2

L=3

L=3

I=1

A=1

M=4

C=3

O=7

R=2

D=4

E=5

R=2

This totals 43, which reduces to 7. Numerologically, the negative side of "7" is associated with over-attention to detail and the misuse of thought.

Andreas Vesalius (1514–1564) was a pioneering anatomist, physician, and medical teacher, but was frowned upon for carrying out the dissections of cadavers taken from graveyards. Numerologically, he works out as:

A=1

N=5

D=4

R=2

E=5
A=1
S=3

V=6
E=5
S=3
A=1
L=3
I=1
U=6
S=3

This totals 49, which becomes 13 and then 4. Numerologically, "4" in its negative aspect becomes repression, enforced conformity, a desire to regulate everyone and everything. It might be argued that there is no more complete control than the control of an anatomist over a corpse that is being dissected! The teaching practised by Vesalius was a very long way from the teaching practised by Arnold of Rugby.

Great and good entertainers like Vesta Tilley can be contrasted with the Marquis de Sade, Donatien Alphonse François (1740–1814), who produced and directed plays in the Charenton mental hospital. Numerologically, de Sade can be calculated as:

D=4
O=7
N=5
A=1
T=4
I=1
E=5
N=5

A=1
L=3
P=8

H=5
O=7
N=5
S=3
E=5

F=8
R=2
A=1
N=5
C=3
O=7
I=1
S=3

This adds to 99, which becomes to 18, and then is further reduced to 9. A misused "9," numerologically, is thought to destroy the personality, and a case can be made for de Sade's personality being destroyed.

Thomas Becket, the martyred Archbishop of Canterbury, provided an example of a brave and sincere religious man who can be contrasted vividly with Grigori Yefimovich Rasputin (1869–1916) who had a profound and dangerous influence over Tsar Nicholas II, his wife Alexandra, and their son Alexei. Rasputin was a Russian Orthodox monk and a faith healer. His moral life was darkly suspect. Numerologically, he can be scored as:

G=3
R=2
I=1
G=3
O=7
R=2
I=1

Y=1
E=5

F=8
I=1
M=4
O=7
V=6
I=1
C=3
H=5

R=2
A=1
S=3
P=8
U=6
T=4
I=1
N=5

This totals 90, which numerologically reduces to 9. The dark side of "9" has already been considered for the Marquis de Sade, and it seems interesting that both he and Rasputin share the number.

This chapter has examined the numerological links and compatibility between certain professions and prominent members of those professions. It has also delved into the dark side, the negative side, of certain numerological characteristics. The question of whether numbers exert influence over characters, or whether they simply serve as indicators and warnings, has also been considered. In the next chapter, the links between astrology, the Zodiac, and numerology will be examined.

18
ASTROLOGY, THE ZODIAC, AND NUMEROLOGY

Just as numerology is a belief in the power of certain numbers to exert their mystical influence over people and events, or to indicate the likely characteristics of certain people and places — perhaps as a warning — so astrology is a belief in the power of celestial phenomena to influence terrestrial phenomena. A great many astrological theories are centred on the belief that the positions of the planets, the moon, and the sun at the time of a person's birth can say a great deal about his or her personality and probable life history.

Astrology and numerology can be combined to expand the information that each is believed to supply. When William Shakespeare was analyzed numerologically, his name came to the total of "5," which meant a visionary character and an expansive adventurer who used freedom constructively. He was born under the sign of Taurus the Bull. Taurus' are thought to have the astrological characteristics of being sensual, pleasure-seeking, and fertile thinkers who are very productive. They are also practical and very energetic. Those characteristics could certainly apply to Shakespeare.

Alexander Graham Bell, the inventor, scored "6" numerologically, which suggested that his characteristics included responsibility, protection, nurturing, care for the community, and sympathy. He was born under Pisces, which suggests a person who seeks higher goals and is compassionate and unselfish. Pisceans are very receptive and sensitive. Bell's Zodiac readings tie in well with his numerological readings.

Andrew Bonar Law had a numerological name reading of "5," associated with expansiveness, visionary wisdom, and being an adventurous man who understood the constructive uses of freedom. His Zodiac sign was Virgo the Virgin. The characteristics for this sign are: living up to duties and responsibilities; a perfectionist approach to life; always seeking improvement; and the ability to change and adapt to life as required.

Sir Frederick Grant Banting also had a numerological name total of "5," the same as that of Andrew Bonar Law. His Zodiac birth sign was Scorpio the Scorpion.

The Scorpio characteristics suggest an intense person with a great deal of self-mastery, and a physical or intellectual hero who breaks free of limitations. This seems very appropriate for a medical scientist who did so much excellent work, especially for diabetics.

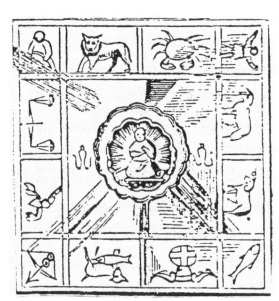

The signs of the Zodiac

King Robert Bruce of Scotland scored "4" numerologically, which indicated that he was a man who could create a sound foundation and implement good order. He was a man, numerologically, who could struggle successfully against limits and then proceed with steady growth. He was born under the sign of Cancer the Crab. This carries the Zodiacal characteristics of nurturing and supporting others, being a good family member and clansman, and being especially aware of ancestry and heritage. All of these factors fit well with Robert the Bruce.

Queen Elizabeth I of England achieved a score of "6," which is associated with responsibility and the protection of her people. Her Zodiac birth sign was Virgo the Virgin — especially appropriate for the Virgin Queen. Bonar Law was also born under this sign, and his characteristics were very similar to those for Queen Elizabeth I. These people live up to their duties and responsibilities. Their approach to life is perfectionism. They are always seeking to improve things. They are the type of people who have the ability to change and adapt to life as required.

Sir Francis Drake scored "1" on the numerology of his name. This showed him to be a pioneering leader and an independent character that succeeds in attaining things. Like Alexander Graham Bell, the inventor, Drake's Zodiac birth sign was Pisces the Fish. The Piscean

Scorpio

characteristics for Bell were seeking higher goals and being compassionate and unselfish. Pisceans are typically very receptive and sensitive, as well as compassionate, empathetic, unselfish, and willing to take care of others. Although Drake's work as a sailor involved him in one battle after another — and in a battle situation he had to be ruthlessly efficient — there was a great deal of unselfish caring and protection required of him as well. He was fond of his Devon crew, and protected them as best he could.

Francis Bacon scored "5" on the numerology name calculations. This gave him expansiveness, visionary adventure, and the constructive use of freedom. His Zodiac birth sign is Aquarius — the same as co-author Lionel. Aquarians are freedom-lovers, free thinkers, unorthodox, and never shackled by outdated ideologies. They also tend to dominate.

Joan of Arc, real name "Jehanne," scored "9" on the numerological scale. This indicated unselfishness and a sense of obligation, a generous, giving nature, and humanitarianism. Her Zodiac birth sign was Capricorn. The characteristics associated with Capricorns are: seriousness; an attempt to create the perfect society; and concern with truth and reality. These are all totally appropriate for Joan.

Madeleine Jarret, the teenaged Canadian hero, scored "6" on the numerological scale. This indicated her great sense of responsibility and protectiveness amid the dangers of the seventeenth century. Like Bell and Drake, her Zodiac birth sign was Pisces the Fish. Like them, the heroic Madeleine took care of people and was very receptive and sensitive.

John Kenneth Galbraith scored "8" on the numerology of his name. This indicated practical endeavours and high material goals. His Zodiac birth sign is Libra. The characteristics associated with Libra are peace, harmony, balance, and social awareness. All of these are appropriate for an outstanding economist like Galbraith.

Guy Fawkes had a numerological name score of "8," which indicates his practicality and pragmatism. Attempting to blow up the building that was housing Parliament certainly demonstrated pragmatism, if not much morality! His Zodiac birth sign is Aries, which is associated with aggression, wilfulness, power, and assertiveness. It is also associated with warrior-type energy and impatience. All of these qualities seem appropriate for Guy Fawkes.

William Wordsworth, the great romantic poet, has a numerological name score of "2," which is associated with cooperation and adaptability, consideration of others, and partnering — as with Coleridge. Like Guy Fawkes, his Zodiac birth sign is Aries, but its characteristics are totally inappropriate for Wordsworth.

Elizabeth Barrett Browning, the poet, has a numerological name score of 1. This indicates someone independent who is capable of initiating action. "One" reveals a pioneering individual capable of attaining things. Her Zodiac birth sign is Pisces — the same as the sign for Madeleine Jarrett. Although Elizabeth Barrett Browning shared Madeleine's innate heroism, she added to it some of the other Piscean characteristics such as escapism and fantasy, as revealed in her poems. Elizabeth also bore the compassion and empathy that is commonly characteristic of Pisceans.

Edgar Allan Poe scored "3" on his numerological name calculations, indicating powers of expression and verbalization. His Zodiac birth sign is Capricorn. Two of the Capricornian characteristics that apply particularly to Poe are ambition and pride in accomplishments.

John Lawrence Sullivan, the boxing champion, had a numerological name score of "4," indicating a struggle against limits and steady growth during his boxing career. His Zodiac birth sign was Libra, which is not compatible with a boxer; Aries would have been far more appropriate for a fighter like Sullivan. Libra is associated with good, steady, enduring relationships, as well as with peace, harmony, and balance. Librans are ideally suited to the counselling professions rather than boxing! Co-author Patricia is a Libran.

Albert Einstein, the brilliant physicist, had a numerological name score of "1," indicating an independent individual, a pioneer and leader — a person who initiates action and attains his or her objectives. His Zodiac birth sign is Pisces. There are numerous Piscean characteristics that are appropriate for him: seeking the highest goals, compassion, empathy, and unselfish work. Pisceans are also very receptive and sensitive.

Charles Lutwidge Dodgson, alias Lewis Carroll, of *Alice in Wonderland* fame, had a numerological name score of "6." This is associated with responsibility, protection, nurturing, and sympathy. His Zodiac birth sign is Aquarius, like Francis Bacon and co-author Lionel. This makes him free-thinking and unorthodox, not shackled by outdated ideology, and having a tendency to dominate.

George MacDonald, the great Christian author, had a numerological name score of "3" — the same as Edgar Allan Poe. This indicates expression, verbalization, socialization, and artistic ability allied to the sheer joy of living. His Zodiac birth sign is Sagittarius. Characteristics from this sign include using talents for the benefit of others, receptiveness to new points of view, and a man who is a freedom-loving idealist. Other characteristics for Sagittarius include enthusiasm, gregariousness, generosity, and a love of ideals. These are all applicable to George MacDonald.

Mark Twain, alias Samuel Langhorne Clemens, had a numerological name score of "5." This suggested expansiveness, vision, adventure, and the constructive use of freedom. His Zodiac birth sign was also Sagittarius, like George MacDonald, and is detailed above.

George Formby, the entertainer, singer, and ukulele player, had a numerological name score of "9." This was right for George, who was a good and kind man. His Zodiac birth sign was Gemini. This indicates a skilled communicator — a very sociable person who greatly enjoys interacting with others. This was certainly true of George Formby.

Elvis Aaron Presley, "the King," had a numerological name sign of "7," indicating knowledge, understanding, and awareness. His Zodiac birth sign is Capricorn, like Edgar Allan Poe. As noted earlier, two of the Capricorn characteristics are ambition and pride in accomplishments.

It can thus be seen that on some significant occasions, the numerological name score and Zodiac birth sign have certain things in common.

Where astrological readings are conveyed to the individual concerned, traces of self-fulfilling prophecies may be detected. To tell someone that he or she will be a great success in politics or the entertainment world, in sport or in business, may well persuade the person concerned to enter the particular field in which success is predicted, and then to proceed with such confidence and enthusiasm that the chance of success is greatly enhanced. To tell someone that he or she has tremendous strength and stamina, and determination and willpower, is likely to encourage that person to live up to the astrological prophecy and to develop those qualities to a greater extent than would have happened without the prophecy.

To the earliest astrologers, there were 7 classical heavenly bodies: the sun and moon, Mercury, Venus, Mars, Jupiter, and Saturn. Astrology has its closest links with numerology in that the core of astrology is concerned with the idea that all mathematical relationships can be shown to exert aspects of energy that can be expressed as numbers. They can be angles, flat or solid shapes, or even sounds. Pythagoras realized that musical notes depend on the length of the string that creates them. He understood that harmony follows certain mathematical rules. His work on the harmony of the spheres argued that the planets all emit specific sounds, and the harmony so produced was reflected

The Twins

on the Earth, and onto earthly life. Francis Bacon, besides being the father of modern empirical science, was also capable of thinking along astrological lines. On page 351 of *De Augmentis*, written in 1623, he argued that there was no "fatal necessity" in astrological predictions. In his mind, the stars could "incline and persuade, but could not compel." Thomas Aquinas had said much the same thing four centuries earlier!

Contemporary Western astrology is mainly concerned with horoscopes. This is a form of divination based on the relative positions of the heavenly bodies at the time of a person's birth. It is concerned with where the planets then appear to move with regard to the Zodiac.

The Zodiac itself consists of 12 signs. Each is 30 degrees apart so that the 12 signs take up the full 360 degrees of the ecliptic, which is the apparent path of the sun. The signs are as follows:

SIGN	SYMBOL	DATES
Aries	Ram	March 21– April 20
Taurus	Bull	April 21– May 21
Gemini	Twins	May 22– June 22
Cancer	Crab	June 23– July 23
Leo	Lion	July 24– August 23
Virgo	Virgin	August 24– September 23
Libra	Scales	September 24– October 23
Scorpio	Scorpion	October 24– November 22
Sagittarius	Centaur Archer	November 23– December 21
Capricorn	Goat	December 22– January 20
Aquarius	Water Carrier	January 21– February 19
Pisces	Fish	February 20– March 20

The constellations connected with the signs of the Zodiac are also concerned with classical ancient history and mythology. The Ram carried Athamas's son, Phrisux, and his daughter, Helle, to Colchis. It was then sacrificed and the fleece was displayed in the sacred grove, where it turned to gold. It later became the target of Jason and the Argonauts. This constellation was well-known to the ancient Egyptians as well as the Greeks and Romans.

The Bull is associated with Zeus, who turned himself into a bull in order to carry off the beautiful Europa, daughter of the King of Crete. The warrior twins, Castor and Pollux, were the brothers of Helen of Troy. They protect ships and sailors.

The constellation of Cancer the Crab is a reminder that Juno sent a crab in an attempt to defeat Hercules while he was fighting the many-headed Hydra. The plan failed, and Hercules destroyed the crab as well. The Lion constellation has 2 meanings: for the ancient Egyptians, the sun was in this constellation when the floods came and made the lands fertile around the Nile; in Greek mythology, it features Hercules again when he slaughters the dreaded Nemean Lion.

The constellation of Virgo the Virgin represents the goddess of agriculture. She can be thought of as Ishtar, Isis, Demeter, and Cybele. She could also be Persephone, Queen of the Underworld. Libra, the Scales, are believed to be the scales used by Astraea representing fairness, balance, and justice. The constellation of Scorpio the Scorpion represents the Scorpion sent to kill Orion after he had threatened to kill all living animals. It is interesting to note that the 2 constellations are on opposite sides of the sky, as though keeping well apart!

The Archer-Centaur constellation in Babylonian astrology represented a demonic entity called Pabilsaq. The constellation Capricorn represents a sea-goat. The goat is sometimes called Amalthea, and is associated with the cornucopia — the horn of plenty. He looked after baby Zeus.

The constellation of Aquarius represents the boy who served the gods their drinks. He is known as Ganymede in some mythologies. The twelfth constellation is Pisces the Fish, actually 2 fish. In some mythologies they are said to be the goddess Venus and her son Cupid escaping from Typhon. In other mythologies they represent Aphrodite and Eros.

The first 9 constellations are associated with the numerological interpretations of the numbers 1–9: Aries the Ram, for example, is connected to the number "1" and is associated with initiating action, pioneering, leading, independence, attainment, and individuality. Sagittarius is "9," and is associated with humanitarianism, giving, unselfishness, a sense of obligation, and creative expression. The tenth constellation is Capricorn and the number "10," taken as a whole rather than being broken down further to 1, in this context stands for completeness. This very special constellation is regarded as the number of the cosmos itself. Capricorn — like the cornucopia — contains all things and makes all things possible. The eleventh constellation is Aquarius, and the number "11," before being broken down to 2, has the meaning of patience, intuition, honesty, sensitivity, spirituality, and idealism. Just as Aquarius is the water-bearer, so "11" in this complete sense is the bearer of light, in both a spiritual and a physical sense.

The twelfth constellation is Pisces the Fish, and "12" also has a very special and unique meaning. Here it stands alone and is not reduced down to 3. "Twelve," in this special complete and separate sense, is the number of energy and vitality. It is also the number of resilience. "Twelve" is an inspirational number, a number associated with love and great and enduring affection.

In the next chapter, Isopsephy and Gematria are examined and analyzed.

19
ISOPSEPHY, GEMATRIA, CELTIC, AND DRUID NUMEROLOGY

The word *isopsephy* is taken from the Greek *isos*, meaning "equal," and *psephos*, meaning "a pebble or small stone." The word refers to the numerological technique of adding up the number values of the letters in a word and arriving at a single number from them. It was customary in ancient Greece to use pebbles for calculations. Gematria refers to the same technique of adding number values, but using the Hebrew alphabet instead of the Greek alphabet.

In isopsephy, each unit number from 1–9 was allocated a separate letter. The tens, from 10–90, were also allocated separate letters, and so were the hundreds from 100–900. This requires a total of 27 letters, but the generally accepted Greek alphabet has only 24. What was to be done about the missing 3 letters? Three obsolete letters were resurrected. These were: *digamma*, which was later replaced by *stigma*, to represent 6; *qoppa*, or *koppa*, for 90; and *sampi* for 900.

GREEK LETTERS AND THEIR NUMEROLOGICAL EQUIVALENTS

Letter	Numerical Equivalent
Alpha	*1*
Beta	*2*
Gamma	*3*
Delta	*4*
Epsilon	*5*
Digamma or Stigma	*6*
Zeta	*7*
Eta	*8*
Theta	*9*
Iota	*10*
Kappa	*20*
Lambda	*30*
Mu	*40*
Nu	*50*
Xi	*60*
Omicron	*70*
Pi	*80*
Koppa	*90*
Rho	*100*
Sigma	*200*
Tau	*300*
Upsilon	*400*
Phi	*500*
Chi	*600*
Psi	*700*
Omega	*800*
Sampi	*900*

The gematria, sometimes rendered "gimatria," is a method of giving number values to a Hebrew word or phrase. When two or more words or phrases score exactly the same number, it is thought by gematrists that there is a connection between their meanings. The word *gematria* is thought by some expert numerologists to be derived from the Greek letter gamma, third in the Greek alphabet, because the number "3" has special numerological power and significance. Other theories suggest that the word *gematria* is derived from the Greek *geometria*, meaning "geometry." A very widely-known example of gematria is the Hebrew word *chai*, which means "life." The letters of *chai* add numerologically to produce a sum of 18, and "18" has become a positive and highly favoured number among followers of the gematria.

The numerical values allocated to Hebrew letters in the gematria are as follows:

Letter	Numerological Equivalent
Aleph	1
Beth	2
Gimel	3
Daleth	4
He	5
Waw	6
Zayin	7
Heth	8
Teth	9
Yod	10
Kaph	20
Lamed	30
Mem	40
Nun	50
Samekh	60
Ayin	70
Pe	80
Sadhe	90
Qoph	100
Resh	200
Shin	300
Taw	400
Kaph-sofit	500
Mem-sofit	600
Nun-sofit	700
Pe-sofit	800
Sadhe-sofit	900

Gematrists use a number of different techniques when they calculate words, phrases, or entire sentences. What is termed the *mispar hechrachi*, or "absolute value" method utilizes the full numerical values of the original 22 Hebrew letters. *Mispar gadol* uses the final forms, known as the "sofit" forms, to calculate the values from 500–900. Another technique, known as the *mispar ha-gadol*, actually spells out the name of each letter and then totals them. Yet another method called *mispar katan*, or *mispar me'ugal*, calculates individual letter values, but leaves out the "0"s. A further method called *mispar siduri* gives every letter a value counting up as far as 22. There are another 10 or 11 different methods, each of which calculates the Hebrew letters differently.

To complicate the gematria methods yet more, techniques such as the *atbash* cipher are used, where the alphabet is doubled back on itself so that the first letter is represented by the last letter. Using an English alphabet, this would mean that the letter "A" would be "Z," "B" would be "Y," "C" would be "X," and so on.

Moving forward from the gematria to Celtic and Druidic numerology, it is relevant to consider the life and work of Taliesin (534–599). He was a gifted bard with mystical insight, and there can be little doubt that he was also an expert numerologist. One of his most mysterious sayings is that he considered himself to be "a word among letters." What might he have meant by that? Was he familiar with gematria and did he calculate the numerological meanings of words from the letters within them, or *around* them? Some gematrial techniques involved using letters from adjacent words, as well as those in the word being analyzed numerologically. Is that what Taliesin was referring to so cryptically? Many of the exciting stories about Taliesin refer to him as the heroic companion of King Arthur and Bran the Blessed.

He is also believed to have connections with the Druids and his Celtic powers of numerology linked in with Druid numerology. The Druids were an ancient order of Celtic priests in the societies of Western Europe, Britain, and Ireland. They were particularly associated with the great stone circles like Stonehenge, and their numerology was associated with circle geometry.

King Arthur

King Arthur's Stone

The Druid numerologists seem to have been particularly interested in the number 6, which relates very closely to circle geometry. Using the modern system of dividing a circle into 360 degrees makes the division of 360 degrees into 6×60 degrees, and these natural divisions seem to have been an integral part of the Druid circles, whether or not those profound ancient thinkers used 360 degrees in their calculations or not. The Druids were renowned as seers and predictors of the future, and their circle geometry and numerology almost certainly played a major part in their predictions.

Stonehenge

The Druid's Stone in Bungay,
England

The Druids were very probably the earliest priests to operate on the Isle of Wight in the UK. The high ridge across the downs on the Isle of Wight seemed to them to mirror what they thought of as the path of the Moon Dragon. This made the island a very special place for them. The 3 holy sites — yet again, the numerologically important "3" is involved — were the pinnacle of Ur, the Longtone at Mottistone, and the Oak Grove of Gabhanodorum. All 3 of these are on the Firestone Ridge, which is dragon-shaped.

In this brief chapter, the Greek and Hebrew systems of numerology — isopsephy and gematria —have been examined along with a summary of Celtic and Druidic involvement in numerology. Whether employed by magicians and mystics from the East or West, the principles remain constant. Names, dates, and places like the Dragon Ridge and Stonehenge all have numerological significance. In the next chapter, the tarot cards are examined in detail along with their numerological connections.

20
NUMEROLOGY AND THE TAROT

The tarot cards are inseparable from numerology. Tarot readings cannot be carried out unless the numerical values of the cards are taken into account. The tarot, which was at one time known as *trionfi, tarocchi*, and *tarock*, was well known in Europe from the fourteenth century onwards, where the cards were used for a set of games. These included the French game *tarot* and the Italian game *tarocchini*. The tarot cards are most widely used today, however, for divination and prophecy. There are traditions that take the tarot cards as far back as ancient Egypt or Babylonia, and some legends link them with the mysteries of the Kabbalah as well. There are 4 ordinary suits in the tarot, each comprised of 14 cards: 4 picture cards and 10 numbered cards. There is also a suit of trumps, which contains 21 cards, and there is a single card known as "the fool." The 21 trumps and the fool are referred to as the major arcana. The other suits are the minor arcana: these suits are usually referred to as coins, swords, clubs, and cups.

The major arcana are considered the most important tarot cards when the deck is being used for divination. The first card in the major arcana is known as "the juggler," "the magician," or "the thaumaturgist." It often carries a picture of a juggler or stage magician. This card represents power behind the scenes: hidden, unsuspected power. It can represent an unsuspected "Mr. Fix-it" type of character, or a grey eminence. In the modern world, this person is a subtle politician or financier. This is the spider in the heart of the web, the networker who influences all the other networkers. Numerologically, card "1" also has the sense of initiating action.

The Goddess

Card "2" is referred to as "the goddess," or as "the female pope." In many tarot sets she is pictured as the goddess Juno accompanied by a peacock. Like card "1," she symbolizes power and influence. The subtle difference between the meanings of card "1" and card "2" is that the goddess works in total secrecy and her activities are unsuspected. The juggler/magician rarely uses his powers openly. The goddess uses her powers even more secretly, and with total concealment of them. This card indicates things that are hidden and unexpected. In a story of espionage, this card would be the kind of spy who is known as a sleeper. For many years this agent is not asked to do anything — then suddenly he or she is at the centre of the action with a critical role to play. The power of this character — the female pope — is like the dagger hidden behind a tapestry on the wall of a medieval castle. Numerologically, card "2" is adaptable. It uses its hidden influence to mediate.

The third and fourth cards are "the empress" and "the emperor." They are depicted in most sets as sitting enthroned in regal splendour. In contrast to the hidden powers of the magician and the goddess, the emperor and the empress are open, ostentatious powers. They occupy prominent, public positions at all times. They are media giants, colourful leaders of commerce and industry, prominent politicians such as presidents and prime ministers, or fierce tribal chieftains. Whereas cards "1" and "2" have real manipulative power, of which others are largely unaware, cards "3" and "4" *appear* to have more power than is really the case. Psychologically, these first 4 cards might be described as introverts and extroverts: cards "1" and "2" are introverts; cards "3" and "4" are extroverts. Numerologically, "3" is vitally important. It stands for expression and verbalization. "Four" represents foundation and order — the order over which card "4" is the apparent ruler.

The fifth card is "the pope." It is sometimes illustrated with an ancient Greek god, sometimes with a religious figure. This card represents holiness rather than power. This fifth card is linked to the ninth card, "the hermit." Together they have the power of morality, ethics, and what might be termed "sincere religion." Becket displayed this kind of power against King Henry II. Men and women with this kind of power cannot be moved by threats or bribery — only by what they truly believe. "Five," in numerology, represents vision, and with the fifth tarot card there is moral, ethical, and religious vision. The ninth card, the hermit, is numerologically associated with unselfishness and humanitarianism.

The sixth card, "the lovers," is mysterious and intriguing. It shows two happy young people totally engrossed in each other. If Sigmund Freud had lived before the tarot was invented, he would have been its most probable designer. What Freud called the libido can be expressed directly through sexual energy, or in thousands of other ways. Freud maintained that the libido can be sublimated when these other forms of expression are used. This sixth card relates to the most powerful of all human motivators. Perfect love is greater than any fear, and greater even than the very powerful desire for self-preservation. Truly loving people in this sense will risk their lives without a second thought to save the people they love. By incorporating this sixth card, the designer of the pack has fathomed the profoundest depth of human nature. Numerologically, "6" is associated with protection, sympathy, and nurturing others. The sixth card fits extremely well with the numerological aspects of "6." The sixth card relates to genuine altruism. When this unselfish, altruistic love is coupled with the great power of sexual love between devoted partners, the result is the emotional equivalent of a hydrogen bomb.

When examining the depth and importance of these first 6 cards of the major arcana, there are two ways of contemplating the mysterious tarot and its meanings. The great religious author George MacDonald was often asked about the meanings of his fantasies and allegories. He replied that the creative power of a reader was just as great as the creative power of an author. He believed that if a reader finds a depth of meaning in a story, one which the author had not seen, then the reader's creative powers generate a structure of meaning just as valid as anything the author might have intended. Following MacDonald's train of thought, does that mean that the tarot is a masterpiece of neutrality? Do the cards have no meanings apart from the meanings that the human mind projects upon them?

The alternative interpretation is that there are curious arcane powers within the cards themselves and the symbols they carry. This is exactly the same question that faces the serious student of numerology. Do the numbers merely reflect the ideas in the minds of those who examine them, or do they have intrinsic powers of their own? If they do have innate powers, what are those powers? Can numbers influence people and their environments, or do they merely reveal what is in people and environments and give warnings about them where necessary?

A third idea might be that the tarot cards have some sort of reciprocal relationship with their readers. It is undoubtedly the case that what people do has an effect on them. A carpenter, a blacksmith, a poet, a composer, a mountaineer, and a racing driver are all affected and shaped to some extent by what they do. A doctor, a nurse, or a professional gangland killer are also shaped by their activities. As the old saying goes: "While I'm making something, it's making me."

There is a significant association between the seventh card, "the chariot," and the numerological significance of "7." Most tarot sets have a picture of a chariot on this seventh card. "Seven" stands for knowledge and awareness, the same knowledge and awareness that can go straight to the heart of a problem and solve it swiftly. Some astrologers believe the chariot to be the missing thirteenth sign of the Zodiac. The history of chess regards the castle, or rook, as a chariot. Its powerful, direct lateral moves represent the work of a chariot on the battlefield. The Old Persian word *rukh* meant chariot. When that seventh card appears, it can represent some physical force such as a storm or flood. Anyone or anything strong could be the chariot.

The eighth tarot card is "justice." It usually carries a picture of scales and a sword. There is a very practical aspect of justice, and the numerological "8" is associated with practical endeavours and high material goals. Card "8" represents balance. The justice card has been said to represent the mathematical parallelogram of forces. It is justice in the sense of a just balance between a raging flood and a massive granite cliff. This card is reason and logic together. This is the card that acknowledges the co-existence of ice and fire in the same universe.

Card "9," which is called "the hermit," carries a picture of a religious recluse. It is allied with card "5," the pope. This card is calmness and meditation. It represents morality, ethics, and true religion. Just as the chariot represents conflict and victory in war, external power and force, so the hermit conquers the inner person. The old proverb suggests that those who conquer themselves are greater than those who conquer cities. Numerologically, "9" is associated with unselfish giving and humanitarianism. The person who has conquered selfishness and cares for others is the true hermit of card "9." The hermit reminds people that there is just as much to explore inside their minds as there is in the external universe.

Card "10" is "the wheel of fortune" — and misfortune. It is usually shown as a wheel with people on it, being rotated by blindfolded fate. It is the roulette wheel of loss and gain. Numerologically, 10 can be reduced to 1. This person is the leader, the pioneer, the man or woman of action. Being in the right place at the right time — or the wrong place at the wrong time — can have devastating effects upon the subject's life. That's what card "10" of the tarot is all about. Disaster can strike the most prosperous and secure man or woman at any moment. It can fall out of the clearest, bluest sky. It works the other way too. The business tycoon on the verge of failure and bankruptcy suddenly wins $10 million in the lottery. Such are the twists and turns of the tenth card — the tarot wheel of fortune.

The eleventh card is "strength," or fortitude of mind and body. It often shows Hercules fighting the lion. Numerologically, the 11 can be reduced down to 2. "Two" is associated with cooperation and adaptability. It could be thought of as referring to the cooperation and adaptability of a strong, determined mind in a strong, muscular body. The authors' favourite cartoon shows a rugged and muscular old bullfrog in the beak of a heron, which is attempting to eat it. The frog has its powerful front webs firmly around the heron's throat and is strangling it with all it's got.

The heron's eyes are bulging like organ stops. The caption reads: "Don't ever give up!" The determined old bullfrog represents the true meaning of tarot card "11." Strength of mind, spirit, and body working together. A *determined* martial artist can defeat a younger, stronger, heavier opponent *if* he or she has greater determination than the opponent who has all the other advantages.

During the First World War, the German battle cruiser *Emden* fired at a small Russian gunboat, the *Jemchug*, and practically blew it in half. As it sank, the gunners in the rear turret of the *Jemchug* swung their gun around, and with a last defiant act of supreme courage and determination, managed to get off just one shell at the triumphant *Emden*. That kind of strength and fortitude goes with the eleventh tarot card. It is the unbeatable spirit of Templarism: *first to attack and last to retreat.*

During the Second World War, Bavarian Gypsies survived in their mountain strongholds against crack Nazi storm troopers because the Gypsy motto was: "*Take one with you.*" From the youngest toddler to the oldest Romany chief, that determination not to die while your enemy lived was etched indelibly into the Gypsy soul — and a simple piece of broken glass concealed in a ragged sleeve was capable of severing the jugular vein of a heavily armed storm trooper. That's tarot card "11." This card demonstrates that motivation without the strength or fortitude to back it up is like an arrowhead with no arrow.

The twelfth card is "the hanged man." The card shows the victim hanging upside-down with a cord around one ankle and the right foot crossed over the left knee, which is straight because it is the left ankle that is secured by the rope suspending the hanged man. This card represents those occasions when nothing is moving. The hanged man is literally pending, in the sense of waiting. The card refers to those occasions when we have to wait for the answer to some important question. Numerologically, 12 reduces to 3, and "3" carries the associations of expression and socialization. The hanged man is pending because of social factors beyond his control. The card expresses the absence of movement.

Marjorie Copeman, the psychology lecturer at Keswick Hall College near Norwich, was a lady of great wisdom and experience. One of her wisest sayings was: "We are all familiar with the traditional flight or fight responses to a stimulus: but there is a third way — we may simply ignore the stimulus and allow it to dissipate on its own."

The hanged man on the tarot cards symbolizes Marjorie Copeman's insight about the third way.

"Death," usually represented by a skeleton wielding a scythe, is the thirteenth tarot card. Numerologically, 13 reduces to 4. The association with "4" can be taken to mean a struggle against limits. However, the death card does not refer to physical death at all. In the Tarot, death stands for change — moving from one kind of life to another. It is not an end, but a new beginning.

The fourteenth card is Temperance. This represents balance, particularly a balance of the appetites. It means drawing back from dangerous and extreme attitudes. Temperance is a defence against fanaticism and obsession. Temperance may be regarded as the flagship of common sense. The picture often shows an angel pouring water into a drinking vessel. Numerologically, 14 reduces to 5. "Five" is associated with the constructive use of freedom, which is what true temperance is all about.

The fifteenth card is "the devil" — as far from the wisdom of Temperance as it is possible to be. It normally shows a woman, representing Eve, weeping because she yielded to temptation, while a demonic entity stands over her triumphantly. This is the symbol of temptation: the urge to neglect what is good and to apply our energies instead to that which is wrong. The demon symbol on the card refers not only to the dark, psychic forces of personified evil like Satan, or Lucifer, but to the evil within us: selfishness and greed. This fifteenth card is the tarot warning that evil lurks frighteningly close to the surface of even the kindest and best-natured human beings. Numerologically, 15 reduces to 6. "Six" is associated with protection, nurture, and sympathy. We need to protect ourselves and one another from evil and temptation.

The sixteenth card is "the lightning struck tower." It shows a tower falling in ruin. It follows the devil, as though indicating that yielding to temptation brings disaster. The lightning struck tower indicates — as does the wheel of fortune on card "10" — the possibility of a sudden change of circumstance. Whereas the wheel of fortune can bring welcome changes as it spins, the lightning struck tower is the warning that fate can deal appalling blows. The lightning struck tower is a constant reminder that security is an illusion. The numerological reduction of 16 to 7 reveals the characteristics of knowledge, aware-ness, and understanding also associated with this card. The presence of the lightning struck tower indicates the need to understand life and to be aware that danger is always lurking.

The seventeenth card is "the star," and it signifies hope. It is the light at the end of the tunnel as well as the light in the sky. In many sets of tarot cards, the illustration consists of a constellation of stars and a beautiful girl. In the fable of Pandora's Box, hope was the only worth-while thing it contained. The star keeps a shipwrecked sailor swimming in a shark-infested sea in the undying hope of rescue. The star shines on the future of the lovers of card "6." Numerologically, 17 reduces to 8, and "8" is associated with endeavour and goal-seeking. It is hope that keeps endeavour alive.

Card "18," "the moon," represents mystery. It could almost be set alongside the first card, the magician. In Shakespeare's *Midsummer Night's Dream* the magic happens by moonlight when Oberon and Titania take over from the sunlit world of reason and common sense. It is the moon card that suggests that there is a mystical, half-visible side to life. The card usually carries an image of the moon looking down on a pair of young lovers. The boy is serenading the girl. Numerologically, 18 reduces to 9, and "9" is associated with unselfishness and creative expression — as in the song the young minstrel is singing to his girl.

The nineteenth tarot card is "the sun." It is illustrated with the sun in the centre of a bright landscape. It represents the practical, everyday world of work. Attractive as the romantic moonlight may be, things have to be done if there is to be any achievement and progress. The ferry will not cross the river unless the ferryman rows hard. The sun card and the moon card together show that life is a balance between working and dreaming. Numerologically, 19 reduces to 10, and again to 1. The number "1" carries the associations of initiating action and getting jobs done.

The Jester

The twentieth card is "judgement." The older tarot packs portrayed it as a colourful scene of Heaven and Hell — or sometimes, even more specifically, as the ancient Egyptian "Book of the Dead." The last judgement card is the card that stands for finality. The twentieth card is the card of accountability. Numerologically, 20 reduces to 2, and "2" in this instance is associated with mediating, in the sense of judging and evaluating.

The twenty-first card is "the universe," or perhaps just planet Earth within it. The Earth supplies food, water, and oxygen to those who live on it and they need to protect it in return. This twenty-first card usually shows all types of life: plants, animals, birds, and fish, along with human beings. Numerologically, 21 reduces to 3. The number "3" is associated with the sheer joy of living.

The last card in the major arcana is not numbered. It is sometimes represented as a fool or court jester: a man or woman concealed behind a persona.

"The fool" is a wild card and represents the wildness within people. The fool represents freedom and irresponsibility — the whimsical, autonomous, uncontrolled, and uncontrollable aspect of human life. Numerologically, the "0," the absence of number, is very powerful and meaningful. It can bring great changes, like the death card, number "13." In one sense, all of life is contained within its sinister circle. For Taoists and Buddhists, it symbolizes the void. In Kabbalism it stands for unlimited light.

These examples strongly suggest a powerful nexus between the tarot and numerology. In the next chapter, the significance of numbers in folklore and mythology will be examined.

21
NUMEROLOGY IN FOLKLORE AND MYTHOLOGY

In almost all the well-known myths, legends, and folklore stories, numbers play a critical role, and those numbers have numerological significance. It is the third of 3 adventurers who rescues the other 2 and finds the treasure, slays the ogre, or kills the giant. It is the third sister — as in Cinderella — who marries the prince. The magical boots take their wearer 7 leagues at a single bound. Snow White is protected and helped by 7 dwarves. In this chapter, numbers from folklore, legend, and mythology will be examined in light of their numerological significance.

Many tales concern single heroes, who fit in well with the numerological aspect of "1." They are fearless pioneers who initiate action. Oisin, sometimes spelled Ossian, the great Celtic hero and poet, provides a relevant example. The King of the Land of Youth was determined to retain his power and authority against all challengers. Every seventh year (another numerological "7"!) there was a contest for the kingship. The cream of the warriors and athletes met at the palace and ran to a hilltop 2 miles away. The first man to reach it became king for the next 7 years. Fearing that he was aging and that a younger man would defeat him, the king asked a wise old Druid for help. The Druid told him that he would keep the crown forever — unless his son-in-law defeated him. The king had only 1 daughter, who was outstandingly beautiful, but he was determined to have no son-in-law, so taking the Druid's magic wand, he struck her and uttered a spell that gave her the head of a pig. Now I shall be king forever, he thought. No one will want her now.

The wise old Druid was greatly saddened by what the selfish king had done to his daughter. He visited the stricken girl in secret and told her that if she married a son of the great Fionn mac Cumhaill of Erin, her own lovely head and face would be restored. The princess made her way to Erin and saw Oisin, to whom she became greatly attracted. She offered to help him carry home some of the game he had recently caught, and he accepted her offer gratefully. When they stopped to rest, the enchanted princess was so hot and tired that she opened her dress to cool down, and Oisin was captivated by her beauty. She explained about the spell her father had cast on her to prevent her from marrying, and told Oisin that only a son of Fionn mac Cumhaill of Erin could restore her former beauty by marrying her.

Oisin was delighted to help her. They were married very shortly after their meeting and the lovely princess was instantly restored to her natural beauty. They went back to her own land and her father's castle, where Oisin raced up the hill a long way ahead of the other runners. He and his beautiful young wife ruled the land together for many years.

Another hero in a folktale from Denmark was a blacksmith who was working late at his forge one night when he heard a woman screaming for help outside in the darkness. He picked up the white hot iron in his tongs to use it as a light and went to see what was happening. A huge troll was driving a heavily pregnant girl down the road. Filled with anger, the burly blacksmith stepped between them and drove the troll back with the glowing iron in his tongs. The troll fled. The blacksmith helped the girl back to his house, where his wife helped her. She gave birth to twins. In the morning, the blacksmith took her and the newly arrived twins safely back to her husband, who was overjoyed to see them.

Numerologically, "2" stands for cooperation and adaptability, consideration of others, partnering, and mediating. Many stories are told of the twins, Castor and Pollux. In the mythology, they are the sons of Zeus, who turned into a swan when he raped Leda, and the boys hatched from the egg that she laid subsequently. In other versions of the story, one of them was conceived by Zeus and the other by Tyndareus, Leda's husband. The boys were very close to each other, and in some versions of their legend, the immortal son of Zeus, Pollux, offered to share his immortality with his human brother. They then became the constellation Gemini. The twin heroes were always regarded as benign and were helpers of human beings, especially sailors. They were also patrons of athletes, especially boxers.

An ancient Chinese fable tells of a young peasant boy who made a scant living from infertile soil with the help of his ox.

Chinese boy

The pair were inseparable friends. One day, the friendly ox told his young master that he was really the Ox Star whom the gods had sent to Earth as a punishment for something he had done wrong. The young peasant boy longed to be married and the ox agreed to help him. He showed the boy where to hide in the undergrowth near a large pool. The ox knew that this was the pool where the heavenly maidens came down from the sky to bathe. The girls duly arrived, laid their beautiful clothes on the bank, and began swimming in the lake. The ox told his young master to hide one heap of clothes, which he did. As the girls came out of the water, the young man emerged from the undergrowth. The girls grabbed their clothes in panic and flew off back to the heavens — all except for the girl whose clothes had been hidden. Without her magical robes, she was unable to fly. She soon realized, however, that the young man meant her no harm, and only wanted to marry her. She agreed, and they lived happily together for many years. She had great skill as a weaver, and this enabled them to become rich. This tale involves the close friendship of the boy and his ox, and how it led to great prosperity and happiness. It illustrates the numerological value of "2" as cooperation and partnership.

The number "3" has major significance in the story of Horatius on the bridge with Herminius, and Spurius Lartius, defending Rome from the Etruscans. The outline of the story is that the Roman King Tarquin was a selfish and greedy tyrant whom the Romans drove out. He then went to Lars Porsena, the Etruscan king, and asked for help. Porsena gathered a huge army and set out with Tarquin to attack Rome. Only the bridge across the Tiber stood between Rome and certain defeat in view of the odds against them. The Etruscans advanced towards the bridge, but at its narrowest, 3 men could defend it against thousands. Horatius volunteered to block the Etruscan advance with 2 helpers. Spurius Lartius and Herminius came with him. The battle raged for hours, but the Etruscans could not get past the 3 great Roman warriors. Finally, the other Romans who were cutting down the city end of the bridge shouted to their 3 heroes to come back before the bridge collapsed into the Tiber.

Herminius and Spurius Lartius made it just before the bridge fell, but Horatius was stranded alone on the far bank facing thousands of Etruscans. Turning his back on them disdainfully, he plunged into the swirling Tiber and battled his way through the raging river safely to Rome. Numerologically, "3," in the case of these Roman heroes, undoubtedly represents the joy of living, having battled successfully against overwhelming odds.

A Japanese story also features the mysterious and powerful "3," in the form of Momotaro and his parents. The couple had been childless although longing for a son. They found a peach floating in a mountain stream. Cutting it open, they found a very tiny baby boy inside it. They named him *Momotaro*, which means "peach child." The couple raised him as their own son, and did all in their power to keep him safe and happy. At the age of 15, Momotaro decided that he wanted to repay his adopted parents and their friends and neighbours in the village for their generosity and kindness to him as he had grown up.

Momotaro the Warrior

A large group of *oni* lived on a nearby island. Oni are hideous monsters from Japanese folklore. They are sometimes referred to as trolls, demons, ogres, or devils. They are usually shown as being gigantic. They have wild, dishevelled hair and long horns. They have multi-coloured skin, often red or blue. They carry iron clubs and are then referred to in Japanese as *oni-ni-kanabo*, which translates as "oni with an iron club." The phrase has come to mean someone invincible and impossible to defeat. They had been raiding the mainland for some years, abducting girls and stealing treasure. Momotaro's mother gave him 3 rice cakes before he set out, and he acquired 3 loyal companions by giving each of them one of his rice cakes. The first was a dog; the second was a pheasant; the third was a monkey. They took a boat to the island where the terrifying oni lived. Here they attacked the oni, and Momotaro — a superb warrior — killed them all.

He and his companions then rescued some girls whom the oni had held as captives. They then filled their boat with the treasure that the oni had stolen and made their way home again. Momotaro married the loveliest of the girls whom he had rescued and sent the others back to their jubilant families, who had never dreamt of seeing their daughters again. He shared the treasure with his parents and their friends and neighbours, enabling them to live in great comfort and happiness for the rest of their lives. Here, once again, the numerological association with "3" is concerned with the joy of living. The fearless young warrior, Momotaro, brought joy to his parents and their friends, to the girls whom he had rescued, and to his lovely young wife.

The numerological associations with "4" include a solid, orderly foundation; a struggle against limits; and steady growth. "Four" is also associated with service. In Norse mythology, Freyja, the goddess of love, magic, beauty, sexuality, and fertility, bought the exquisite necklace, Brisingamen, from the 4 dwarves who had created it, by spending a night with each of them. The love goddess and the 4 dwarves each kept their part of the sexual bargain.

Ancient Egyptians used 4 canopic jars to represent the 4 sons of Horus. These jars were placed around the sarcophagus containing the mummified corpse. A jar containing the stomach was placed to the east. The lungs went in the northern jar. The liver jar was placed to the south. The jar containing the intestines stood to the west. Again there was a specific order and pattern to the way in which this was done. The mummified corpse and the jars were part of the struggle against death, an attempt to enter the afterlife and grow there.

In Chinese mythology, there are 4 legendary dragon kings who live in palaces made of crystal. They control the north, south, east, and west. They rule over the 4 seas. Their armies consist of crab generals and shrimp soldiers. The dragon kings rule over the clouds and the rain, as well as the oceans. When angered or aggrieved, the dragon kings can send floods to destroy their enemies. The northern king is Ao Shun. The southern king is Ao Qin. The king of the east is Ao Guang, and the west is ruled by Ao Run. This idea of rule by the 4 dragon kings fits well with the numerological associations with "4": orderly foundations and struggle against limits.

In numerology, "5" is associated with expansiveness, vision, adventure, and the constructive use of freedom. The first 5 books of the Bible, known as the Pentateuch, are Genesis, Exodus, Leviticus, Numbers, and Deuteronomy. Genesis, in particular, contains the visionary adventures of the ancient patriarchs.

A very interesting folktale from the Isle of Man tells how the Manx fairies would capture human beings and take them away for years at a time. In one of the many versions of these stories, a citizen of Kirk Andreas was captured by the fairies and kept by them for 5 years. During this time, he was nevertheless able to observe what was happening to his family and friends back in the normal human world. They, however, could not see him. After the 5 years of his entrapment in the Manx fairyland, he suddenly found himself back in the normal human world again, feeling as if he had just woken up after a long sleep.

To prove his account of his strange imprisonment with the fairies to his family and friends, he told them what he had seen them doing on particular days and at particular times. He asked if they remembered passing a large thorn bush on their way to market at Ramsey. He also asked if they remembered hearing a sharp, loud, metallic impact as they passed the bush. They did remember it clearly, as the sound had startled them. The man who had been imprisoned by the fairies said that as he and the fairy who was guarding him had been sitting beside the bush having a meal from the iron plates that the fairies used, his fairy guard had suddenly put his food down and raised his bow to shoot at one of the prisoner's brothers on the far side of the bush. The prisoner raised his plate and deflected the arrow just in time — that was the loud sound that the travellers had heard as they journeyed to Ramsey. The 5-year imprisonment in fairyland was certainly a visionary adventure.

Ancient Chinese mythology contains many stories of the 5 emperors, who were gods that had descended to Earth. The Yellow Emperor, Huang Ti, was the strongest and most important of the 5. He loved people and animals and strove to rule the world in peace. The other 4 emperors, however, were less benign than Huang Ti, and he was forced to fight against them periodically. The Red Emperor was Chih Ti, half-brother to the Yellow Emperor. The White Emperor was Shao Hao. The Black Emperor was Zhuan Xu, and the Green Emperor was Tai Hou. The numerology of "5" relates appropriately here, especially concerning adventure and the constructive use of freedom.

Numerologically, "6" is associated with responsibility, protection, nurturing, and sympathy. In the Biblical story of creation, God made the universe in 6 days. Human beings were created on the sixth day. The problems that subsequently confronted Adam and Eve in legend as well as in the Biblical accounts were similar in some ways to the problems that confronted a famous thirteenth century Turkish wise man named Nasreddin Hodja. He could always find a way around a problem, and there are elements of wit and humour in all of the legends and folktales in which he is featured. As a prosperous Turk he had 6 wives, whose company he greatly enjoyed, but they were constantly asking him to tell them which one he loved best. He always told the wife who asked him when they were alone together that she was his favourite, but still they questioned him. At last, he bought

6 beautiful rubies from the jewel merchant, and when he was next alone with one of his wives, he gave her one of the precious rubies and told her never to tell anyone about her gift. It had to remain an absolute secret between them. When each girl had received her ruby and promised never to tell, the wily Nasreddin Hodja announced that he had given a ruby to his favourite wife. After that there was peace and quiet in the harem.

Although he was prepared to bend the truth on occasion, under Nasreddin Hodja's craftiness and his cunning methods of solving problems, he was basically a kind and caring man. In that way, his association with the qualities of the numerological "6" showed responsibility, protection, nurturing, and sympathy.

The numerological significance of "7" relates to analysis, understanding, knowledge, awareness, and studiousness. The seven wonders of the ancient world were listed as: the Great Pyramid of Gizeh, the Hanging Gardens of Babylon, the statue of Zeus at Olympia, the Temple of Artemis at Ephesus, the Mausoleum at Halicarnassus, the Colossus of Rhodes, and the lighthouse at Alexandria. Each of these stretched human knowledge and understanding to its limits.

According to the Japanese creation myths, the earliest of the gods were referred to as the Kotoamatsukami, followed by the 7 generations of Kami, who are referred to as Kamiyonanayo — literally meaning "the 7 generations of the gods." The gods were credited with great wisdom and understanding, which accords with the numerological associations with "7."

In Chinese folklore and mythology, the 8 Immortals, or *Pa Hsien*, have prominent places. They were a group of Taoist deities from the thirteenth century who became the central figures in many popular legends. They lived together in what was known as the Eastern Paradise on the islands of Peng-lai. The 8 Immortals represented every type of human being: young, old, male, female, poor, and wealthy. Chinese craftsmen and artists depicted them everywhere as pictures, statues, tapestries, and pottery. The most celebrated of them was Li Tiehkuai, meaning "Li with the Iron Crutch." One story associated with him is that he sent his soul up to Heaven while a young disciple guarded his body until he returned. Tragically, this young disciple's mother was terminally ill and he rushed to her bedside. Not wishing to leave Li's body unprotected, however, he cremated it. When Li returned he found only a pile of ashes! Looking for another body, he came across that of a beggar who had just died and he entered that — realizing afterwards that it had only one leg. His celestial master therefore sent him an iron crutch from Heaven, hence his name. He went to the home of the disciple who had cremated his body and restored the boy's dead mother to life. Li became the immortal who was concerned with healing. Another of the 8 Immortals is Han Chung-li, who was an expert alchemist who converted base metals to gold and silver, which he gave to the hungry, homeless poor in order to preserve their lives.

Numerologically, "8" is associated with practical endeavours and the 8 Immortals used their powers in practical ways to help the poor and others in grave need. The significance of "8" in folklore and mythology transfers to the spider because of its 8 legs. There is a very old Cherokee story that tells how Grandmother Spider brought light into the world. The buzzard and the possum both tried to bring light but had no success in their ventures, then Grandmother Spider volunteered. She made a clay bowl, then with the advantage of having 8 legs she rolled it to where the sun was sitting resting on the far side of the Earth. She carefully manoeuvred the sun into her fireproof clay bowl and rolled him along, leaving a web as she went. She brought him all the way from the east to the west and his light shone all around the world.

The Torah contains a story of how King David was escaping from Saul's soldiers and hid in a cave. A spider spun a web across the cave entrance. When Saul's men saw it, they said that there could not be anyone inside the cave because the web covered the entrance. So the spider helped David to escape from his pursuers. Numerologically, "8" relates to practical endeavours, and the spider who brought light, together with the spider who saved King David, were both extremely practical.

One example of "9" in folklore and mythology relates to the 9 muses. These goddesses of art and literature were the daughters of

Zeus and Mnemosyne, the goddess of memory. She and Zeus spent 9 days and nights together when the muses were conceived. The muses help and inspire human beings to create various art forms and types of literature. In alphabetical order, Calliope is the muse of epic poetry and eloquence; Clio is the muse of history; Erato inspires the lyre and poetry concerned with love; Euterpe is the muse of musical instruments, especially the flute; Melpomene is the muse of tragedy; Polyhymnia inspires sacred songs and impersonations; Terpsichore is the muse of dancing; Thalia is the muse of comedy, and, rather surprisingly, of science as well; Urania is the muse of astronomy and astrology. Numerologically, "9" is the humanitarian number: it stands for unselfishness, giving, and creative expression. It is the ideal number for the 9 muses, who give so much to the human race and inspire creative expression.

In this chapter, links have been sought between numerological associations and numbers in folklore, mythology, and legends. There do seem to be several significant connections. In the next chapter, numerology and music are examined.

22
NUMEROLOGY IN MUSIC AND FOLK SONGS

Experts in musicology and music theory tend to regard mathematics as the basis of sound. One essential aspect of the link between music and numbers is the use of rhythm and meter. A rhythmic structure means that there are certain repeated pulses, accents, and phrases within a piece of music, and the durations of the notes have to be measured relative to other notes and silences. A composer of music is in some ways like an architect planning a building.

What is referred to as a musical scale is a set of pitches. In contemporary Western music, the diatonic scale is most frequently used. It originated in ancient Greece, where there were 3 traditional ways to tune the lyre. These 3 methods were called diatonic, chromatic, and enharmonic. They produced sequences of 4 notes that were known as tetrachords. *Tetrachord* means "4 strings." Numerologically, "4" is associated with an orderly foundation, and musically that's what a tetrachord was. A diatonic tetrachord consisted of the notes AGFE and the intervals were 2 whole tones and a semi-tone. Scales are repeated each octave. An octave is 8 notes and, numerologically, "8" has the significance of practical endeavour. When the sounds of the notes are calculated in terms of their frequencies in hertz (named after the German physicist Heinrich Hertz (1857–1894), then each successive octave has twice the frequency range of its predecessor.

There are 3 particular folk songs, "Green Grow the Rushes-O," "The Twelve Days of Christmas," and "One, Two, Buckle my Shoe," that are especially interesting from a numerological point of view.

The first, "Green Grow the Rushes-O," begins with "I'll sing you one-o" and goes on to say what that "1" is. It is "1," all alone, and is numerologically the initiator of action. Most interpretations of the secret meanings behind the words suggest that this "1" is God, but in the Jewish or Islamic sense rather than the Christian idea of the Trinity.

The "2" in the second verse is numerologically associated with co-operation and adaptability. Some theories suggest that the "2" refers to Castor and Pollux, the benign heavenly twins who help human beings. Other theories suggest that they are John the Baptist and Jesus. A third group of theories suggests that they are the Holly King and the Oak King. It was also customary in the Middle Ages to put rushes around 2 statues of saints at religious festivals — so this may be the reference.

Co-author Lionel amid the rushes

The "3" rivals in verse 3 may refer to the Greek goddesses Hera, Athena, and Aphrodite, and the judgement of Paris, meant to determine which of them was the most beautiful. It has also been thought that "rivals" may be a corruption of "arrivals" and so refers to the 3 wise men, the Magi, who brought gifts to the stable in Bethlehem at the first Christmas. The 3 synoptic gospels written by Matthew, Mark, and Luke may be thought of as giving slightly different accounts of the life and work of Jesus, and so be rival biographers in that sense. Numerologically, "3" is associated with expression, verbalization, and the arts. The gospels express the life of Jesus in words.

In verse 4 there is little room for doubt that it refers to all 4 of the gospel writers: Matthew, Mark, Luke, and John. "Four" is numerologically associated with an orderly foundation, a struggle against limits, and steady growth. This is relevant for the history of the early Church and the role that the 4 gospel writers played in its development.

The 5 symbols at the door in verse 5 probably refer to the medieval custom of inscribing a pentagram on the door to ward off evil spirits and dark magic. Other theories relate it to the Pentateuch, the first 5 books of the Bible. Numerologically, "5" is associated with visionary adventure and the constructive use of freedom. The householder marking a door in this way is an adventurer in what he sees as a dangerous world, using his freedom to ward off evil.

There are theories that the 6 proud walkers of verse 6 go back many centuries to a band of 6 fearless Anglo-Saxon warriors who walked around the boundaries of their fiercely defended territories until they were finally defeated by the Norman Conquest in the eleventh century. "Six," numerologically, is associated with responsibility and protection, and would be appropriate for those fearless Anglo-Saxon defenders.

In verse 7, the 7 stars in the sky almost certainly refer to the Pleiades, or Ursa Major. In the book of Revelation, chapter 1, verse 16, there is a reference to 7 stars in the hand of Jesus. "Seven," in numerology, refers to analysis, understanding, knowledge, wisdom, and awareness. The earliest astrologers and astronomers were men and women of great ability who learnt many things from the stars that they watched and studied so meticulously and assiduously.

In verse 8, the April rainers probably refer to the Hyades constellation, which became visible in April with the sun. In classical Greek times it was believed to be the source of the April rains. Numerologically, "8" refers to practical things, and it is logical to associate a constellation that apparently brings rain with that kind of pragmatism.

The 9 bright shiners of verse 9 may refer to the sun and moon and what were in older times the 7 known planets. They could also be the 9 orders of angels and archangels. It is also possible that the reference is to 9 particular saints who were noted for their kindness and generosity to the poor — saints, like the wealthy Nicholas, whose gifts changed so many lives for the better. Numerologically, "9" is associated with humanitarianism and unselfish giving.

"Ten" is as straightforward as was the reference in verse 4 to the gospel makers. "Ten" refers to the Ten Commandments given to Moses on tablets of stone. "Eleven" is equally straightforward in referring to

A partridge

the 11 disciples who remained faithful after Judas Iscariot's betrayal of Jesus, and "12" is for the original situation with the disciples before Judas left their number.

There are a number of interesting numerological suggestions for the meaning of the song about the 12 days of Christmas. Some theorists believe that Jesus himself is the Partridge of verse 1, and the tree is the cross.

Traditionally, partridges, like pelicans, were thought to be so unselfish that they fed their young with their own flesh when there was no other food available. Numerologically, "1" initiates action, and the action here is the action of salvation. The 2 turtle doves of verse 2 represent the Old Testament and the New Testament. The numerological association with "2" is co-operation and partnership, and the truths of the Old and New Testaments reinforce each other in that way. The 3 French hens of the third verse are the 3 wise men, the Magi. Numerologically, "3" is associated with the joy of living and they were filled with joy as the star led them to Jesus. Verse 4 refers to 4 calling birds. These are thought to be the 4 gospels, calling their readers to God's truth. Numerologically, "4" is an orderly foundation, and these gospels are the foundation of Christianity. Verse 5 is about 5 gold rings, and these are thought to signify the first 5 books of the Bible, known as the Pentateuch. Numerologically, "5" is visionary adventure and the constructive use of freedom. The patriarchs and heroes of the Pentateuch were certainly adventurous, and they used their freedom constructively in the development of their religious thought and practices. Verse 6 refers to 6 geese a-laying, and these are interpreted as the 6 days of creation. Numerologically, "6" represents responsibility and protection and is appropriate for the geese protecting their eggs and later their goslings — examples of the life that had been created.

The 7 swans swimming in verse 7 represent the 7 gifts of the Holy Spirit: these are represented by the design of St. Josaphat's Cathedral at Edmonton in Canada, which has 7 copper domes. St. Thomas Aquinas listed the 7 gifts as: wisdom, understanding, counsel, fortitude, knowledge, piety, and fear of the Lord. These harmonize perfectly with the

325

numerological interpretation of "7," which is associated with meditation, studiousness, understanding, knowledge, and analysis.

The 8 maids in verse 8 refer to the 8 beatitudes of Jesus. They are recorded in Matthew's gospel, chapter 5, verses 3–10. Each begins with a blessing. Numerologically, "8" refers to practical endeavours — things to be done in this material world. It fits well with the beatitudes, which explain what type of earthly behaviour will lead to spiritual rewards. The first blesses the poor in spirit, who shall participate in the Kingdom of Heaven. The second blesses mourners, who shall be comforted. The third blesses the meek, who shall inherit the earth. The fourth blesses those who hunger and thirst after righteousness, and promises that they shall be satisfied. The fifth blessing is for the merciful, who shall obtain mercy. The sixth blesses the pure in heart, who shall see God. The seventh beatitude blesses the peacemakers, who will be called the children of God. The eighth and final benediction blesses those who are persecuted for the sake of righteousness. Like the poor in spirit in the first blessing, they too shall participate in the Kingdom of Heaven.

Just as the 7 maids of the seventh verse referred to the 7 fruits of the spirit, so the 9 ladies dancing in verse 9 are interpreted as the 9 fruits of the spirit. In Galatians, chapter 5, verses 22 and 23, these are listed as: love, joy, peace, longsuffering, kindness, goodness, faithfulness, gentleness, and self-control. Numerologically, "9" is associated with humanitarianism, unselfishness, and giving. This fits in well with the 9 fruits of the spirit.

Ten lords leaping in the tenth verse refers to the Ten Commandments. Eleven pipers piping are the 11 true and faithful disciples, and the 12 drummers drumming are the 12 points of the Apostles' Creed. These are: belief in God as maker of Heaven and Earth; belief in his son Jesus; belief in the virgin birth; belief in Christ's crucifixion, death, and burial; belief in his resurrection on the third day; belief in his ascent into Heaven; belief that Jesus sits at the right hand of God the Father; belief that he will return to judge the Earth; belief in the church and the fellowship of saints; belief that sins can be forgiven; and, finally, belief in resurrection and eternal life.

The song "One, Two, Buckle my Shoe," is more obscure than the 2 earlier ones and harder to interpret.

> *One, two,*
> *Buckle my shoe;*
> *Three, four,*
> *Knock at the door;*
> *Five, six,*
> *Pick up sticks;*
> *Seven, eight,*
> *Lay them straight:*
> *Nine, ten,*
> *A big fat hen;*
> *Eleven, twelve,*
> *Dig and delve;*
> *Thirteen, fourteen,*
> *Maids a-courting;*
> *Fifteen, sixteen,*
> *Maids in the kitchen;*
> *Seventeen, eighteen,*
> *Maids a-waiting*
> *Nineteen, twenty,*
> *My plate's empty.*

One suggestion is that it refers in summary form to a young man reaching early adulthood and buckling his shoes to set out in life. He then starts what seems to be agricultural work. He knocks on the door of a prospective employer and is taken on by him. His work consists of gathering firewood and stacking it, looking after poultry and digging the garden. As his life develops he meets a girl and begins to court her. In the days when the rhyme was composed, marriages would have taken place with young brides of 14 or 15. As part of a young married couple, his wife would work in the kitchen while he was doing the agricultural work outside. The waiting seems to refer to the young wife's pregnancy, followed by the arrival of a family and their hungry children emptying their plates — in other words, it was not easy for a poor working couple to buy enough food for their children and themselves.

If this interpretation is correct and the song does refer to the general progress of life for a working couple in the seventeenth and eighteenth centuries, it would absorb all the numerological meanings of the numbers from 1–20.

23
THE ULTIMATE SIGNIFICANCE OF NUMBERS

Scientific progress and technology would be impossible without numbers. There could be no understanding of history without using numbers for years, centuries, and millennia. Geography and architecture — navigating seas and oceans, crossing continents, exploring new lands and then raising stately buildings on them — all depend on numbers. Plumbing the depths or surveying stars and galaxies — raising satellites and space stations — all depend upon numbers. Molecules and atoms have to be understood numerically. Dark matter, dark energy, and the mysteries of black holes can only be solved with numbers. It is no exaggeration to say that numbers are the keys to the universe and everything within it. Those are the uses of numbers as calculators — but what of their *other* mysterious powers?

Numerologists are interested in 2 other aspects of numbers: their predictive powers and their controlling powers. Some numerologists believe that numbers can reveal what is likely to happen; that they can give warnings about unwelcome, negative events on the horizon. It's possible that they can also foretell what needs to be done to get into the path of welcome and positive events. But over and above their predictive, guiding, and warning function, some numerologists believe that numbers can exert control over people and events, can reshape the environment, and refashion the future. If there are a number of probability tracks ahead of us in an undetermined future, some numerologists suggest that the right numbers can steer us onto good and positive tracks if they are used correctly.

To try to understand this aspect of numbers as *shapers* and *controllers*, it is necessary to analyze cause and effect in general. Why do things happen as they do? A bullet leaves a sniper's rifle and brings down an enemy soldier. What made those events happen? Somebody manufactured the gun, somebody made the ammunition for it, somebody declared war, armies were organized, and officers deployed their

Healing herbs and medicines

troops. The sniper aimed and fired. His target lay dead. A long chain of causes and effects led to that event.

A miraculous new drug was injected into a dying man. It cured his disease. He went home strong and well again and went back to work to create a good income for himself, his loving partner, and their children. Somebody studied the disease that was killing him. Somebody experimented with complicated new drugs. One painstaking test after another pointed the way to a miraculous new form of therapy. The dying man lived, to the indescribable delight of his wife and children. What influenced his recovery? It was an entire chain of events, a spark of medical research genius followed by years of hard work.

One event influences another. Every cause creates an effect. The end processes can be death from a sniper's bullet or renewal of life from a magnificent new therapy. Whether it is a rung on the ladder that leads to the sniper's bullet, or to the new life-saving medicine, the cause and effect processes have strange, parallel qualities.

The creation of rifles and bullets and the political circumstances that lead to wars and death and the creation of wonderful new therapies via years of patient and determined clinical research that lead to new life are both subject to influences of various kinds. Some of these influences are obvious and direct — others are invisible and, often, totally unsuspected. The stressed-out military leader drank heavily and in secret the night before a critical battle. His tactics and the orders he gave were riddled with errors. Men were killed unnecessarily. No one realized that it was the previous night's alcohol that had influenced their commander's judgement.

The brilliant medical scientist had a greatly loved friend who died of a particular disease. The researcher regarded that disease ever after as a personal enemy on whom he sought revenge. Thirty years of unremitting work in his dead friend's memory finally produced the miracle cure. The secret influence that terminated the disease was the researcher's psychological determination to finish it. Alcohol for the general? A deep psychological determination for the medical researcher? Secret influences that bring about results; secret causes that produce dramatic effects? The greatest mysteries of all are the mysteries of the human mind.

Some numerologists believe that numbers can exert invisible and unsuspected influences just as powerful as alcohol and as unswerving psychological fixations. If those numerologists are right, just how do the numbers do it? Alcohol has a biochemical effect on a person that can be measured and assessed. A psychological fixation can overcome boredom, exhaustion, or feelings of frustration, failure, and depression. Its powers are not as susceptible to measurement as the biochemistry of alcohol — but they are very real and effective. A professional psychotherapist can detect and analyze them.

Numerologists who follow this school of thought believe that by gathering the right numbers around us — or around someone we are trying to help — the secret, invisible, unknown powers associated with certain numbers can actually change environments and events for the better. These numerologists believe that the right numbers used at the right time and place can influence people and things. If this is true, numbers are not merely predictors — they are influential change-makers.

What are the benign numbers that can be used in this way? They are different to some extent from the lists of number associations that we have already studied. Numerologists who believe in the positive powers of numbers, and their ability to influence circumstances in a positive way, would begin with the number "1." It can be seen to have an individualistic and aggressive power. It gives strength and energy to the subject.

Mysteries of the Mind

If the way ahead is blocked by negative factors and the subject does not have the aggressive energy necessary to sweep the obstacles aside, then the numerologist will recommend the influence of the number "1." Look at a card such as the ace of hearts, admire a clear and unimpeded sunrise with the one great orb shining alone in the eastern sky, or look at a full moon alone in a cloudless sky. These are the symbols of "1." The flame of one candle in a dark room will also focus on *oneness*.

"Three" also brings power according to the theories of this branch of numerology. Three words: "I shall overcome." Arrange 3 coins in a triangle, especially if it is a financial problem that is causing difficulties for the subject. The subject can light 3 candles and sit on a 3-legged stool as he or she meditates on the power of "3." The desired goal can be written on a sheet of paper and folded 3 times, then carried in a pocket or handbag until the problem is solved or the goal is achieved.

"Seven" is also a particularly benign, protective, and helpful number recommended by numerologists who follow this theory. Repeat the desired solution to the problem 7 times. Wind a piece of ribbon 7 times around the seventh finger, counting from the little finger of the left hand. This is the index finger of the right hand. The subject can write the desired objective or solution on a sheet of paper, put it in an envelope, and seal it with 7 seals using old-fashioned sealing wax. The subject can also light 7 candles and look at them as he or she meditates.

"Nine" is thought to be the most powerful of all the proactive positive numbers when used in this way. The subject can light 9 candles, arrange 9 coins in the outline of a figure "9," write the problem, or sought goal, on a sheet of paper, put it in an envelope, and seal it 9 times. Ribbon can be wound 9 times around the ninth finger — the third finger of the right hand when counting begins with the little finger of the left hand as before. If these actions can be performed at the ninth hour of the ninth day of the ninth month, it is believed that their strength is considerably reinforced.

If a subject is asking a numerologist for help because of perceived threats from negative circumstances, the number "6" is felt to offer the most effective protection. The subject may be recommended to meditate on a 6-sided fortification, like a hexagonal tower. Hexagonal jewellery can be worn, especially a ring with a hexagonal stone. A hexagonal crystal may be thought to be especially effective. A watch can be stopped at 6 o'clock and worn on the wrist or carried in a pocket. Cricket umpires often carry 6 small pebbles, which they use to make sure that they are getting the 6 balls of an over-correct. The subject can do this, too, by pocketing 6 small stones and going over all 6 while waiting in a bus queue, or sitting in a restaurant waiting to be served. Six protective circles can be drawn around a photograph of the subject and 6 protective candles can be lit.

These attempts to use numbers as influences to attract good things and to protect against negative things are very interesting, but are open to the question of whether — when they seem to work — they are actually self-fulfilling prophecies. If the subject believes that "1," "3," "7," and "9" are helping him or her to defeat problems and realize goals, the subject's confidence increases, performance improves, and the goal is achieved. If the subject believes that "6" is offering protection, he or she can relax confidently under that believed-in protection and behave accordingly. Anxiety and stress are reduced and the subject gets through the problem.

So the fascinating mysteries and secrets of numerology yet remain to be solved.

BIBLIOGRAPHY

Berlitz, Charles. *World of Strange Phenomena*. London: Sphere Books Limited, 1989.

Blashford-Snell, John. *Mysteries: Encounters with the Unexplained*. London: Bodley Head, 1983.

Bord, Janet and Colin. *Mysterious Britain*. Great Britain: Paladin, 1974.

Briggs, Katharine M. *British Folk Tales and Legends: A Sampler*. London: Granada Publishing, 1977.

Camilleri, George. *Realms of Fantasy: Folk Tales from Gozo*. Gozo: Gozo Press, 1992.

Cavendish, Richard (ed.). *Encyclopaedia of the Unexplained*. London: Routledge & Kegan Paul, 1974.

Clark, Jerome. *Unexplained*. Michigan: Gale Research Inc., 1993.

Du Sautoy, Marcus. *The Number Mysteries*. London: Fourth Estate Publishers, 2011.

Duane, O.B. *Celtic Myths and Legends*. London: Hodden Headline Group, 1998.

Duane, O.B., and N. Hutchison. *Chinese Myths and Legends*. London: Hodden Headline Group, 1998.

Dyall, Valentine. *Unsolved Mysteries*. London: Hutchinson & Co. Ltd., 1954.

Eysenck, H.J., and Carl Sargent. *Explaining the Unexplained*. London: BCA, 1993.

Fanthorpe, Patricia and Lionel. *The Holy Grail Revealed*. California: Newcastle Publishing Co. Inc., 1982.

_____. *Secrets of Rennes-le-Château*. Maine: Samuel Weiser Inc., 1992.

_____. *The Oak Island Mystery*. Toronto: Hounslow Press, 1995.

_____. *The World's Greatest Unsolved Mysteries*. Toronto: Hounslow Press, 1997.

_____. *The World's Most Mysterious People*. Toronto: Hounslow Press, 1998.

_____. *The World's Most Mysterious Places*. Toronto: Hounslow Press, 1999.

_____. *Mysteries of the Bible*. Toronto: Hounslow Press, 1999.

_____. *Death the Final Mystery*. Toronto: Hounslow Press, 2000.

_____. *The World's Most Mysterious Objects*. Toronto: Hounslow Press, 2002.

_____. *The World's Most Mysterious Murders*. Canada. Hounslow Press. 2003.

_____. *Unsolved Mysteries of the Sea*. Toronto: Hounslow Press, 2004.

_____. *Mysteries of Templar Treasure and the Holy Grail*. Maine: Samuel Weiser Inc., 2004.

_____. *The World's Most Mysterious Castles*. Toronto: Hounslow Press, 2005.

_____. *Mysteries and Secrets of the Templars: the Story Behind the da Vinci Code*. Toronto: Hounslow Press, 2005.

_____. *Mysteries and Secrets of the Masons*. Toronto: Hounslow Press, 2006.

_____. *Mysteries and Secrets of Time*. Toronto: Hounslow Press, 2007.

_____. *Mysteries and Secrets of Voodoo*. Toronto: Dundurn Press, 2008.

_____. *Secrets of the World's Undiscovered Treasures*. Toronto: Dundurn Press, 2009.

_____. *The Big Book of Mysteries*. Toronto: Dundurn Press, 2010.

_____. *Satanism and Demonology*. Toronto: Dundurn Press, 2011.

Forman, Joan. *Haunted East Anglia*. Great Britain: Fontana, 1976.

Fowke, Edith. *Canadian Folklore*. Toronto: Oxford University Press, 1988.

Guerber, H.A. *Myths and Legends of the Middle Ages*. London: Studio Editions Ltd., 1994.

Guirdham, Arthur. *The Lake and The Castle*. United Kingdom: Cygnus Books, 1992.

_____. *We Are One Another*. United Kingdom: Cygnus Books, 1992.

_____. *The Cathars and Reincarnation*. London: Spearman, 1970.

Lambert, R.S. *Exploring the Supernatural*. London: Arthur Barker Ltd., 1955.

Lampitt, L.F. (ed.) *The World's Strangest Stories*. London: Associated Newspapers Group Ltd., 1955.

Larousse Encyclopaedia of Mythology. London: Paul Hamlyn, 1959.

Mack, Lorrie, et al. (ed.) *The Unexplained*. London: Orbis, 1984.

Manley, Bill. *The Penguin Historical Atlas of Ancient Egypt*. London: Penguin Group, 1996.

Michell, John, and Robert J.M. Rickard. *Phenomena: A Book of Wonders*. London: Thames & Hudson, 1977.

Page, R.I. *Reading the Runes*. London: Trustees of the British Museum, 1987.

Pennick, Nigel. *Mazes and Labyrinths*. London: Robert Hale, 1998.

Playfair, G.L. *The Unknown Power*. London: Granada Publishing Ltd., 1977.

Porter, Enid. *The Folklore of East Anglia*. London: B.T. Batsford Ltd., 1974.

Pott, Mrs. Henry. *Francis Bacon and His Secret Society*. London: Sampson Low, Marston & Company, 1891.

Rawcliffe, D.H. *Illusions and Delusions of the Supernatural and the Occult*. New York: Kessinger Publishing, 1959.

Raymond, Andrew. *Secrets of the Sphinx*. Hawaii: UNI Productions, 1995.

The Reader's Digest Association (eds.) *Folklore, Myths and Legends of Britain*. London: Reader's Digest, 1973.

_____. *Strange Stories, Amazing Facts*. London: Reader's Digest, 1975.

Rolleston, T.W. *Celtic Myths and Legends*. London: Studio Editions Ltd., 1994.

Russell, Eric Frank. *Great World Mysteries*. London: Mayflower, 1967.

Saltzman, Pauline. *The Strange and the Supernormal*. New York: Paperback Library, Inc., 1968.

Scott, Michael. *Irish Ghosts and Hauntings*. Great Britain: Warner Book, 1994.

Sharper Knowlson, T. *The Origins of Popular Superstitions and Customs.* London: Studio Editions Ltd., 1995.

Snow, Edward Rowe. *Strange Tales from Nova Scotia to Cape Hatteras.* New York: Dodd, Mead & Company, 1946.

Spence, Lewis. *Ancient Egyptian Myths and Legends.* New York: Dover Publications Inc., 1990.

_____. *Introduction to Mythology.* London: Senate, 1994.

Spencer, John and Anne. *The Encyclopaedia of the World's Greatest Unsolved Mysteries.* London: Headline Book Publishing, 1995.

Sullivan, K.E. *Viking Myths and Legends.* London: Hodden Headline Group, 1998.

Wallis Budge, Earnest Alfred. *Egyptian Language.* New York: Dover Publications, 1983.

_____. *The Book of the Dead.* New York: University Books Inc., 1984.

Wilson, Colin. *The Psychic Detectives.* London: Pan Books, 1984.

Wilson, Colin and Damon. *Unsolved Mysteries Past and Present.* London: Headline Book Publishing, 1993.

Wilson, Colin, Damon, and Rowan. *World Famous True Ghost Stories.* London: Robinson Publishing, 1996.

Wilson, Colin and Dr. Christopher Evans (eds.) *The Book of Great Mysteries.* London: Robinson Publishing, 1986.

Young, George. *Ghosts in Nova Scotia.* Nova Scotia, 1991.

_____. *Ancient Peoples and Modern Ghosts.* Nova Scotia, 1991.

BY THE SAME AUTHORS

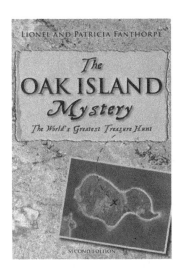

The Oak Island Mystery
The World's Greatest Treasure Hunt
9781554889945
$24.99

In 1795, three boys discovered the top of an ancient shaft on unin-habited Oak Island in Mahone Bay, Nova Scotia. The boys began to dig, and what they uncovered started the world's greatest and strangest treasure hunt. But nobody knows what the treasure is. Two hundred years of courage, back-breaking effort, ingenuity, and engineering skills have failed to retrieve what is concealed there.

Theories of what the treasure could be include Captain Kidd's bloodstained pirate gold, an army payroll left by the French or British military engineers, priceless ancient manuscripts, the body of an Arif or other religious refugee leader, or the lost treasure of the Templars. The Oak Island curse prophesies that the treasure will not be found until seven men are dead and the last oak has fallen. That last oak has already gone, and six treasure hunters have been killed.

After years of research, the authors have finally solved the sinister riddle of Oak Island, but their answer is challenging, controversial, and disturbing. Something beyond price still lies waiting in the labyrinth.

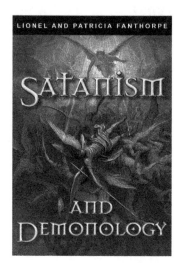

Satanism and Demonology
Mysteries and Secrets
9781554888542
$24.99

Satanism has been known around the world by many names over the centuries and has involved the shadowy deities of ancient pagan religions. During Christian times, Satanist sorcerers frequently tried to invoke the Devil to make their black magic work. In *Satanism and Demonology*, the great central questions behind the legends are explored: does Satan, or Lucifer, really exist, and if he does, what dark, anomalous powers does he wield?

Authors Lionel and Patricia Fanthorpe begin with an examination of what Satanism is, then explore its earliest prehistoric history. They track Satanism from the Middle East and ancient Egypt to the European witches and sorcerers of medieval times, and then on through the Renaissance to our present day. The bizarre, uninhibited satanic rituals, liturgies, and sexual practices are all examined in detail.

VISIT US AT

Dundurn.com
Definingcanada.ca
@dundurnpress
Facebook.com/dundurnpress